IVAN AND THE OPRICHNIKI

With a secret society known as the Oprichniki ("The Sur-rounders"), Ivan the Terrible launched one of history's most appalling reigns of terror. Riding in the dead of night on black horses in black monk's hoods, they raped and looted at will. They stripped men and women, driving them out into the icy cold. Insatiably sadistic, they penned their victims up and starved them until they ate the flesh of their own dead.

Their brutality and ruthlessness is rivaled only by the Inquisition itself.

HAROLD LAMB'S MAGNIFICENT RETELLING
OF THE GROWTH OF THE RUSSIAN EMPIRE

Books by Harold Lamb

- TAMERLANE
- OMAR KHAYYAM
- ALEXANDER OF MACEDON
- SULEIMAN THE MAGNIFICENT
- CHARLEMAGNE
- HANNIBAL
- THE CRUSADES
- CYRUS THE GREAT
- THEODORA AND THE EMPEROR
- BABUR THE TIGER
- GENGHIS KHAN

Published by Bantam Books, Inc.

The March of Muscovy

IVAN THE TERRIBLE AND THE GROWTH OF THE RUSSIAN EMPIRE 1400-1648

by Harold Lamb

THE MARCH OF MUSCOVY

*A Bantam Book / published by arrangement with
Doubleday & Company, Inc.*

Bantam edition published April 1966

*Bantam Books are published by Bantam Books, Inc., a subsidiary
of Grosset & Dunlap, Inc. Its trade-mark, consisting of the words
"Bantam Books" and the portrayal of a bantam, is registered in the
United States Patent Office and in other countries. Marca Registrada.
Bantam Books, Inc., 271 Madison Avenue, New York, N. Y. 10016.*

FOREWORD

TODAY Russia is omnipresent in the consciousness of the world. We are apt to think of her as an enormous, expanding entity, almost monolithic in hardness, and as enduring as the mountains of the earth.

To understand this hardness and this quality of endurance, it is necessary, perhaps, to look not at what Russia is today but at what she was in the beginning. What was that beginning?

This book attempts to tell the story of the expansion of Russia during the period corresponding to the pioneer days in America. In the beginning there was only a town on a river, and not a very notable town, at that. Upon that town of Moscow certain forces acted, and around it outward events took shape, resulting in migration and colonization across the breadth of the Eurasian continent, and even bridging the sea to the New World. What were those forces? Why did such a mass movement take place? And why did it move to the east of Muscovy, and then to the north of east?

About the middle of the seventeenth century, a chronicler in Moscow put the question in this way: "What man ever thought or divined that Moscow would become a kingdom, or what man ever knew that Moscow would be accounted an empire?"

His question is as difficult to answer as it is fascinating to try to do so. For Moscow first emerged from obscurity toward the end of the Tatar dominion, to become in two centuries the Russian Empire.

This book is concerned with the happenings of those two centuries, not to explain them but to relate the visible events as they have been recorded by dependable eyewitnesses—by foreign visitors and merchants, by exploring Cossacks, fact-finding ambassadors of the time, by wandering and exiled priests, and in the comments of that most acute observer of his own people, Ivan called the Terrible.

It so happens that Ivan's life extended through the main movement of his people to the east, as Elizabeth's extended through the earliest movement of the English navigators across the high seas. But Muscovy began, and the advance from Moscow started, in the lifetime of Ivan's grandfather.

To understand the age in which the two Ivans lived, it is necessary to look briefly at the land called Rus before the incoming of the Tatars.

CONTENTS

The fundamental factor of Russian history has been migration or colonisation . . . all other factors have been inseparably connected therewith.

V. O. KLIUCHEVSKY

MOSCOW, THE LAND AND THE PEOPLE, IN THE YEAR 1200 A.D.

Where the Rivers Led

THE river ran swiftly. It was a smallish river that could be forded easily by a tall man, in the shallows. Still, it was deep enough to float the flatboats, or at need the rafts when the water was low in the autumn.

It wound like the track of a snake through sandy, wooded country. Only the poorer sort of fish seemed to be in it. The boats or canoes that navigated its shallows carried their cargoes a long way, into a larger river which in turn flowed into one of the great waterways of a continent. The men who poled and sailed the boats sometimes voyaged in this fashion for a thousand miles, or several thousand miles; sometimes their journey ended in one of the outer seas.

Because of its swift, disturbing current, the river was named the Moskva, for troubled waters.

Where a stream entered the Moskva, both the river and the stream wound around a height covered with pines. Boatmen passing below the height could send an arrow arching up among the pine trees; anyone standing in the grove above could, however, send an arrow hurtling down with much greater force. So the wooded height had been a natural position for defense, and good for observation also.

It was known as the Hill of the Pines.

For this reason, the people coming down the trail from the north to the Moskva had built a blockhouse on the pine hillock. This served them more as a halfway house on their journey down to Kiev of the Golden Heads than as a frontier observation post; but it was that, too.

Men said that in the year 1155 a certain Yuri (George) Dolgoruky ringed in the blockhouse with a log stockade at the west corner of the hillock where the slope was steepest over the stream, called the Neglina. This stockade protected

1

the enclosure against raiders. After a warehouse was added to the blockhouse for storage, and huts spread out through the trees, a church was built by the gate, the Gate of the Pines. Thus fortified, the stockaded habitations became known as the Kremyl, or Kremlin, the fort.

Although frequently attacked and sometimes burned, the Kremlin stood for a long time. It was a simple enough task to rebuild it out of the timber of the surrounding groves. Grave-yards grew up around the church—that of the Saviour of the Pines—and other churches made their appearance. Quite a town spread over half the hundred-odd acres of this natural height which had ceased to be a frontier strong-point and had become a trading town at the juncture of the north-south landway with the east-west river route. The town kept the name of Moskva, which was to be pro-nounced by visitors from the far western end of the conti-nent "Moscow."

It was a small town and unimportant.

By the beginning of the thirteenth century Moscow had no particular reason to exist, except as a convenient stopping point for wayfarers on the long journey south, or as a ware-house where goods could be exchanged in small quantities. Great men, nobles or merchants coming from elsewhere, en-joyed the comparative coolness of the height with its canopy of pines during the stifling heat of summer. They also feasted vastly with their followers in the long halls of the Kremlin.

The river froze hard in winter. The barrier of snow over the earth and ice upon the water did not stop the traffic that passed by Moscow in this winter cold. The boats, of course, were laid up, the carts had their wheels removed and runners fastened on. Sledges and pack horses found their way over the ice.

Important merchants moving with their trade goods and guards along the river route from west to east, and back, stopped over at Moscow only to avail themselves of the protection of its wooden wall or perhaps to exchange some goods for the necessities of their journey. They traded lengths of woolen cloth or bits of ironwork, ingots of silver, or casks of wine—products of the more thriving towns situated elsewhere on the more thronged trade routes—for Moscow's local produce of the forest and earth. Moscow had plenty of hewn wood, turpentine, wax, tar, meat and beer, or honey mead.

Of furs, Moscow had as yet no more than the skins of animals in the surrounding woods, fox, otter, squirrel and beaver. The far-ranging traders carried in their packs sables and the unblemished white and black furs of the colder north.

Since the slightly rolling countryside of the Moscow area had no ranges of hills or dense forests—as in the north— its sandy soil was easily cultivated by the sharply pointed wooden plows made of a tree branch. The scattered growth of pines and birch and beech did not interfere with cultivation, and the soil never lacked for water. During the short summer the cattle herds grazed on abundant grass.

Only, the short duration of the summer heat made the task of farming arduous. There was no rest for the Muscovites between the first plowing of the muddy, clayey soil and the last hurried harvesting when grain and corn and hay were stored under roofs, and mead and beer brewed, and finally the cattle herds driven in. The greater part of these herds were slaughtered, their carcasses kept frozen out of doors until the meat was needed.

This town had risen on the bank of the river to meet the needs of passers-by; its growth had been shaped by the nature of the country around it. At this point and for a long time it remained isolated from the greater forces shaping events elsewhere.

Look at the *place* itself. It had no natural advantage, except that two minor lanes of travel crossed there in medieval days. The wooded Kremlin height was not a good defense against siege, like, for instance, the sheer rising rock Acropolis of Athens. It succumbed quickly enough to the attack of raiders experienced in war.

Nor did its inhabitants dominate either the headwaters or the mouth of the meandering Moskva River. It did not possess the peculiar advantage of the Acropolis height, of being within sight of a bay that opened into a most important sea. There was no strategic advantage in being upon a river unless you controlled its outlet.

The site of Moscow offered no such security as Venice had, within its network of lagoons which provided protection from invasion and immediate access to the great thoroughfare of the sea.

No, the characteristic of the Moscow plain was its openness; except for its comparative isolation it offered no security to its inhabitants. There were hundreds of similar sites upon the dozens of rivers that bisected the great central plain of Eurasia—Kiev, in the far south, built upon a high bluff overhanging the mighty Dnieper, not very far from the sea, had been the leading city of that plain.

The *country* around Moscow offered no advantage except its moderate fertility. It had, instead, one decisive disadvantage. It lay without natural barriers well within the central continental plain which had served as a thoroughfare for invaders. This plain extended through the rolling hills of the Ural range far into the eastern steppes from which the horse-nomad hordes had appeared in waves as regular as waves of the sea, to sweep against the settlers in the mid-region.

This countryside along the Moskva apparently contained no advantageous mineral resources such as the silver and iron of the Urals. It had, therefore, no natural wealth—even in the way of fisheries—to be mined or exploited in trade.

Nor did it lie adjacent to some great strategic crossroads of the medieval world, as Constantinople, the ghostlike survival of the earlier Rome, lay between the straits that divided two continents where civilization had waxed and waned for two thousand years. The men of Moscow, who still spoke two languages, knew Constantinople as Mikligaard (The Great Enclosure) and Tsargrad (City of the Caesars). Little wonder that in such an advantageous spot that imperial city was hemmed in by triple walls seventeen miles in circuit, guarding its immeasurable wealth.

Not far to the north of the Moscow countryside began the dense forest belt, mostly spruce growth that yielded in the further north only to the frozen swampland that bordered the ice-fringed narrow seas opening toward the Arctic. These northern regions were sparsely inhabited, for good reason.

A little way to the south, the country changed to the marginal feather-grass steppe, which in turn yielded quickly to the expanse of open grasslands known to the Muscovites as the green steppes, wherein lay the black earth region, so fertile that population thronged into it, and the conquering hordes of the east had sought it out long before. Beyond, fertility ended in the dry earth region, the brown steppes entering the deserts bordering salty inland seas, the Black Sea and the Caspian. In all this vast sweep southward there was no natural barrier before the true mountains, the Caucasus, which seemed to the Muscovites to form a continuous wall between the seas, dimly perceived on the horizon.

These remote hinterlands, immeasurably beyond their reach, offered no advantage to the dwellers within Moscow. Yet all of them as time went on exerted an influence *upon* the inhabitants of Moscow. Just as the north wind passing over the ice seas and frozen tundras intensified the cold of

winter, and the prevailing south winds brought in summer the
hot breath of the parched steppes, the human forces shaped
by the remote frontiers made themselves felt within Moscow.
Pagan tribes migrating from the land under the rising sun
intruded on Muscovite pastureland; hordes settled around
the southern seas, and sallied up for portable plunder, to
carry off the cattle, horses, slaves or tribute money.

Lacking Athens' defensible citadel, or the protective lagoons of Venice, or Constantinople's inland waterways, Moscow remained fully exposed to such destructive visitations. It
lay unguarded, a huddle of wooden houses in the inhospitable
plain.

So the only frontier known to Moscow at first were the
steppes of Asia.

The dwellers within Moscow had, as we shall discover, an
awareness of those far frontiers. The great plain lent itself
to a familiarity with distance; its abundant grass and water
and game allowed horsemen adapted to the land to make
journeys in summer of thousands of miles more easily than
a rider could travel hundreds of miles in western Europe,
between inns.[1]

Upon the rider of the steppes was impressed the immensity
of space, and at the same time the manifold life nourished at
the grass roots, by the soil. Even after seven centuries of time
this impression persisted, on entering the green steppe. "Never
had plough passed over the immeasurable waves of wild
growth; only the horses hidden in it as in a wood trampled it
down." So one writer exclaims. "The whole surface of the

---

[1] Europe did not exist as a political entity at that time. It was
the seabound western peninsula of the land mass of Eurasia, marked
off from the main continent by a different civilization, inherited
from the Roman Empire. In this peninsula Latin and Greek were
still the languages of common culture.

This "Europe" lay west of the Constantinople-Riga axis. It con-
tained well within it the loose-joined skeleton of the Holy Roman
Empire. Its dominating cultures were the growing Italian and
Germanic, with the remnant of the Byzantine.

Along the Constantinople-Riga axis stretched the natural barriers
of the Carpathian Mountains and the Pripet marshlands. This axis
marked roughly the limit of infiltration of the horse nomads of the
east—although groups like the Magyars and the Bulgars had driven
wedges past it. It marked also the western limit of the great central
plain and the true steppes, and the approximate limit of the in-
vasions of the Huns, Magyars, Khazars and the Turkish Betchenaks.

In the peninsula west of the Constantinople-Riga axis, population was fairly dense (conjectured to be twenty-five to thirty
persons in a square kilometer). East of it, population was still
scattered (conjectured to be less than five in a kilometer).

earth was a green-gold ocean splashed with millions of different colored flowers . . . blue and lilac cornflowers. . . . Partridges, protruding their necks, pecked under the delicate roots." [2]

And at night, "The steppe draws easy breath; the grass raises a gay, youthful rustling which you do not hear during the day . . . its unvaried music lulls you. And sometimes you hear the bird the steppe people call the *sleeper* crying out 'sleep, sleep' and another one laughs or bursts into hysterical wailing—that is the owl. . . . There is the smell of hay and scorched grass and faded flowers, and the smell is heavy, luscious, and sweet." [3]

The People of the Rivers

These men of Moscow craved land, but not any *one* land. What they wanted was the soil that could be plowed with the wooden hook plow, or grazed over—that would have them as owners. Such ownership they understood; they had had no experience with a country that belonged to a nation. Their love of a homeland runs through the wording of the early folk epic, the *Word of Igor's Arming*.

"Then Igor looked up at the bright sun, and saw all his fighting men covered with shadow beneath it. And Igor said to his fighting men, . . . 'Let us mount, brothers, on our swift horses and look upon the blue Don. . . . I wish to bend down my head and drink of the Don in my helmet.' "

When Igor reaches the open plains, he is as aware of the night's life around him as the visitors of later times. "Night groaned to him, and roused him . . . the carts creak at midnight like swans released. . . . O land of Rus, already thou art beyond the frontier hills."

When the song describes a battle it is in terms of harvesting: ". . . the sheaves are laid up with heads; men thresh with flails in hedgerows; on the barn floor they spread out life; they winnow the soul from the body."

And afterward: ". . . Seldom did the ploughman cry *gee up,* but often did the ravens croak as they took their choice among the bodies."

Igor and his mates had left their bodies along the Don from which they had so desired to drink. In common with many other men of Rus they had been overcome by the

[2] Gogol, *Taras Bulba.*

[3] Chekov, *On the Steppe.*

horse nomads who were then unquestioned masters of the steppe.

The very rude eloquence of the song of Igor's arming reveals that he and the other dwellers in the isolated towns had been farmers as well as warriors. Although they had kept to the forests, or at least to the wooded plain like the environs of Moscow, they had not been reduced to a forest economy. That is, to existing by fishing and hunting and cropping the clearings, or spaces where the spruce was burned and the ground fertilized by ash. In this they differed from the natives of the forest and woodland belts, the Finnish tribes.

As early as Igor's expedition the women of Rus had lamented, "Henceforth we can no longer think with our thoughts of our dear loves . . . nor amass gold nor silver— nay, far from it!"

The men of Rus did gather in gold and silver by trade as well as mining. An observant Arab traveler who ventured later into that little-known region—he called it the "land of darkness"—said of them, "They are all Christians, with red hair and blue eyes and heavy-boned faces. They are shrewd. You carry out of that land *saoum,* that is, silver bars that they have mined and with which they buy and sell."

The intelligent Arab (Ibn Batuta) had mentioned these barbarians as Christians rather than as a people. The men of Rus spoke of themselves in the same way, as *krestianin.*

Other observers describe them as rudely clothed and equipped, wearing protective armor of padded leather or iron link, using wooden dishes, and bearskins for coverlets, and their saddles for pillows.

They hunted persistently. In the early Ancient Chronicle a prince, Vladimir Monomakh, was careful to enter some of his feats as a hunter in his last testament: "Here is what I have done at Chernigov; in the open steppe I have roped ten or twenty wild horses, and in the length of Rus I have caught wild horses with my hands. Two wild bulls have crushed me down with their horns—my horse and I. I have been battered by the horns of a stag, and trampled by an elk, as well as gored. A wild boar has carried off my sabre in its side, and a bear has chewed my knee, but God preserved me from injury."

This same Ancient Chronicle relates "a wonder of the land of the Slavs." In heated wooden bathhouses, people stripped themselves and lashed their bodies with withes until they were almost unconscious, when they poured cold water over themselves to revive. "And this they did without being compelled thereto by anybody, calling this not torture but washing their bodies."

These ruddy, strong-boned men and women of Rus had appeared to be barbarians to the cultured Arab merchants and the visitors—the very few visitors—from Constantinople. They had seemed to be more *traders* than merchants, more *headmen* of tribes than princes. And they had developed other peculiarities than bathing themselves with almost religious zeal in steam-filled huts during intense winter cold.

For one thing, they were mobile. From the forest they moved their households to better soil, or in pursuit of vanishing game. With their heavy, hafted axes they could provide themselves with log cabins in a few days. They rode their work horses, without bit or spur—using only snaffles and whips. They journeyed over deep snow on rude skis and sledges, in Scandinavian fashion, or like the native tribes.

Vladimir had urged his children, "Don't do damage when you travel, in the villages or open lands . . . be careful to honor any guests who come to you, of whatever sort. For such travelers will make you known in every land, for good or for harm."

Evidently a guest would be necessarily a person making a journey. Those who stayed at Moscow were usually on the way elsewhere. And, like the settlers, they tended to follow the watercourses, often keeping their boats in convoy for protection. Where the current was swift against them, they landed on the bank to haul the longboats by ropes. Where the river dwindled to a stream, they would usually unload the craft and carry them on men's shoulders to the next watercourse. Over long gaps between water, or up steep gradients, the voyagers had to leave their vessels and transport their goods piecemeal to other boats on the far side.

Such portages had become familiar to them; they had traced out the waterways and managed, somehow, to get through. At some of the long portages (*voloki,* the men of Rus called them) the native folk waited to supply animal transport, or provide shipping for the through traffic. For this service a regular toll was charged, and a truce arranged, during which the guards of the portage would be responsible for the goods of the wayfarers.

So the men of Rus had a high degree of mobility even in the early times. More than that, they were nearly amphibious. River travel offered several vital advantages; it offered the best passage, winter and summer, through the dense northern forest belt; it traversed the scattered populated centers like Moscow; and in the open steppe in the south it provided a degree of protection against the formidable horsemen of the pagan hordes.

It so happened that there was not only a portage but an area of portages a few days' travel to the west of Moscow, beyond the headwater town of Mozhaisk. Ordinary boats could navigate only eighteen miles beyond Mozhaisk. On the uplands here the voyagers could return by stages down the Moskva to the broad current of the upper Volga; a portage led them to water connecting with the great Dnieper. Streams near Mozhaisk also connected with tributaries leading north and south directly.

This made the portages a minor junction for the through traffic. It did not avail Moscow anything as yet, but it was there.

Over this junction point Moscow's finest importations had come, beautiful silk stuff, brocades, perfumes of Arabia, seductive gold and silver vessels, pictured manuscripts in Greek, and thin steel weapons, chemicals—extraordinary products of Byzantine artistry, from Constantinople. These luxuries passed into the hands of the rich only, but they set a standard of life—they were harbingers of splendor, trinkets from the longed-for reigning city of the Autocrat who wore a cap of gold rimmed with bright carnelian, himself heritor of the authority of the Roman emperors. Constantinople was also the only contact of the people of Rus with an advanced civilization.

One Byzantine, Constantine Porphyrogenitus, has left an account of the southern voyage of the traders and headmen of Rus—"a voyage troubled in all its length by danger and accident"—down the Dnieper to the imperial city. The convoys assembled below the terminal city of Kiev, a safe stronghold. They were not the canoes or hollowed log boats of the northern tributaries but timber-built, with masts for sails, holding thirty or more men and the cargo.

The great hazards of the Dnieper were the cataracts of its eastern bend where the river narrowed between cliffs. Ledges of rock along the shore here made the quieter water innavigable, unless the boats were towed by hand between the rocks. In midstream, the current raced through a series of rapids, to each of which the voyagers had given a name— the Sleepless, the Insatiable, the Laughing Water and the Boiler, and so on.

At these rapids guards of fighting men were thrown out against any raid by the steppe horsemen, in this case the Betchenaks, a Turkish people. Slaves unloaded the larger craft, which were floated down and loaded again in quieter water.

Off the Dnieper estuary, the survivors of the convoy gathered at an island where the ships were refitted for sail and navigation at sea. From this point they skirted the shore of the Black Sea, followed along the land by tribesmen who attacked them when they were driven ashore by heavy weather or need of fresh water. In turn, the convoy was apt to attack an ill-defended port of the Byzantines on the way to the great metropolis of the world. When the prospect of loot appeared more lucrative than any advantage from trade, they did so. In fact they had often tried their strength against the defenses of Constantinople herself, in their trade-or-raid voyages—the Ancient Chronicle mentions ten organized "expeditions" of this kind in the space of a hundred and eighteen years.

These voyagers of Rus had an amazing knowledge of the outer world as it could be reached by *sea*. They knew that the coast of the Land of Silk (China) could be reached to the east, and that Britain was an island beyond the western lands, inhabited by children of Japhet; they understood that if you sailed past Constantinople, you passed in time from the Middle Sea (Mediterranean) to the outer ocean over which a long way led past the isle of the Britons up northerly into the Sea of the Variags, whence by river and portage in the land of Rus the voyager could return to the Dnieper again, by the road "from the Variags to the Greeks." [4] So says the Ancient Chronicle.

The knowledge displayed by such chroniclers among a barbaric people is surprising enough. It extended to what most Europeans knew as the "sea of darkness" barred by ice. It made clear that the peninsula of Europe itself could be

[4] The Chronicle IV. ". . . there was a road which led from the country of the Variags to the Greeks, and from the country of the Greeks to the Variags, along the Dnieper; and above the Dnieper there was a portage for boats over to the Lovat; by the Lovat the way enters the great lake Ilmen; out of this lake flows the Volkhov which falls into the great lake Neva, whence it flows out to the sea of the Variags. By this sea one is able to go to Rome, and from Rome (again) by sea to Constantinople and from Constantinople to the Black sea into which discharges the river Dnieper. For the Dnieper rises in the forest of Okov and takes its course south; the Dvina rises in the same forest and takes its course north and discharges into the sea of the Variags. The Volga which takes its source also in this forest, takes its course eastward."
This forest lay about two hundred miles west of Moscow, in the highlands of the portage region.

circumnavigated by land as well as by sea. It stretched far beyond their knowledge of their own great continental plain. The land even beyond the Volga they called the Unknown Land. Yet for a time the trade route "from the Variags to the Greeks" was the most important in Europe.

All that is not so surprising as the mobility of the peoples of Rus. They did not migrate in a mass, they simply kept on moving. This restlessness found a voice in the sayings of a later day, "A man in the saddle knows no brother," or "The sky is our rooftop." It was the restlessness of settlers, of small human groups faced with an immense terrain. By necessity they followed after water, timber, fishing, game, trade routes, better soil for grain. As very soon they were to follow after fur-bearing animals, silver, iron and gold ore.

Even then they had a saying, "Where man comes the water goes." Faced with such a contingency, European peoples had dug wells or built aqueducts. The people of Rus moved on to new water.

It is not at all clear whether such moves were planned by leaders—by the headmen, priors of churches, powerful traders—or required by the needs of the family groups. Yet it is very clear that *something* impelled these intractable groups to thrust outward toward new land. Attempts to confine them within bounds later on caused serious conflict.

This silent urge to seek better conditions was leading the ordinary folk of Rus outward, along their now familiar boulevards of the rivers, and so inevitably toward the outer seas. It was becoming an urge to the sea.

It was outmatched, of course, by the high mobility of the steppe folk, the horse-riding peoples of the south, those more efficient wagers of war who grazed their animal herds and exacted tribute from settlers over a vast area.

In this characteristic of mobility both the folk of Rus and the steppe dwellers differed utterly from the sedentary peoples of Europe proper.

There, west of the imaginary Constantinople-Riga axis, frontiers were more or less fixed, towns built of permanent stone had risen on the ancient sites of the Roman world, towering cathedrals drew human congregations into parishes, the hereditary authority of kings, dukes and princes restrained the action of peoples in feudal fashion. So, presently, would the authority of new republics restrain them. Trade guilds would maintain a hivelike activity within permanent factories, military-religious orders such as the Teutonic Knights and Livonian Knights would garrison fortifications, monasteries still serve as unchanging schools, and even the fishermen sail from the ancient ports of their ancestors.

True, throughout the European zone—the "western lands" as the men of Rus thought of them—individuals traveled readily enough along highways and footpath-ways or ancient Roman roads, but they were individuals making a journey for some purpose—couriers of lords, pilgrims shrine bound, mountebanks seeking a living, minstrels and mendicants wending by easy stages from hostel to hall to inn, paying or begging their way. *"Peregrino, quasi mendicano,"* Dante, a wandering poet, wrote in his time.

So on land; on sea it was another matter, for only merchants or masters of passenger craft faced the hazards of blue water, from port to port, after invoking St. Christopher.

Even the seafaring Arabs had taken permanent residence in Granada. The most restless groups lay close to the eastern edge of Europe—the Hungarians (Magyars), Vlachs, Bulgars, recent arrivals from the eastern steppe.

In this limbo of the east no frontiers had been clearly delineated, the few older cities like Kiev had been demolished too often to be either secure or permanent. There was no restraining authority of either Church or State to keep people confined. There was nothing at all to restrain movement except natural or human obstacles.

For a reason that will soon appear the men of Rus could not penetrate easily into the western lands of Europe. But they did have a tendency to wander as individuals. They were forever wandering down toward the Black Sea which they called at times the Sea of Rus. After being converted to Christianity—the last racial group of Eurasia to be so converted—the *krestianin* promptly began to make their way as pilgrims toward Constantinople, and by sea to the Sepulchre at Jerusalem. A certain Daniel, a prior of Kiev, making this pilgrimage very early, found a countryman living as a hermit in "the cell of Mar Saba," a cave overlooking the gorge of the Kedron; and four other pilgrims from Rus joined Daniel at the Sepulchre.

The men of Rus never lost this penchant to wander off somewhere.

The Invaders

The country around Moscow had been Finnish in the first place, especially to the northeast, along that favored wooded plain lying between the Oka and the upper Volga (the fertile Mesopotamia of Rus). The older names here, like that of the river Oka, are Finnish as well as Slavonic.

For a long time the Finnish peoples had been more numerous than the incoming Slavs. Keeping to a forest life— they had drifted here from the dense forest belt of the far northeast (modern Siberia)—they had resisted and then had become more or less reconciled to the advent of the more intelligent Slavs who had refused to be bound by the limitations of a forest economy.

But there had been no mass killing of the native population by the newcomers. There were no fields strewn with skeletons here as in the southern steppe. Neither the Finns nor these eastern Slavs were *warlike*.

(Long since, the Slavs whose ancestral homeland had been close to the Pripet marshes—in the center of the invisible line that divided "Europe" from Eurasia—had separated, for unknown reasons, into three groups. The first, the western Slavs, had edged back toward the Vistula River. The second, the middle Slavs, had worked its way south through the Carpathian barrier. The third, the eastern branch, had progressed east across the Dnieper, reaching the headwaters of the Don, keeping to the fertile margin between the forest and the true steppe, mingling with the native folk rather than dispossessing them.)

Their conflict had been for possession of the land, and this slow and stubborn contest had been waged under the necessity of maintaining life on this inhospitable plain. They had adapted themselves to that necessity rather than to the transitory gain of warfare, in which they had little skill.

The Slavs themselves had edged rather than drifted eastward into the lands of Rus. It is not easy to picture them because they left little record of themselves, either in building or in writing, during these early stages. Apparently they were small-boned, rather short and dark, with long heads— folk more apt to imagine things than to come to grips with reality. Their gods had been natural and terrifying, the Bright Sun (Dajbog), the Thunder (Perun), with an accompanying host of the spirits of the woods and streams, and swamps— to the swamps lovely women shining in obscurity enticed human beings to death in quagmires. These seductive eastern lorelei were *lieshi*—"of the forests."

Certainly the Slavs, adhering together in tribes, fearful of their druidical priests, built no temples. The effigies of Perun and Dajbog had stood on earth mounds overlooking the plain.

Into this plain the eastern Slavs had progressed slowly

MOSCOW and the WEST

☐ STRATEGIC HIGHLAND AREA GIVING ACCESS
   TO RIVERS LEADING TO ALL OUTER SEAS
   AND TO EASTERN EURASIA
■ TOWN   ☐ OSTROG (BLOCKHOUSE FORT)
🛦 APPROXIMATE LIMIT OF NORTHERN FOREST BELT

from their homeland around the Pripet marshes, a wide inland water region, the source of many rivers, rich in fish and marsh grass only, but yielding some degree of security from attack. In doing so they had moved beyond reach of the nascent Germanic culture, and of the slow awakening of the European peninsula through the stages of feudal life, the code of chivalry, the recapture of classical knowledge. They had moved beyond European civilization, such as it was.

Yet they had kept some contact with their western brethren, the western Slavs, beyond the Pripet marshes. The Ancient Chronicle calls this brethren the Poliani (Poles) or People of the Plain. Apparently the writers of the Chronicle felt these Poles to be superior folk, both "wise and industrious."

More than that, the Chronicle mentions the other outthrusts of Slavs into the western lands: "The Slavs, spreading outward, have taken names from the places where they have settled—thus those settled on the river Morava call themselves Moravians, while others are termed Czechs; there are still others, the white Croats, and the Serbs." [5]

However that might be, the easternmost Slavs in Rus had changed little—remaining an isolated agricultural group clinging to waterways, activated only by old tribal customs —until the advent of the men of Rus, who quickly dominated them without in the least suppressing them.

The folk of Rus came in from Scandinavia by way of the sea.

And it was these men of Rus who gave their name to the lands, although they left no explanation of the meaning of the name. The Byzantines who knew them called them the Rhos.

Certain it is that they came in from Scandinavia, and that they were for the most part Swedish. Variags, the Slavonic writers called them, "from beyond the sea of the Variags"— from the Swedish coast. They were few in number, compared to the Slavs. Skilled navigators of the rivers, they had found their way to Lake Ladoga and past Novgorod, down to the great portage center west of Moscow's hillock, whence they reached the headwaters of the Dnieper and Volga, pushing south in their red boats with the carved dragons' heads,

[5] Tenaciously, the three groups of Slavs held to the memory of a common origin, even while they began to differ in language and customs. At least the eastern Slavs in the lands of Rus repeated the legend that they had descended from one of three brothers, Czech, Liakh (Pole) and Rus.

past the settlements of the Slavs, sailing down into the fertile steppe, crossing there over the portage from the Don to the Volga, hearing of and seeking the warm southern sea and its strange peoples. There, in the words of Igor's song, "the fair maidens of the Goths sang on the shore of the blue sea, tinkling in Russian gold."

After some two generations of this voyaging overland by ship the Variags, known as the "sons of Rurik"—the legendary Rurik—had stopped to remain there as overlords of the Slav towns, especially Kiev with its gleaming Byzantine cupolas, the Court of the Golden Heads.

The west knew them rather as Vikings or People of the Fiords—of those mist-shrouded inlets of the sea where the early Scandinavians maintained their homesteads under blaze of the northern lights. They had set out over the long ways of the sea to raid and trade and settle in kindlier lands. The Viking seafarers thrust outward early enough to the island they named the Ice-land, and to the further Green-land.

One branch, the Norse or Normans, invaded the island of the barbaric Britons. Other Norman groups gained similar footholds in the Mediterranean. But still other Scandinavians hired themselves out as mercenaries to the emperor in Constantinople—in the Varangian Guard.

The skill of the Viking folk lay in husbandry, in cattle breeding, in navigating their ships with the dragon-headed prows. By nature they were neither merchants nor warmakers. They were shrewd, practical minds, bartering for goods, enriching themselves with spoil. Their ability to organize ended at the point where they had fitted out a fleet to take the sea, or planned the economy of a small town through an approaching winter.

These Variags who had pushed east into the Slav lands, then, were warlike, but more skilled in farming than in making wars. Apparently they were invited to fortify the small Slav settlements, and having done so, they made themselves overlords of Rus. Few in number, they dominated the equally barbaric Slavs. Their own name for Rus at that time was the Land of the Towns, and to those towns they brought only a rude order.

The Russkaya Pravda or Law of the Rus—the nearest approach to the subsequent law of the land—held vestiges of the strict Scandinavian sense of property, and the right of the individual to claim damages for injury to his person—of the right of jury trial, of the price to be paid in money for a murder, the penalty for non-payment of a debt.

The code of the Pravda, however, remained theoretical; the Variag chieftains who had installed themselves as lords of the towns scattered along the rivers of Rus profited more by raid than by lawful trade. They had great physical courage, berserk tempers, and the Chronicle leaves a clear record of their bickering feuds. Of Vladimir the Splendid, grandson of Igor, it relates in curt words:

"In the year 982 Vladimir went with his Variags to Novgorod and said to the justices of Yaropolk [his brother], 'Go to the residence of my brother and tell him Vladimir is about to go against him—let him prepare for combat.' And he settled himself down at Novgorod. Then he sent to Rogvold at Polotsk this message: 'I wish to take your daughter to wife.' Rogvold asked his daughter, 'Are you willing to marry Vladimir?' She replied: 'I am not willing to be pursued by the suit of Vladimir, the son of a serving woman.' Rogvold had come from beyond the sea to reign at Polotsk. . . .

"The messengers of Vladimir went back and told him what had been answered by Rogneda, daughter of Rogvold, prince of Polotsk. Thereupon Vladimir assembled a host of Variags and Slavs . . . and marched against Rogvold. At this moment they [at Polotsk] wished to marry Rogneda to Yaropolk. Yet Vladimir went to Polotsk and killed Rogvold and two of his sons and took his daughter to wife and marched against Yaropolk."

This feud between two Variag families was carried on by a handful of fighting men on either side, and its chief consequence was that the towns changed masters, enriching the victors. Actually, after besieging Yaropolk and killing him in Kiev, Vladimir installed himself there as overlord of the best section of Rus, that around Kiev. The feud, however, did not end with that. A certain Variajko, an officer of Kiev, escaped to the Betchenaks in the steppe and carried on guerrilla raids against Kiev until Vladimir managed to make him return to loyal service under oath. Nor was Vladimir's mastery of Kiev untroubled. "Then Vladimir possessed himself bodily of his brother's wife, a Greek [Byzantine] woman; she got pregnant and gave birth to Sviatopolk. Thus out of the root infected by evil grew bad fruit; for the mother of Sviatopolk was a religious woman and Vladimir had her without marrying her . . . and had no love for the son."

His own followers displayed a spirit as unruly and preda-
tory as their feudal lord's. "Then his Variags said to
Vladimir, 'This town belongs to us because we captured it;
we wish that it be bought back from us at the rate of
two *grivnas* [a small silver coin] for each inhabitant.' And
Vladimir told them: 'Wait a month until the marten skins
are gathered in.' They waited a month, and he gave them
nothing. And his Variags said: 'You have tricked us—show
us the road towards the Greeks [Byzantines].' He bade
them 'Go' and he picked out from among them some good
men, intelligent and brave, and gave to these land holdings.
The others went on to Constantinople. And he sent envoys
in advance of them to the emperor to relate: 'There are
Variags on the way to you; do not keep them in the city,
for they will work mischief, as they have here; disperse
them in different places and do not let one of them return
here.' "

In this miniature epic is reflected the weakness of the
Scandinavians who had migrated from small homesteads to
dominate the vast plains of Rus for a few generations. Independent and careful and just by nature, they entangled
themselves in internecine feuds, matched trickery against
armed force for small gains. Except for their magnificent
conquest of the river routes, they displayed no ability to
cope with this immense frontier.

Instead, they built up their towns, designing small white
cathedrals crowned by delicate gold-bulbed domes; into their
towns they welcomed the eastern folk, learning the while the
varied tongues of the east; around them gathered the rude
culture of Kievan Rus.

Theirs had not been a conquest of the Slavs as a people;
they blended with the larger mass of the Slavs, leaving their
names and the tradition of leadership as tangible heritage.

The song of Igor relates: 'Now at once arose a weary
time . . . the quarreling of the princes destroyed them
against the pagans. For brother spoke out to brother—'This
is mine, and that is mine as well.' And the princes began
to dispute much of a paltry thing—'This is great.' And to
forget feuds among themselves against themselves, so that the
heathen advanced from all sides into the land of Rus."

This internecine strife of Variag family against family
became a heritage of the masters of Moscow, very soon
thereafter.

Beside the quarreling, the wording of the song of Igor reflects the weakness of the Scandinavian-dominated Slavs

against the pressure of the "pagans" who ranged the open grasslands—the corridor of the steppes—from the headwaters of the Don to the Black Sea. Always the strongest of the migrating peoples, emerging from mid-Asia, had sought this righ black earth belt, watered by its network of rivers. The Magyars, and then the Khazars (moving up from the Caucasus), half-cultured Turkish people, followed by other Turks from the eastern steppe, Betchenaks and Kumanians had lorded it over this southern frontier, pressing the milder Scandinavian-Slavs northward, coming in, as the song has it, "from all sides."

Once the Don had been known as "the river of the Slavs"; once the far-wandering Variags had held the Don's mouth, on the blue sea where they left the remnant of a town, their Asgard (Az-gorod, which became Azov), with others on the lovely shores of the Crimea where remnants of them still clung, with remnants of elder folk, Goths and Magyars.

So at the beginning of the thirteenth century, the barbaric Turkish clans were still penetrating eastward along the open plains. Their ruling chieftains were still the kagans, or kha khans, the great khans of Asia. Their pressure upon the folk of Rus, however, was that of numbers and vitality rather than the conflict of war; in blood and customs, they blended with the "sons of Rurik" and their dependent Slavs, who had withdrawn to the bluff of Kiev, cut off from the sea by the Asiatic hordes.

For two centuries the most powerful neighbors of the men of Rus had been these eastern nomads, and that long association was to have its effect upon the Scandinavian-Slavs retreating now to the northern forest belt.

The Spectral Voyage of St. Andrew

Christianity came to the land of Rus in the time of the brief overlordship of the Variags, the sons of Rurik. It did not, however, serve to unite these people exiled in the east more closely with the Christians of western Europe—who had known the authority of the Church for nearly five centuries. In fact it served to widen the breach between them.

The folk of Rus became converted to the ritual of the eastern Church, which centered in Constantinople, while the Europeans proper, including the western Poles, had followed the rites of the Catholic, administered from Rome. But more than this semipolitical cleavage was the difference that the Slavs accepted the Christian religion only by slow degrees and then in a way of their own.

Just as the deities of the pagan Scandinavians had not replaced but had merged insensibly with the nature gods of the Slavs—shaped not a little by the superstitions of the Finns —so the concept of Christianity was merely added at first to the old religion. You might say that these men and women of Rus could not be converted; they had to be convinced. And they were convinced in the early stages more by works than by faith. The *power* of the new deities had to be demonstrated by performance. The power of the old gods residing in trees and stones, in running streams and in the depths of the forest, was too apparent to be denied overnight. What in the new faith was to prevent the supernatural destructive force of an early frost that blighted the corn crop, of a murrain among the cattle, or a dry season that brought famine into the land? The folk of Rus believed stubbornly in the *old*, except when a miracle happened.

Vladimir the splendid and unruly, the overlord of that day—who held most of the towns of Rus but could not organize them into any workable whole—apparently commanded that images of the old deities be burned, and the people be baptized in the new faith, but his command accomplished little.

The Chronicle relates how Vladimir arranged a demonstration of the impotency of Perun, the thunder deity, whose wooden image stood on a mound. "He ordered [them] to fasten Perun to the tail of a horse and drag him . . . to a stream; and he instructed a dozen men to beat *him* with their staffs, not that he thought the wood had any feeling, but to mock the demon within. . . . While they dragged him thus along the stream down to the Dnieper, the *pagan folk wept for him*. Then after he had been dragged in this manner, they cast him into the Dnieper."

This tradition repeats that Vladimir and his immediate followers waded first into the river, up to their chests and necks, to be baptized, while the common folk argued that, "If this faith is not good for them, the prince and his boyars would not have accepted it."

(The boyars were the men who served the princes, at once companions and fighting men, the *druijina* of Igor's host. They held themselves superior to the mass of Slavs, the *smerdi* or "simple" folk, yet there were Slavs among the boyars, and even a few Finns, as there would soon be Turkish families, and Lithuanians.)

The folk of Rus had had no difficulty in identifying the

Scandinavian thunder god, Thor, with the ancient Perun; but only after a long time did they manage to merge this dual pagan deity with anything Christian, and then it was quite inexplicably with the prophet Elijah. St. Basil (Vasily) was also accepted as a wonder-worker, along with St. Nicholas.

On the whole they found it easier to accept the demons of medieval Christianity than the saints. In their imagination—and the Slavs had very active imagination—the malignant powers lurking in swamps and gorges, even in stables and around sickbeds—mostly spirit women and vampires—had not ceased to assail them. They were impressed by the splendor of Byzantine liturgy, by magnificent vestments and glittering paintings of the new saints, all of which made a church something of a dream world. But they were more moved by pictures revealing the torments of the Last Judgment.

These superstitions were shared by the sons of Rurik themselves. In this land where Church and State had no authority, the people clung obstinately to old beliefs, distrusting what was new; the princes themselves merely carried out old customs. Power resided only in the incalculable forces of nature, more destructive than beneficial.

It was a strange, primitive mental trauma, and it set the folk of Rus apart from more enlightened westerners for centuries. It did more than that. In some manner, clear only to the Slavic mind, it made any ruler over them henceforth appear to be only the intermediary of divine power.

With the churches, the Slavic mind accomplished a transformation quite as unexpected. The clergy, from monks to priors, appeared to be the servants of the same divine power. Henceforth their task would be to aid cultivation, to interpret omens and to ward off evil powers. And especially at harvest and planting time to bless the soil for the people—to bring forth their wonder-working images out of the churches into the country in times of the direst trouble.

So in clumsy fashion but inexorably the Slavic mind formed a concept of ruler and priest to fit the land itself. This concept would influence happenings in the future very greatly. For when the folk of Rus did believe in the Orthodox faith, they made it peculiarly their own and believed blindly.

For the present old superstitions prevailed. A monastery was built where lightning had struck a certain rock overgrown by trees; small holy pictures, *ikons,* were set up in the niches by the cabin doors where birch twigs sacred to the old gods had hung over a lighted candle. A legend came into being, no one knew how, that in elder days the apostle Andrew had visited Rus by way of Constantinople, and the Dnieper to Novgorod. St. Andrew, it seemed, had followed the very road of the Variags.

Sorcerers collected followers easily by a display of miraculous powers. The Chronicle tells of one, named Simon. "By enchantment, he made dogs speak with human voices, and he changed old people into young." At Novgorod in the time of the Variag prince Gleb, a magician claimed to have power in him to walk over the Volkhov River. He mocked the Christians and gained a following among those who believed him to be inspired, until they prepared to kill their bishop. "The bishop took up a cross, and put on his vestments, and spoke: 'Let those who believe in the magician go over [to stand] by him. Let those who have faith come around the cross.' At that they divided into two companies. The prince, Gleb, and his armed escort passed over to the bishop, and all of the people followed after the magician. And grave troubles arose between them. Gleb, holding an ax under his coat, went out to find the magician, and said to him: 'Know you what will happen tomorrow—and today, before evening?' He said: 'I know everything.' And Gleb said: 'Then you know what is going to happen today?' He said: 'I will work great miracles.' Gleb pulled out his ax and killed him; he fell dead and the people dispersed."

Miracle workers, interpreters of dreams, people inspired by voices, voluntary exiles in the forest, naked fanatics with hair uncut—all these were to appeal to popular credulity for a long time, until, for example, Rasputin.

There was little *rule* to the Church on this eastern frontier that knew neither monastic orders, disciplined friars, nor organized crusades. The Eastern Church, Byzantine in its origin, never formed a link between its human servants and its inhuman imagery of ascetic saints and Days of Judgment. It remained insensible to the changing thought of the west.

(In the west a Jean de Meung could jest at sacred cows in a *Roman de la Rose,* while a Dante combined Virgil's Inferno with Christian imagery, and a Thomas Aquinas, aware of Arabian philosophy as well as the arguments of nascent science, could defend Christian belief as an ultimate truth in his *Summa Theologiae.*)

In Rus, little was written except ritual, and that in Greek penned by the few churchmen who could read and write. In the west Latin was becoming the common language of Church,

State and Science. It was spoken more and more, for instance by the western Slavs now known as the Poles.

All this widened the breach between the eastern Slavs of Eurasia and the peoples of the west, not because the Slavs in Rus had changed but because the peoples of the west were changing rapidly in a renaissance.

Yet the people of Rus did wreak a transformation in the stultified Eastern Orthodox Church bequeathed to them by Constantinople. (Just as they had transformed their local rulers into an odd combination of guardians and landowners.) While the churches themselves remained copies of the Byzantine, small and dark, many-cupolaed, gleaming with patterned paintings and mosaics, the *monasteries* expanded to meet the needs of the frontier.

These monasteries grew into great rambling log structures with outwalls and fortified towers, filled with increasing garrisons of human beings who were not learned scholars but beekeepers, grain growers, wine brewers, physicians of sorts and moneylenders, who also lent seed for planting and gave out food in famines. And among them were artists who put life into the stiff imagery of Byzantine painting.

On its part the Orthodox Church supplied the scattered peoples of Rus with a common bond, a mutual dream and a fear. To that extent, it united them for the first time.

Curiously enough the influence of Christianity and especially of Byzantine customs seemed to act to reduce women in Rus to inferior beings. In the elder Slavic tribes women had appeared to enjoy much freedom and some protection. They had always worked the soil equally with the men. Now a vogue of witch-hunting arose to harass them. Woman, it seemed, was the natural enemy of asceticism.

"What is she," a religious tract inquired, "but a net in which to draw men by attraction of eyes, and flesh?" Even the Chronicle reflects this conviction. "Diabolical spells are worked by women who are weak and beautiful." Villagers held, in agreement, that the evil spirits of the wasteland were feminine—the *vourdalaki* (vampires), *lieshi* (marsh sprites) and a *viedma* (witch). If a Joan of Arc had appeared in the villages of Rus she might have been driven forth to the forests to consort with the spirits that had given her visions; she could not have been entrusted with authority because there was no concept among people or ruler of a maid who could advise them.

These easterners differed from their western brethren in another way. They lacked the stimulus of life and the sharpening of minds found in the great western cities, such as Cordoba, Ravenna or Constantinople itself. Few people stayed within their small towns. In fact, there was here no separation between town and country life. Their word *gorod* for "town" signified only the fortified knoll of a region, in which the people might take refuge.

They developed another peculiarity, as time went on. Deprived of their slender contacts with the west (along the old avenues of trade to the Baltic, and to Constantinople), they came into increasing contact with the far southeast, that is, with the Persian-Arab culture of the Caspian region, by way of the Volga. Arab coins appeared in the market places. In the small cathedral of St. Vasily of Kiev purely Persian paintings turned up on the walls of the stairways. Weights of the weighing scales—iron coated with thin bronze so that no one could cut them down without the cheat becoming apparent—were Persian in standard, not European. The very churches themselves, the newest ones, had figures carved in their stonework that were Armenian or Persian in origin.

This influence of the east did not reach the folk of Rus directly but through the peoples of the marginal lands, not so much through the Laps and Finns, who were isolated in the north, as from the Bulgars of the upper Volga, the neighboring Mordvas and Cheremiss, and the steppe nomads of the south—the Khazars, Betchenaks and Polovtsi. The settlers adopted some of the weapons and much of the way of life of the tribal folk, and the conflict between them was rather the attrition of a new frontier than organized war. "A Polovtsi rides in," the chronicles explain, "to where a peasant works his fields. With his javelin the rider kills the man, and carries off the woman and children from the cabin, which he burns with its byres."

Such captives would be sold as slaves. Between raids, trade went on. At times the more warlike steppe dwellers held southern Rus under tribute. The intelligent Khazars, converted in great part to Judaism, took a sword from each house for tribute, and the story runs that they were disturbed by finding these two-edged swords better than their own scimitars. Then again payment of a squirrel skin was made to the masters of the steppe by the owner of each house—little more than a token tribute.

Subject to such influences, the folk of Rus grew into something unlike any human entity in Europe. Almost leaderless, held together by no national tie, the future of this *Russian people* remained uncertain.[6]

For a space, even while it gathered together, the Russian people almost disappeared from the sight of Europeans—as if it had sunk into the seemingly limitless expanse of forest and steppe to the east. It had become lost and inert. Although Christian, it had departed so far from the ritual of European Christians that it was often called pagan.

Only in the extreme northwest and southwest did irregular contact continue with the homeland—called vaguely by the Russians "the western lands." In the north the city settlement of Novgorod (New City) had thrived on fur and fishing, and had developed alone into a merchant oligarchy, sturdily independent of the rest of the land. Here trade contact was maintained with the Baltic region, through the Hanseatic merchants.

In the south Kiev almost formed a state of its own, highly disordered but stimulated by intercourse with the Black Sea region and the rising kingdom of Poland. We find mentioned at this time two dim bastions within the wilderness of Rus— "Lord Novgorod the Great" and "Kievan Rus."

The mid-region, that of the great central plain, almost disappeared from view. True, names of feudal areas appear in

[6] How the Russian character was formed by its environment is well told by V. O. Kliuchevsky (*History of Russia,* translation by C. J. Hogarth, Vol. I, p. 217).

Of the Great Russian during this formative phase, Professor Kliuchevsky says, in part: "We can see him contemplating his surroundings, and thinking how best he can identify them with the names and festivals of his saints, since it was the Church's calendar which served him both as note book of nature-observation and diary for the register of his thoughts concerning his daily toil. . . .

"The natural features of the country led to the adoption of habitation in small, isolated hamlets. Naturally this did not teach the Great Russian to act in compact masses. . . . It was a silent, secluded struggle in which he was engaged, which left him no time to think of the community nor yet of his relations toward his fellow men. This made him self-centered, cautious and diffident in public. . . . Hope of success (to this day) arouses all his energies, but attainment of success leaves him cold again. . . . The Great Russian belongs to that type of humanity which deteriorates from the moment that it first becomes aware of its own powers. . . .

"The changes and chances of life early taught him to look back whence he had come rather than forward whither he was going . . . and [to be] attentive to consequences rather than to their prevention . . . his mental process leads him to make straight for his goal (ill-considered though the goal often be); he does so looking to either side of him as he goes. Circumstances and the forces of nature have combined to teach the native of Great Russia to try all roads when making for a given point, and to think and act as he goes along."

the chronicles—Smolensk, Suzdal, Riazan, Chernigov—but without semblance of unity, force or even culture. (In the "western land" adjacent to this mid-region beyond the Pripet marshes, the kingdom of Poland had developed around Kracow, with a well-defined noble class speaking Latin and able to read—very soon there would be a university at Kracow. Already these Poles spoke of the vanished eastern Slavs as Russian barbarians, and Asiatics.)

Deep in this mid-region the sprawling wooden town of Moscow and the Moskva River had been lost to sight.

Nothing new or unusual had happened *within* the lands of Rus, dislocated as they were by feuds and by partitioning off the land among sons and retainers of landowners. No inner force whatever had manifested itself in this time of stagnation.

This stagnation had been caused by happenings elsewhere beyond the frontiers. And those forces from outside drove the scattered nuclei of the Russian people toward the central plain, around Moscow.

II

HOW THE TATAR YOKE WAS BROKEN:
1238—1462

The Outer Forces

IN THE beginning of the thirteenth century the men of
Rus had been losing in their contest for the steppe. Toward the Black Sea the moribund framework of the Byzantine Empire clung precariously to the shores.

Then a convulsion of the peoples in the west paralyzed
Constantinople itself. The first crusaders, almost as dangerous a threat to the Byzantine city as to the Moslems in
Jerusalem, drew the energies and attention of the Byzantines
southward. Trade up the Dnieper almost ceased.

On the heels of the crusaders appeared the fleets of the
Italian merchant republics—Venetian and Pisan at first.
These shrewd traffickers, armed like the earlier Vikings for
combat but much preferring the profits of peace, channeled
the grain and hide and slave trade of the Black Sea[1] westward.

After a space the Venetians managed to divert one crusad-
ing expedition to the capture of Constantinople itself. This
foray of Christendom devastated the imperial city, and crippled what remained of the Byzantine network of trade. Almost immediately both Venetians and Genoese began to
build competitive *comptoires* at the mouths of the Back Sea
rivers.

The Russians, far from reaching the Black Sea now, seldom appeared in the steppe. Simultaneously the outer forces
closed other avenues to them.

---

[1] Called by the Greeks who first explored it the Euxine or Pleas-
ant Sea, because it was pleasanter to navigate than the Mediterranean.
Constantine Porphyrogenitus named it simply Pontus (The Sea) at a
time when the Variags held it to be "Our Sea." It was actually darker
than the Mediterranean, and the first Russian name to stick was
Charnomore or Dark Sea.

Segments of Turks driven onward by propulsion from within central Asia began to occupy Asia Minor and the Mediterranean shore. Baghdad and Persia ceased to be centers of luxury trades, and the traffic up the Volga dwindled.

Armed Muscovite boyars, early sixteenth century. The quilted jackets protected against cold. (From contemporaneous sketch reproduced in Sigismund von Herberstein's *Rerum Moscoviticarum Comentarii*, edition of 1571)

To the north, pressure was exerted along the Baltic by twin organizations arising in the west during and after the crusade movement. A trade monopoly strongly armed, the Hansa League, extended its *kontors* from the German rivers toward the eastern Slavs. The walled warehouses of the Hansa advanced rapidly from Dantzig at the mouth of the Vistula to the Dvina, and thence to thriving Novgorod. Keeping pace with the trade monopoly, the militant Order of Teutonic Knights moved more cautiously east, building fortified commanderies out from Marienburg and Konigsberg beyond Riga, which became the base of this German move to the east.

The ostensible objective of the Teutonic Knights (soon

combined with the Livonian Knights of the Sword) was to convert the then pagan Prussians and Lithuanians. But behind the military order and the merchants' monopoly followed Germanic colonization and industry.

Against this penetration, the different Slavic people reacted sharply, intensifying in so doing the long racial conflict between Teutons and Slavs. In turn Poles and Lithuanians (then both together) resisted the League and the Knights. Novgorod—Lord Novgorod the Great—although aided at first by an increase in its westbound traffic, also made a stand against the invaders. The German organizations gave to their thrust toward the resources (the timber, wool, fish, flax and hemp) of the Baltic's end the name of a crusade against the *pagan* and barbaric Russians.

Whether pagan or not, the men of Novgorod fought off the invaders, driving the Swedes back from the mist-filled mouth of the Neva, and breaking the strength of the heavily armed Teutonic Knights on the ice of Lake Peipus. Out of these combats Alexander Nevsky gained his fame. The chroniclers say that the ice could not be seen for the darkness of blood upon it, yet they saw the phantom bark of their hero saints, Boris and Glebe, sailing to their aid.

Moscow within the Second Mongol Zone

Moscow, in the middle plain, had been isolated and remote from this German advance into the northeastern frontier of Eurasia. The Oka-Volga valley stagnated with its half-formed settlements until the advent of a force that was cataclysmic.

The Mongol armies from the far eastern steppes overrode the lands.

To the men of Rus these armies of disciplined horsemen, moving over the ice of the rivers in midwinter and cutting roads through the forests, seemed to be an apparition from another world. Scattered in their towns, the *kniazes,* the princes of Rus, proved to be incapable either of uniting or of resisting.[2] "It was too late," the Chronicle of Novgorod explains, "to oppose the wrath of God."

To these communities—since they intended to establish permanent dominion over this portion of the continent—the

[2] Details of the Mongol campaigns of invasion are given in *The Earth Shakers: The March of the Barbarians,* and *Tamerlane* by Harold Lamb. And in *L'Empire des Steppes* by René Grousset, Paris, 1938.

Mongols offered generous terms of submission—"demanding from them," the Novgorod Chronicle explains, "one tenth of everything: of peasants and nobles and horses and goods, of everything one tenth. And the princes without letting them into their towns went forth to meet them, saying, 'Only when none of us are left alive, then all will be yours.'"

And so it happened. Many of the princes of Rus resisted and met a "bitter and violent death." Some fled headlong to safety in the west; a few bowed their heads to the invaders.

Of Moscow, the Chronicle says bluntly, "And the men of Moscow ran away, having seen nothing." That is, they escaped into the woodlands before the arrival of the dreaded Mongol horsemen (winter of 1237–38). The wooden wall was burned, with most of the town. Moscow, poorly built and undefended, had little attention from the invaders.

The larger and richer towns of the region were defended. Riazan was stormed and left burning with its people tortured and bleeding in the streets; Vladimir, where stone churches housed famous images, served as a refuge for the countryside, until it was broken into, and the frantic people who packed themselves into the cathedrals were burned with the buildings.

When the Mongols turned south, the southern cities and Kiev suffered as severely. Only Novgorod far in the north escaped capture. A Mongol column working toward Novgorod became disgruntled in the swamps and continued rain. It came within fifty miles of the rich merchants' republic but turned back through the forest, obscured by mist.

So Novgorod was spared the Mongol invasion. With its fur and fish dominion it remained as it was to wage its alternate war and trade with the Christian powers holding the Baltic.

For two years (1240–41) the Mongol wave of invasion swept westward, after engulfing Kievan Rus, to the southwest.

In their advance, they dislocated the populations in many of the western lands. Fragments of the occupants of the southern steppe, like the Bulgars and Betchenaks, had been driven ahead of them into the refuge of the Balkan highlands; regions like Silesia, Moravia and the Hungarian plain became almost depopulated and were settled thereafter by German-speaking peoples. The western Slavs beyond the Pripet swamp area had fared little better than the Slavs of Kievan Rus.

So heavy had been the impact this time that the heads of

state of western Europe expected a renewal of the attack upon the dwindling area of Christendom. The saintly Louis, king of the French, assured his anxious mother, "When the *Tartars* come, we will either drive them back to Tartary or we will be elevated ourselves to the blessedness of the chosen souls."

This spirit of fatalism in the west did not for long obscure the truth that the Mongols had prevailed over all resistance by expert handling of trained armies. Frederick of Hohenstaufen, head of the Holy Roman (or German) Empire, and a discriminating observer, understood this. "This ferocious and barbarous nation . . . have a head whom they venerate and whose orders they blindly obey, calling him the God of earth. . . . Up to the present time they have had no other [metal] armor than rough and ill-joined plates of iron. But already—and we cannot utter it without a groan—they are beginning to equip themselves better from the spoils of Christians. These Tartars are mounted on the finest horses and . . . they now dress richly and with care. They are incomparable archers."

Both the King of France and the Roman Emperor expected the Mongol armies to resume their advance into western Europe. But the invaders had planned otherwise. At the line of the Danube they had progressed more than forty-five hundred miles from their homeland beside Lake Baikal; they had also passed beyond the limits of the steppes. After raiding around Vienna and down to the shore of the Adriatic, they began their great withdrawal to the territory they intended to occupy.

Abandoning the Hungarian plain, the Carpathians and the Balkans, they moved back toward the Russian plain.

In withdrawing they took with them the movable spoil of southeastern Europe—the cattle, human captives, wheeled vehicles loaded with grain, cloth and utensils. Most of the richer cities like Kracow were burned, and the agriculture destroyed, so that famine and typhus followed the retreating armies.

This destruction was part of the Mongol plan. They had extended outward by creating concentric zones of conquest. The first had been the one they intended to occupy themselves. This was the Russians' Unknown Land beyond the Volga, where the ruling Mongols had wedged themselves among peoples now allied to them, the Turkish Kipchaks, Bulgars of the Volga, and the Bashkirs who were descendants of the earlier steppe nomads.

So they retired from Europe to the left bank of the Volga,

at the edge of their zone of occupation, making the Volga River their true frontier.

Next to this, in their plan, lay the second or *subjected* zone. Here the towns—or the remnants of them—were not occupied but laid under tribute. The population kept its own rulers, but paid tribute to the Mongol conquerors in food-stuffs and furs—there was little money, and the Mongols at first did not want coin—and supplied a yearly draft of the younger men for military service. By this constant draft of fighting men, the Mongols insured themselves against armed strength rising in the subjected zone, which was also laid under rigid obligation to keep the peace. Disobedience within this zone might bring a retaliatory raid of the dreaded Mongol horsemen. Rebellion would draw a punitive expedition, to destroy dwelling places and transport the population to be sold as slaves.

The observant friar, John of Plano Carpini—the first west-erner to arrive of his own will at the remote court of the Great Khan in the east—caught something of the significance of these outer zones. "No one kingdom or territory," he explained in his report, "can resist the Tartars, because they gather men for war from every land that is *subjected* to their dominion. And if any *neighboring* region refuses to join with them, they invade and lay it waste, slaughtering the inhabitants or carrying them off into captivity."

So in the third or hostile zone the Mongols had struck heavily against the Poles, Teutonic Knights, Hungarians, and had scorched the earth as they retired to make it a wasteland through which any other Christian armies from the west would have difficulty in passing. They had retired across the second, subjected zone to the security of the inner occupied zone where they intended to remain.

Actually they halted and settled down along the left or eastern bank of the river Volga.

So their second, outer, zone extended from the line of the Volga to the line of the Dnieper—the old river road of the Variags. Along this latter line, according to their methodical plan, full destruction had been carried out. West of it the lands and peoples were marked for action as against enemies.

By accident of geography, the town of Moscow lay almost in the center of the new Mongol second zone, of subjection.

Certainly no living person in half-burned Moscow had had anything to do with this ordering of their future by these outer forces. At the first impact the inhabitants of settled places had fled to the woods and to the smaller hamlets of the *smerdi*, the "stinking ones," sheepskin wearers, fishers and hunters. Sheltered in huts, they were able to plant and harvest enough food to supply themselves, avoiding town sites and traveled roads, through which agents of the new military occupation were perpetually passing. Friar John speaks of the "overseers, secretaries, scribes and agents" of the Mongol military commanders.

After their withdrawal beyond the Volga, the Mongols made it their policy to treat all the subjected zone—which included most of the Russian lands—leniently enough. Subjection being complete, they wished only to draw a profit from these lands.

To do so, they made a census of all observable households, and fixed a tax rate of five pelts (ranging from white bearskins to beaver and skunk) upon each house. Even the merchants of Novgorod paid a token tribute.

Over the primitive Russian roads new activity surged. Under direction of the Mongol *darugashis*, or road managers, convoys of laden carts moved eastward; couriers bearing Mongol mail passed through at headlong pace, the chiming of bells on their reins heralding their coming to the relay stations where fresh horses waited.

At crossroads, or town gates, control stations were established. Here a careful record was kept by diligent Chinese scribes of travelers passing through. Staffs of other Chinese industrialists studied the breeds of cattle, the furs, herbs and products of an area, to discover what had most value, for taxation.

So complete was this domination of the land by the agents of the new authority that the first visitors said it was like coming into another world. Friar William of Rubruk, passing through as envoy from St. Louis, relates that he was warned by Mongol officers to consider if he could stand the journey to the Great Khan at Karakorum in the east, for the cold in winter "is extreme enough to break down trees, and crack stones asunder."

After inspection, Friar William was provided with an outfit of clothing—sheepskin-lined coat and trousers, felt foot socks and boots, and a leather hood. "Each day we went as well as I could guess about as far as from Paris to Orléans, and more, according to the relays we had. Some days we would change horses two or three times . . . they always selected a strong horse for me because I was corpulent. . . . In the morning they gave us something to drink or

34

boiled millet, after which we had nothing until evening when meat was issued us, with good broth . . . in all the journey we only rested one day, when no horses were available."

Close behind the stout friar followed the brothers Nicholas and Maffeo Polo upon the same route, cared for in the same manner, to be followed later by young Messer Marco Polo—all three of them enterprising merchants from Venice. Neither Venetians nor Genoese had lost any time in establishing, from their ports around the Black Sea, trade relations with the all-powerful Mongols.

The new Mongol post roads, used for military transport as well as trade, ran necessarily west to east, keeping entirely to the land. Their route from the lower Volga southward circled the Caspian and passed through the Caucasus range. Partly for practical reasons and partly from superstition the newcomers from the steppes avoided rivers and seas, disliking even to pass through running water. Throughout Russian territory the old river routes fell into disuse, while travel overland to the far east became possible for the first time.

Friar William relates that when his party crossed the Don they were ferried over, carts and all, by Russian ferrymen; but when he asked the Russians for horses they told him to go to the Mongol post station.

Farther west the Poles christened these new land routes the "black roads" because they were used so often for Mongol raiding expeditions that swept into the country at great speed and then fanned out, to devastate and pillage the countryside as they withdrew. But the Polish lands were in the frontier or enemy zone.

Mongol management tended also to keep the restive Russians within communities where they could be reached easily for tax assessment. After the first exodus from the towns, the bewildered people were held to work in their own fields or shops, as peasants, bound after a fashion to the land.

Meanwhile, in spite of the new controls, a drift of population was going on. Whole communities migrated up from the devastated southern plain, boyars riding with the carts of peasants. By degrees these refugees settled in the midlands, around Moscow and in the fertile Oka-Volga valley. This drift had begun with the decline of traffic through Kiev; it was increased sharply by the Mongol invasion of the steppe. Around Moscow the thick woods offered some security, and the soil was better here than in the northern forests occupied by the Finnish peoples.

As time went on, this midland population increased, and

still inchoate, was taxed, tabulated and conscripted for war by Mongol control, which formed of it a single human mass. Enduring, and skilled in adapting itself to agriculture, which was almost its only means of subsistence for the time being, it became the human entity known as the Great Russians. Moscow lay near the center of this gathering of human beings.

The most probable outcome of this reshufflement of human beings on the Russian plain would have been a Mongol-Russian state based on the agriculture of the plain, and antagonistic to the western powers.

Nothing of the kind, however, came to pass.

Sarai, and the Law of the Khan

What did happen was more amazing. The Great Russian people, leaderless, without national ties, impoverished by the invasion, powerless to resist by military force, still held together as a people, Orthodox in religion and "owners" of the soil they worked. They endured, and so survived. But in surviving they were subjected to influences not only Mongolian but Asiatic, from which they never quite freed themselves.

They had to endure Mongol control—even if it became more and more remote control—for two centuries. For the first century and a quarter of this period of subservience, the Russians were isolated from western Europe by the newly created frontier of devastation along the line of the Dnieper (which of course soon ceased to be devastated but became a north-south corridor crossed by raiding expeditions of Asiatic and European powers).

Friar John declares that the plains around Kiev were strewn with skeletons more numerous than the living folk he met with.

Thus for more than a century the Russians were barred from active intercourse with the west while exposed to forces from the east.

For the first time the Great Russians knew inflexible authority. This authority was vested in the person of one man, in Batu Khan and those who succeeded him. It was different from the shadowy authority of the remote Byzantine emperors who were, after all, *guardians*—of the Church as well as the people. Batu was a quite human dictator, whose wishes had to be carried out like military orders. "Tsar Batu," they called him, in memory of the Roman Caesars.

"Not a dog can bark in all the lands without the permission of Tsar Batu," they added.

Not that the Russians obeyed willingly. They had a superstitious dread even of being listed in the census. Those who obeyed the Mongol orders they called "those who served." Still, the necessity to obey was impressed upon them by vicious punishment that took no account of ordinary laws. A town that had rebelled against an order of a Mongol *baskak*, or tribute gatherer, was razed so thoroughly by Batu's command that its site became overgrown with forest and vines, and it was only rebuilt after three centuries by command of Ivan the Terrible when people had returned to hunt in its forest.

A merchant or householder who failed to pay the *vyhod*—the impost tax—would find his children seized in penalty and perhaps sold down the rivers to the Italian merchants in the Crimea trading ports.

No, there was no escaping census, tax and submission to the patient, intelligent and covetous masters of the land of Rus. Yet at times, by artifice and cunning, it was possible to avoid punishment. By degrees it became important, in the minds of these silent Slavs, to manage to comply with the commands of the agents of the khans openly while secretly holding out against them. And just as slowly a concept came to the Russians, of a single, common enemy, *the* Tatar.[3]

This brooding over their foeman, the Tatar, found a voice in the cradle song of a later generation:

> Small child, sleep: dream you are fierce and brave.
> To take your arms from the wall,
> And go!
> To bind and kill the godless Tatar,
> And all his Tatarchiks.

There is something implacable in such a cradle song. But not for long were the Great Russians to take their arms and go against the godless Tatars.

[3] So the Russians in common with the European chroniclers called the Mongol-dominated peoples of Eurasia. The actual Tatars had been a small tribe between the Mongols and the Great Wall. Carpini is authority for the fact that the Mongols looked on the Tatars as inferiors, and disliked to be called by the name. The Chinese of that time also applied it to the steppe dwellers, as to stupid, doglike folk. How Europeans picked it up remains a mystery, except for the fact that the Mongol-commanded armies to invade Europe were a mixture mainly of Turkish people with some Tatars and very few Mongols. (Batu had been awarded no more than four thousand Mongols to serve him at the death of Genghis Khan.)

Just as the new overland roads opened up the fastness of Eurasia to Europeans who ventured thither for the first time, so the power of the Kha Khan or Great Khan of the steppes appeared to be limitless in its scope—extending over lands and peoples of the east unknown to the Great Russians. The very names of Cathay, Hind (India) and Nippon (Japan) had not been known to them. That the authority of one man could extend outward toward such remote corners of the earth seemed incredible. The clergy spoke of this Tatar yoke as *Bozhi batog,* the cudgel of God.[4]

For the first time the unruly princes of Rus were compelled to humble themselves before a stranger who was not of the Church. They had to greet an agent of the Khan with a gift of a goblet filled with gold, and to kneel while they listened to a message from the Khan. On entering his presence they had to "beat their forehead before his feet," that is, on the ground. A candidate for a fief in Rus, even the son of the late holder, was obliged to go in person to ask the Khan's consent to his appointment.

One, Mikhail, prince of Kiev, received a warning and a summons from Batu. "It is not fitting that you should live in the land of Kha Khan and of Batu without doing homage to them."

When the obdurate Mikhail did go to Batu at the court beyond the Volga, he was required to pass between two fires and to bow to images placed in the portal of the pavilion before being admitted to the presence of the Khan. This he refused to do, believing that the images were pagan. When his action was reported to Batu, the Khan declared, "If he will obey, he will receive his princedom from my hand, but if he refuses, he will die."

Told of this, Mikhail made answer, "To the Tsar I would

---

[4] Even in the lifetime of Genghis Khan, it had been Mongol policy to allow religious freedom within the conquered lands. In Islamic countries, however, the Church headed the resistance movement against the nomad yoke, and the Mongols soon became bitter antagonists of Islam as such.

In Rus, the conquerors exempted all churchmen, "black or white," from personal levy or taxation, on themselves or the property of the Church. In return, they availed themselves of the clergy as intermediaries, almost as collaborators, because they requested public prayers for "Tsar Batu." It was the common folk who inveighed against the "godless Tatars" until the resistance movement gained national strength, late in the fifteenth century.

By fostering the Church, making suppliants of the princes and taking yearly military drafts from the young manhood of Rus, the Tatars kept Rus leaderless rather than enslaved for more than two centuries.

bow, since God hath granted him sovereignity, but to these other things I shall not bow."

He was warned by the officer of the guard: "Mikhail, take care. Thou art dead."

When the prince of Kiev remained silent, the guards threw him down and stamped on him with their boots until they stopped his heart.

Other executions of leaders of Rus were carried out secretly. (The "Tatars" had a superstitious dread of shedding the blood of a highborn person.) Carpini believed that a duke of Suzdal was poisoned at the court of the Great Khan. "Yaroslavl, the great duke of Suzdal in Russia, was invited by the mother of the emperor, as if to honor him. After receiving meat and drink from her hand, he became sick at once upon returning to his lodging, and died after seven days' illness. Since his whole body turned a strange blue, it was believed he had been poisoned so the Tartars might gain possession of his land easily."

Alexander Nevsky, the victor in battle over the Swedes on the Neva River and the Teutonic Knights in the frozen lake, understood the futility of resisting the commands of the Tatars (as the Russians had come to call the Mongol-commanded invaders). He stood almost alone in his endeavor to make the people in Vladimir and Novgorod submit to Tatar taxation and regimentation. His son cried out publicly against a father "who put the chains of slavery upon freemen."

By abasing himself before Batu and the Great Khan, Alexander managed to keep the good will of the Tatars and to spare his cities a purge. But the burghers of Novgorod, infuriated by the imposition of the *vyhod*, stormed against the nobles "who keep rank and riches while we simple men lose what we hold most dear in life."

There was no pretense in the arrogance of the easterners who held their magnificent tent court moving up and down the east bank of the Volga, following the growth of grass. To the riders from the steppe, the man who worked in the soil or kept shop was an inferior being, bound to the toil of his hands. Defeated in war, he had become no more than a vassal who might live as he chose as long as he paid the Tatars for his living.

Among his own people Batu was named Sain Khan, "the Splendid." He had summoned Alexander Nevsky with the words, "Come to me yourself, that you may see my glory."

And glory he had. Master of the Golden Horde—the *Altyn Ordu*, Golden People, so named either because they were ruled by the imperial house of Genghis Khan or because their mobile court of great pavilions gleamed like gold on the green plain—his orders were obeyed from the northern forests to the heights of the Caucasus, the inland sea of Aral, the red deserts around Samarkand, as far as the river Irtish in mid-Asia.

This dominion stretched beyond the farthest horizons known to the men of early Rus; it had become an empire formed around the heartland of Eurasia, having at that time few cities—Sarai, the capital city of Batu, was built of mud bricks and endless lines of tents along the flat left bank of the lower Volga, but it quartered throngs of merchants, envoys, hostages, and churches were building beside mosques. William of Rubruk called it a "moving town." Encamped here on the Volga, Batu and his court were actually on the *western* frontier of an almost unlimited domain that extended to the east.

This, then, was the only empire with which the Great Russian princes and people had had experience. They had known little more of the Rome of the Caesars than the name; hardly more of the Germanic Holy Roman Empire; their contact with the Byzantine empire had come remotely through the Church. But Batu's dynamic imperium of organized armies controlling allied or subject people, drawing its sustenance from the soil of a continent, worked by inferior laborers, taking its wealth from the trade and plunder of the outer zone of civilization—under this the Great Russians were forced to exist as best they could for two centuries.

It has been said too often that these Russians were held apart from the peoples of western Europe under the "Tatar yoke" in the continuing darkness of the middle ages for those two centuries. In reality the Tatar control rested lightly on the individual Russians, interfering little with their way of life. What it did impose on the Russians was despotism.

They had been in contact with the steppe people for long generations, and had borrowed certain customs and the use of certain weapons from them; they had been overmatched before by the power of the steppe and had had to migrate at times out of the grasslands into the protecting forests. But this time they were subjected to iron despotism, and made to fear it.

The Tatar khans exacted obedience through fear; the greater the fear they inspired, the greater the obedience accorded them.

The ordinary peasant actually saw less of the Tatars than

of the earlier steppe dwellers, and he certainly intermarried less with them; but his actions—even the money he got for his grain—were subject to the compassion or anger of the invisible Tatars. He had plenty of time to ponder this because, at least around Moscow and the Oka-Volga valley, a Tatar peace had been imposed on the land. The incessant feuds of Kievan Rus were no longer allowed by the despots of Sarai.

Now the princes of Rus not only had to journey to "beat with their foreheads" before the feet of the khans to be allowed to hold their rank; they had to petition the khans for permission to wage a local war, and for two generations at least that permission was hard to get.

Since the princes were making constant journeys to and from Sarai, and often remained like Alexander Nevsky comfortably housed as a hostage at this court of the khans, they became well accustomed to the ways of the Tatars—sometimes marrying women of the Horde—and to the new despotism. This was not true of the ordinary peasantry, who had to look more to leaders of their own class and by degrees to find champions *against* Tatar exaction. So the legendary hero of the ordinary folk had become a fellow like themselves, an Ilya of Murom who "trampled the Tatars with his horse, and pierced them with his spear."

This was no more than a wishful fancy as yet, a song to be sung at remote campfires in the forest. The strength of the Tatar yoke was in the military organization behind it.

The Migration and the Monasteries

The Golden Horde itself was no more than a quarter of the immense empire of the Golden family of Genghis Khan, but it was organized as a whole within itself—the Khan reigning at Sarai was the military leader, head of the blood kin, the ever increasing family of the descendants of the conqueror now spoken of as the "great ancestor." Beneath the Golden family was the council of the Mongol generals, with the heads of the allied tribal people such as the Bulgars, and Kirghiz (the Turkish strain predominating in the Horde) and the possessors of great herds of horses and cattle. Beneath the general council rested the mass of this pastoral aristocracy, the "people who dwell in tents," now affluent enough. Beneath this favored class came the rank and file of the armies, and the huge mass of subjected peoples who lived in obedience to the will of the khans, and who yielded contributions of young men to the armies.

The Great Russians had to supply their quota of men, who served in the armies of the Great Khan to the eastward, as well as under the commanders of the Golden Horde. Being enduring, and brave enough, these Russian conscripts learned much of war under skilled commanders, and became accustomed to Tatar discipline and efficiency.

During the same time the Moscow region was spared the crushing impact of the large-scale raids that were launched from the Volga westward across the open steppe, along the invasion roads—the *czarny szlak,* or black roads of the Poles —south of ruined Kiev, against the still belligerent Christian forces in Volhynia, Poland and the rising Lithuania.[5] Contingents of the men of Rus joined the Tatars in these raids.

For nearly the first full century and a half, Moscow, unnoticed in this kaleidoscopic shifting of peoples, suffered no attack. It was allowed to germinate under the Tatar peace.

During that time, insensibly at first, it was drawn closer to the governing Tatars.

"When Batu rides forth, a small canopy is carried over his head on the points of spears," good Friar John of Carpini stated, "and the same thing is done with all the reigning

[5] At this time it was the western Slavs, the Poles, Galicians, and their allies the Lithuanians who opposed the invaders by active combat, not the eastern Slavs of Rus. Kliuchevsky, the splendid historian of the Russian people, is deceptive when he claims in his summing up under "Moscow's Service to Europe" (Vol II, p. 321): "Fate set the Russian nation at the Eastern gate of Europe to guard it from violation by the nomad brigands of Asia and for centuries the nation spent its forces in withstanding that pressure of Asiatic hordes. . . . Meanwhile Western Europe, relieved of Mohammedan attacks, turned to the New World beyond the ocean."

For the first century and a half after the Mongol conquest there was no armed resistance by the Russians as a whole. During this time, beginning with the attempt of Daniel of Volhynia to launch a crusade of Christian Europe eastward against the pagans and ending with the abortive expedition of Vitoft, Duke of Lithuania, the western Catholic peoples maintained what we would call an active front against the Asiatics.

The chart in the Moscow Historical Museum, showing the larger expeditions launched by the Golden Horde from its base at Sarai— 1260–1399—shows only one directed against the Russians at Moscow (at the end of the fourteenth century) while no less than six were launched westward across the Dnieper, three of these against the Polish capital of Kracow, and eight against the Genoese trading cities clinging to the Crimea.

What is entirely true, as Kliuchevsky no doubt meant to point out, is that the Russian people on this eastern frontier took upon itself the full impact of the invaders from the eastern steppes for centuries, at a cost in life and suffering that no western people had to meet.

Tartar princes and their wives. Batu is extremely kind to his people, yet he is held in great awe; he is exceedingly sagacious, cunning in war, and inexorably cruel in battle, in which he has had a long experience."

When Alexander Nevsky prostrated himself before Batu's golden throne by the Volga, he seemed to be an uncouth figure beneath the "Splendid" Khan. The leader of a small host of *druijina*, of men-at-arms, overlord of three towns which may have counted ten thousand houses between them, he was in fact a feudal vassal doing homage to an emperor who commanded almost unlimited power.

"I see well," Batu assured him, "that you are superior to all other princes of this land."

The grandson of Genghis Khan had been informed by spies of the situation throughout Rus; he had traveled over most of Eurasia; separating himself by degrees from the tie of obedience to the homeland in the Gobi, he had managed to bring order of a kind into this new empire of his own. He spoke three languages, and could listen to the advice of astronomers from Persia as well as to the Mongol military experts. Of the two men, he was actually the man of culture, and Alexander the barbarian.

His son, Sartak, was a Christian; there was a Christian chapel in his cosmopolitan city of Sarai. It needed only a little time, perhaps, to weld the leading class of Tatars with that of the Russians in religion, and to create a single government of the two peoples. The Russians lacked the intelligence to maneuver for this, and the Orthodox Church did not show the insight of the Roman in trying to appraise and convert the Tatar khans, who still remained pagans. Batu's younger brother, Birkai, was converted to Islam, and may have poisoned the other heir to leadership of the Golden Horde, Sartak.

Although the aristocracy of the Horde did not follow Birkai's example at first, within two generations of Batu's death, Islam had won a grip on the Horde, and Christians were in increasing disfavor.

Another force, more intangible, worked a change within the Horde, and in consequence among the subject Russians. Freed from more than a semblance of control by the great khans of the east, independent now, and with its territories fairly well reconverted after the wars of invasion, trade increased with the Black Sea region, and the Persian cities, as well as over the main continental caravan routes now in full operation. The Tatar frontier along the Volga became a merchants' paradise.

Marco Polo relates how his father and uncle, who traveled up from Sudak in the Crimea to the court of the Volga khans, presented themselves before Birkai, who "was delighted at the arrival of the two brothers, and treated them with great honor; so they presented to him the whole of the jewels they had brought with them. The prince was highly pleased, and accepted the jewels, making a return to the brothers of twice the value of the jewels."

Birkai himself habitually wore precious stones in his gold earrings, and others in his green leather girdle; he had all a Tatar's taste for splendor. Actually, the adventurous Polo brothers had done the customary thing in turning over all their stock in trade to the Khan, who gave them back goods worth twice as much to the Italian merchants.

The Tatars had set up rigid frontier inspection of imports, which paid a customs duty. The khans could, as in this instance, claim the whole of a merchant's importation, and pay back either currency or kind. They were in trade themselves.

They had established, besides, a monopoly of liquor and the manufacture of weapons, all of which must needs be bought from the imperial agents. This in turn added to the immense wealth of the treasury at Sarai.

Not content with Batu's Sarai, Birkai had built a new and finer capital of his own at the strategic spot where the Volga in its bend to the west comes closest to the eastern bend of the river Don. (Where, on the right bank, Stalingrad now stands.)

Later, even the sophisticated Arab traveler, Ibn Batuta, was impressed by the size of Birkai's Sarai, as he heard it named. "It has fine markets and great streets. The houses stand side by side, next each other, without ruins or garden space between. We mounted horses early one morning to make the circuit of the city and discover its extent, and we did not arrive at the other side until after the noon hour . . . it has thirteen large mosques for the Friday prayer. . . .

"Sarai is inhabited by people of several nations, chiefly by the Mongols who are masters of the country and only in part professing the Moslem religion . . . the Russians and Greeks [Byzantines] are wholly Christians. . . . Each different nationality occupies a separate part of the city. Merchants and visitors from the two Iraks and Syria and Egypt have a quarter to themselves which is walled in to safeguard their wealth of merchandise."

So this intelligent Arab, a century after the death of Batu, found Birkai's Sarai a truly cosmopolitan city, where foreign merchants carried on a massive trade under the loose protection and supervision of the Mongols.

The khans also held a monopoly of the land itself. The treasure of the empire gathered at Sarai was at their disposal to be given out piecemeal to those who served them.

With this entirely new personality of a khan who was *served*, of an emperor who was at once military dictator, merchant in chief, holder of monopolies, dispenser of land and treasure, the dwindling number of Russian princes were in close contact for generations as they paid their duty calls at Sarai or were kept hostage there.

And at Sarai they also made acquaintance with the forces revolving around this new swift accumulation of wealth— with conspiracy, and buying and selling of privileges. They found that by bringing valuable gifts to the feet of the khans they could obtain a *yarlig* or imperial order granting them more valuable rights or lands within Rus. The elder Polos had made a *gift* of their stock of jewels to Birkai; they had been *rewarded* with other goods.

But having once made such gifts to their covetous masters, similar payments were expected of the princes of Rus at every visitation. Then, too, even the intelligent and realistic Mongols were becoming softened by luxury, if not bewildered by the administration of wealth beyond their dreams; by degrees they were entrusting management of taxes and finance to experienced southerners, Persians, Arabs, Armenians. So the Russians found that a varying scale of payments needed to be made to these ministers who now came between them and the personality of the Khan.

Insensibly, by the very mechanism of the empire of the Horde, dealings between the Russians and Sarai changed to money transactions. A distinguished prince like Alexander Nevsky was no longer held superior to his fellows; the Russian petitioner who could pay the most profit to the Khan, or his ministers, was often granted precedence.

And more and more, by dint of money paid in, recognition was given to visitors from the unknown city of Moscow.

A change had taken place quite naturally in the Tatar administration, within Rus itself. It had come to be, as peace prevailed, simply the collection of tribute, while the armies collected loot from the belligerent peoples of the west.

The Tatar regime at Sarai no longer had need of the products of the Russian lands, of the more ordinary furs, timber, tar, hemp, flax, honey and grain. It was both simpler and more profitable to take the *vyhod* or house tax in coin. Since the Russians had no serviceable currency of their own, the practical Tatars minted coins for them at Bolghar up the Volga. The new siler coinage was called *dengi*, from the Mongolian *ding*. (Many Mongolian and Turkish words crept into the new commercial activity: such as *bazaar* for market, *tovar* for goods, *puto* for copper money.) This silver coin still had stamped on it the name of the distant Kha Khan of the Mongols, who in theory still ruled the lands of Rus through his subordinate Khan of the Golden Horde. In that century (1238–1338) all of Eurasia faced toward the point in the Gobi Desert where stood Karakorum (Black Sands), the capital city of the Kha Khan.

Quite naturally, too, the preoccupied Tatars had farmed out the tax collections in Rus to their agents, Moslem and Armenian dealers. These foreign folk rode into the villages, account books in hand, accompanied by a Tatar officer, and the Russians named them "the Squeezers." They were cruelly intent on extracting every coin or skin or bit of cloth due from the households, and when payment was not made, the *baskaks* could carry off a human being to be sold down the river into slavery, to other foreign dealers. Usually they tried to take half-grown boys and girls. And often this stirred up the villages to resistance with crude weapons. Once a *baskak* who had been a renegade priest was killed by such a mob and left to be eaten by the dogs.

As the rigid military supervision ended, and the control of later khans in Sarai relaxed, continued raids for slaves were engineered from the Volga. Such human merchandise brought a good price from the Venetian and Genoese dealers at Sudak or Kaffa in the Crimea. Yet the Russians persisted in escaping and trying to make their way back over the steppe. This stubbornness lowered their market price, and a slave dealer from the rivers would lead a captive through the covered market street of Sudak, crying aloud, "He is of the Kingdom, not from the Principality." And by this the dealer meant that his slave was a Pole, not a Russian, and so less apt to escape from a purchaser.

At the same time other Russians were escaping from bondage. Conscripts serving in the Tatar military posts had a way of vanishing by groups into the steppe. Even as early as the journey of Friar William to Karakorum, the monk-emissary reported danger along the steppe road at river crossings from outlaw Hungarians and Russians, in bands of twenty or thirty.

These half-trained deserters haunted the wastelands, avoiding the towns. In their own stubborn way the common folk of Rus resisted the dominion of the easterners, forming partisan groups in the wilderness and especially along the rivers where they could escape capture.

This mute popular revolt was mildly encouraged by the Church, which was obliged to protect the peasantry against the pagans across the Volga. In a more active and quite involuntary fashion, the Orthodox monks joined in the escape from authority. The new-built monasteries extended outward within the northern forest zone.

From the first the Tatars had spared the monasteries. Bewildered, it seems, by the lack of any central authority within the lands of Rus, the ingenious Asiatics had turned to the Church as a possible link between their government and the mass of the subject people. Churches and monasteries had no tax imposed on them. "White and black priests," as the Tatars called them, suffered no interference.

The natural consequence of this exemption was that fugitives and homeless folk took refuge within the sturdy log walls of the monastic sanctuaries. Once there, they stayed, to labor and enjoy freedom from the troubles of the towns outside. And the monasteries grew into something very much resembling fortified towns themselves.

In the old, beloved Rus of Kievan times, the monasteries had tended to follow the "road of the Variags to the Greeks," that is, the river route from Kiev to Novgorod. Elsewhere, they tended to abide close to cities like Vladimir and Suzdal, residences of wealthy princes and patrons. Now, whether reacting to the Tatar impulse or following some unvoiced impulse of their own, the monasteries began to leave the city areas and to build within the unbroken forests, far from contact with the older communities.

At times they seemed to follow the drift of the peasantry northward, and again the peasantry appeared to settle around the log buildings of a new center of ascetics, to share in the growth of the monastery within the "desert," as they called it. But nearly always the movement was led by some man with a passion for seclusion, who became on that account saintly in the eyes of his followers.

This restless plunge of monastic life into the wilderness; as restless as any other movement of the moody Slavs— drew young people along with it as well as the older monks. It set monks and peasants to work clearing and burning forest growth, plowing, building and planting, in new centers of isolation.

It drew them into the seclusion of the forest belt north of

the inconspicuous town of Moscow—a slow stream of *smerdi*, hermits, farmers without farms, peasants who turned hunters perforce, children who had lost their parents, boyars who, deprived of their estates, paid the heads of the new monasteries to be taken in and fed bodily if not spiritually in peaceful seclusion. All these elements formed an inchoate mass. Except for the spiritual guidance of the monasteries, it had no directing force.

It moved to the north of Moscow because it could not go anywhere else.

On the other three sides formidable powers lay, not ringing in Moscow so much as passing and repassing over the central plain. By the end of the thirteenth century, the Golden Horde of Batu's descendants stretched both east and south; west and south the wild horsemen of Lithuania pressed, half pagan still, making sacrifice to the god Perun in the swamplands. To the west also flew the White Eagle of the Poles, in conflict with the armored Teutonic Knights, who shared power with the merchants of the Hansa, who in turn still clung to Novgorod, where great trading companies and boatmen-pioneers ruled the river routes.

In the presence of such kaleidoscopic powers the town of Moscow might have become again a trading post, or halfway point on the river road; instead, it gained strength and was in a fair way to becoming a wealthy city.

Moscow's Peaceful Cunning

After the Mongol conquest, Moscow disappeared for a while. At least the town escaped written notice. But in the silence of the century after 1238, it was growing in size and wealth. This happened largely by a strange accident of geography, but it happened also because of what the chroniclers call "money and wit."

Obviously the churches and dwellings burned in the first rush past of the Mongol armies were rebuilt as usual after a fire. And the people flocked back from the outlying villages. The Muscovites had not resisted the armies of the east, so they were neglected in the general scramble that followed throughout the lands of Rus. Just as obviously, the Muscovites paid the *vyhod* to their Tatar overlords.

Then geography began to have its effect. On the small Moskva River, the town lay almost in the center of a ring of cities that had been more powerful—Smolensk, Tver, Vladimir, Riazan, the chief of them. For long generations before the Tatars, Moscow had been protected against damaging raids by this outer circle of more warlike centers. Vladimir had been the leading center for a while, with its miracle-working holy picture. Now these great towns had been half devastated by the Mongol conquest, and when they roused intermittently in rebellion, they suffered the more. Neglected in the center of all this, Moscow had paid its tithe and farmed its poorish soil, in peace and therefore in a relative prosperity.

To protect the outlying farms, Moscow had built block-houses along the rivers where the farmers could find shelter in a raid. Around these strategic centers villages grew up.

Now the few villages attached to Moscow—we hardly know their names—stretched outward along the Moskva River and its scanty tributary streams. They made a haphazard pattern along small waterways tending toward the richer Oka-Volga valleyland. This pattern, useless for defense, aided both trade and farming. Crops and herds increased along Moscow's network of villages, and with them grew the "treasure" of the Kremlin—money, furs and jewels.

With that the Muscovites had been buying up the lands between their waterways, especially around the more compact holdings of the once great Vladimir and Tver.

The neglected center had grown more prosperous than its shattered outer ring.

Early in the fourteenth century the rulers of Moscow began to foster this policy of expansion by "peaceful cunning." Here also accident played a part. The lords of the Kremlin were not among the great families of Rus.

True, a son of the notable Alexander Nevsky, Daniel by name, had been named *kniaz* (prince) of Moscow. At the time this had seemed to be little enough of an honor. The heads of the city who followed this Daniel remained obscure. One was removed by the Tatars to Sarai. Another, nicknamed the Bully for good reason, swaggered into Mozhaisk and Kolomna at the two ends of the river. But so little honor was attached to the rule of the Kremlin that Moscow at times lacked a prince and had to borrow one from another city.

These princes of Moscow, inferior to the great families that had ruled virtual kingdoms in Kiev and Vladimir, lacked title or prestige. They were upstarts, but they were growing wealthy—scheming, and hoarding the new coins that came from the Tatar mints. By usury and by trickery, they wrested land from the circle of great princes around them. Peasants began to call them "gatherers of the lands."

Now those great princes of the elder lineage had been not so much liquidated by the Tatars—who desired nothing more than the peaceful well-being of their new vassals—as bankrupted by their own quarreling and incompetence. On the other hand the growing Moscow territory, although becoming poorer in soil and thinner in the forests, was fairly well cultivated, and policed against raiding.

Nor could the scions of Kiev and Vladimir enrich themselves now as formerly by summoning their boyars and raiding a wealthy neighbor. The Tatars had laid an interdict upon such wars.

The astute Muscovite princes seemed to be the first to realize how greatly they could advance their fortunes by intrigue with the all-powerful Tatar khans at Sarai. One Yuri (George) married the sister of a reigning khan—distributing gold freely among the "Squeezers" at Sarai—and returned to Moscow with a certificate from the Tatars that he was "Great Prince" of the lands of Rus.

This opened wide the feud with the more distinguished princes of Tver, which, on the headwaters of the Volga, had dominated the Moscow region until then. In this strange and ruthless feud the princes of Tver took to their weapons in desperation, and were defeated by the arguments and bribes of the Muscovites at the court of Sarai.

When Michael of Tver fought openly against Yuri and a Tatar *baskak*, he was summoned to Sarai, accused of treason, and assassinated there by Yuri's henchmen. His heart was torn out of his body, which was left lying in the street until a Tatar *baskak* demanded, "Do you leave the body of a kinsman in the dirt?"

This blood feud ran its course in spite of the Tatars. Yuri was killed by Michael's son. A lord of Tver burned the house of a Tatar *baskak*. A Tatar army rode against Tver. The Orthodox Church, obedient to its Tatar overlords, excommunicated the allies of Tver. Four princes of Tver lost their lives in this futile struggle against the Muscovites, who took refuge in the armed strength of the Golden Horde. Finally the great bell that had hung in the cathedral of Tver was sent to the Kremlin as a token of submission.

No lord of Moscow knew better than the first Ivan (John) how to profit from this policy of subservience to the khans at Sarai and extortion from his rivals of Rus. Ivan Kalita (John the Purse) they called him, who could argue over kopecks with beggars at the Gate of the Pines, and could endow a monastery. He drew up one of the first laws of the city—

for it was a city now—the Landlord Law, from an archaic
Byzantine model, suitable to the personal whims of John
the Purse. But above all such law, John the Purse placed
the *yarlig,* the decree of his sponsors at Sarai.

So much gold and silver did John the Purse accumulate, so
much land did he buy or extort that he became, with his
family, the greatest of the princely landowners. More he
wrested from bankrupt boyars. Still more he gained by trading "gifts" at Sarai for *yarligs.*

Yet, laboring over his account books in the Kremlin, this
first Ivan managed his lands well, with profit.

The lands needed workers. Ivan bought back slave captives
from the Horde to work his acreage.

Unobtrusively, this man who had no heart for war made
clever suggestion to the *baskaks* of the Tatar khans. Could
not more tribute be had by increasing the *vyhod?* Could not
more wealth flow into the treasury of Sarai if the Persian
and Armenian collectors were dismissed? After that it was
not at all strange that Ivan Kalita should be appointed
chief tax collector of the Khan. Nor was it surprising that
his family should be granted permanently by *yarlig* the title
of Great Prince of Rus.

This family had had no share in the aristocracy of ancient Kiev or the rude democracy of Novgorod merchants.
Its rivals called it the "Money Bags."

Oblivious of mockery or hatred, the Muscovites continued
to serve as treasurers of the khans, to gather land and to
avoid war under the protection of the Tatars. They had no
traditions of past glory. Old Slavic law might hold elsewhere
but the Muscovites, in acting as the agents of the Tatars,
carried out the laws of Sarai.

Among the palaces of the Kremlin there was one of wood
reserved for the envoys of the Tatar khans. When an envoy
from Sarai appeared on the outer road, the prince of
Moscow went out on foot to take the rein of the envoy's
horse, and to feed it. While Tatars dwelt in the Kremlin, the
ceremony at banquets and audiences was that of Sarai.

More than that, Moscow was beginning to take on the
semblance of Tatar Sarai. Muscovite princes were to hold
monopolies of the making of liquor and weapons as the
Tatar khans had done; they were to rule through depart-
ments, *prikazi,* like their conquerors; they were to take over
the Tatar census rolls and horse-post transport; they were to
claim all Muscovite land as their own, to make new laws replacing the old *Russkaya Pravda.* In doing so, they were to
subject all classes of society to the authority of the Kremlin

as all classes had been subject to the court of the khans, and they were to enforce their new authority by fear.

Moscow more than any other city came under Tatar influence. And the great princes after John the Purse were the first to perceive that the power of the Golden Horde was fragmenting.

At this time, toward the middle of the fourteenth century, the power of Moscow was increased by two different happenings. They were almost accidents yet resulting from the policy of peaceful cunning of the Muscovites. First, by extending their holdings along the connecting rivers the wealth-hoarding Muscovites obtained control of the portages and trade routes stretching easterly on the upper Volga (past embittered Tver). In the west Lithuanian pressure wrested away Smolensk and the great north-south portages.

Thus Moscow's landholdings ran easterly rather than west; while still small, on the face of the vast Eurasian continent, they had grown from the insignificant five hundred square miles owned by the first Daniel to as many thousand.

Perhaps because the Moscow area remained more or less orderly, refugee princes from the south settled there. Peasantry tended to drift in also, and boyars followed the land workers. The once obscure princes of the Kremlin found themselves surrounded by a restless nobility, often of higher lineage than their own.

That in turn meant an increase of residential palaces within the Kremlin's walls—for the most impoverished princes held to their right to be part of the court. By degrees the Kremlin height, losing its pine grove, was filling with palaces, reception courts and churches—John the Purse, for one, tried to make it something of a metropolis by building the new Usspensky Sobor of stone.

And that brought about the second happening. Princes lay buried in the stone churches. The new cathedral impelled the Metropolitan to visit it, from Vladimir. The Metropolitan Peter was said to have said to John the Purse: "God will raise this town above all other towns. Saints have been buried here, and here shall my bones be buried."

Certain it is that other metropolitans moved to Moscow to stay; the miracle-working image was carried thither from Vladimir; a holy man, Sergius, started building a monastery in the forest forty miles northeast of the city; John the Purse aided him with a money grant and swiftly rose the broad brick and earth walls, the nine defense towers, of the Troitsko-Sergievsky monastery, to serve Moscow.

This made Moscow something of a religious center by the mid-fourteenth century. As yet it had none of the ancient glory of Kiev, or even the prestige of Vladimir. Although its people and land were known as Great Rus it was as yet only a metropolis growing beside a river, managed skillfully by men of small countinghouse minds, tallying wealth in fur coats, silver candlesticks, gold plate and cattle, mindful of the maxims of their fathers, and having no thought of dominion other than to increase the fortunes of their family.

Then the Tatar dominion broke down.

In far Cathay the descendants of Kubilai Khan had been driven out. Throughout mid-Asia conflict increased, great tribal groups clashed and coalesced in kaleidoscopic change. Mongol supremacy, shattered, resolved itself into resistance against the more barbaric groups of the interior. Hordes unknown to the Muscovites pressed against the Golden Horde.

In this swift reversal of forces, the city of Moscow was relieved at once of the Tatar overlordship, and deprived of Tatar protection.

For some time the center of the Golden Horde had been shifting to the south, toward the grass steppes beyond the Don, the black earth belt across which ran the great caravan route from central Asia to the Balkans.

Until then, of all the segments of the Mongol dominion, the Golden Horde had kept most closely to the old Mongol way of life. (Batu Khan, the son of a bastard, had looked on himself as an exile from the Golden family, and had exerted himself to set up an independent domain, breaking off contacts with the others of his kinsmen as soon as feasible, and refusing to act as a spearhead for another attack upon western Europe. His successors had followed this policy in the main for a century, until the death of Birdi Beg in 1359, when the Horde was drawn toward more luxurious living in the southlands.) Now a portion of the Horde had settled permanently in the natural fortress of the Crimea, close to the Italian trading ports of Sudak and Kaffa.

Here in the southern steppe European trading ports—Venetian, Genoese and Byzantine—ringed the strategic Black Sea, while population increased rapidly, and new trade terminals rose at the river mouths, Azov on the ancient site of the Variags at the mouth of the Don, Hadj-tarkhan or Astrakhan in the Volga delta.

This plain with its melting pot of peoples was to be known as the Ukraine, or Borderland.

In abandoning the line of the Volga for the more fertile Ukraine, the Golden Horde had left remnants behind it. A Moslem khanate remained settled around Bolghar on the upper Volga, and another mass kept to nomad life in the eastern steppe, the Nogais.

During its move south, the Horde had contended with kindred Mongols in Persia, the Il-Khans, for the rich prizes beyond the barrier of the Caucasus and the seas—the cities of the southern caravan route, Hamadan, Trebizond, Baghdad and Tabriz, with the incalculable wealth of India and Egypt beyond. Around Tabriz, the trade terminal of the Caucasus, this conflict had centered.[6]

"To Tabriz," an exploring friar named Oderic relates, "all the nations may resort for trade. Christians here declare that the Emperor of Persia [the Mongol Il-Khan] gets more tribute from this city alone than the king of France from all his dominion."

This conflict had drawn the strength of the Golden Horde from the line of the Volga, leaving only the remnants behind. And upon those remnants pressed the barbaric tribes of the interior like the White Horde, still Turkish and still pagan, pushing toward the civilization of the outer regions.

Inevitably, this twofold conflict broke down all semblance of the Mongol empire which had, after its fashion, made one world of Eurasia for more than a century.

When it ended, the transcontinental traffic ended also, the post stations ceased to be manned, the turnover of world trade dwindled. With the collapse of the intricate system of command, the staffs of interpreters ceased to function, the finance—such as it was—broke down. Understanding between the central peoples lessened. Embassies to the Tatar khans from as far away as Rome ceased; kings of Armenia and Georgia and dukes of Rus no longer kept in touch with the capital of the conquerors; the flood of adventurers like the Englishman who appeared with the Tatars in Moravia, to

---

[6] In their futile attempt to crush the Il-Khans, the khans of Sarai made one of the strangest mutual-assistance pacts of history. Largely Turkish themselves, they reached agreement across the sea with the Turks from the Aral region who then occupied Egypt, the so-called Mamluks. The Mamluks used young male slaves—as the Othmanli Turks would do after them—to recruit their army. The khans of Sarai made a point of shipping them such slaves, taken from among the Slavs, by the transport of other allies, the Venetians. But this strange alliance could not manage to crush Persia, which in the end survived both the Mamluks and the Golden Horde.

The Il-Khan dynasty, however, was absorbed by the population of Persia, and won over by her culture, as that of Kubilai Khan had been conquered by China.

act as interpreter, the goldsmith from Paris who befriended William of Rubruk—the human wave that had pushed or had been drawn toward the east receded. The new Catholic missions established beside old Nestorian centers along the caravan routes, even in the mountains of the mid-continent, under enterprising spirits like that of John of Monte Corvino, were left isolated.

Drafts of Russians no longer journeyed to the east for military service. Nor did the Muscovite princes continue to pay tribute to Sarai.

Kulikovo

The last thing to be expected was an army emerging from Moscow, the city that had been favored by the khans of Sarai, and had been in charge of the Tatar "Squeezers." Moscow itself had not contemplated such a happening; circumstances brought it about.

During the retreat of Tatar authority, the aspect of the "western lands" had changed. The frontier beyond the Dnieper, devastated so often by the Tatars, no longer existed. Polish colonists were pushing across that no-man's land, in company with strong armies of Lithuanians, the half-pagan folk from the damp forests between the Pripet marsh area and the Baltic. They occupied Smolensk, and availed themselves of the portages by Mozhaisk.

At the same time Moscow had ceased paying tribute to Sarai. This circumstance, coupled with the wealth now gathered in the treasury of the Kremlin, brought the advance of a Tatar army in retaliation during the summer of 1380. The Khan commanding, Mamai, had reached an agreement —of the kind then being made with the western neighbors of the Horde—with the Lithuanians. The Lithuanian grand duke, Jagellon, marched his nearest forces to join the Tatars on the river Oka, near Riazan, which submitted to the two armed powers in advance. Moscow did not follow Riazan's example. It offered a token payment to the Tatars, no more.

The headstrong young prince of Moscow, Dmitri, departed from the policy of his predecessors. An army was mobilized hastily with the aid of the northern cities, and joined by a contingent of Volhynians from the frontier zone. It was actually an allied force, but it followed the black standard with the gold symbol of Moscow; it assembled around the Kremlin and was blessed by Sergius of the Troitsko monastery.

This makeshift force, stiffened by veterans who had served with the Tatars, did one thing boldly enough. It marched out, across the Oka and across the Don where so many Russians had died. It advanced to meet the Tatars, whose forces had been drawn from the Volga and Ukraine. It *attacked* the Tatars, before the Lithuanian riders appeared on the plain.

For the first time, the Muscovites went over to the attack. What happened then is obscure; apparently the Muscovites copied the tactics of the Tatars, because the rush of battle covered miles of the plain, and the Volhynian force attacked from cover somewhere. But certainly the Slavs lost heavily, and certainly they held the plain near the village of Kulikovo, after looting the Tatar camp, on the "field of Kulikovo."

The effect of Kulikovo, psychologically, was enormous in all the lands of Rus. A Tatar army had been defeated and driven to flight before Russian horsemen under the banner of Moscow. Dmitri was given the hero name of *Donskoi,* of the Don.

To the Russian peasantry it seemed at last as if the mythical Ilya of Murom had "taken his spear and slain the Tatar." Whatever the cost, the nightmare of a century and a half had been lifted, and the Great Russians had a new song to sing.

What happened afterward was disastrous. Within two years a large Tatar army appeared from the northeast, its passage marked by burning towns. It was commanded by Toctamish, who had emerged from mid-Asia to dispossess Mamai. It forced the gates of Moscow, now defended by stone walls, and burned and sacked the city, searching out all hidden wealth. Dmitri had taken refuge elsewhere.

The calamity stirred up the other princes and boyars to cry, "We were more unlucky than our fathers who won no victories over the Tatars."

Dmitri returned to pay out of his own purse for the burial of twenty-four thousand bodies left by the Tatars.

So Moscow, in ruins again, paid the price of its one victory in the field over the Tatars. It did pay an actual price, because payments to the Volga khans had to be resumed. At least, tradition relates how the sons of Dmitri Donskoi journeyed to the Tatar encampment on the Volga with empty hands, to protest that no treasure remained in their city with which to pay the *vyhod.*

Not for a century after Kulikovo did a field army emerge again from Moscow to challenge the Tatar military supremacy.

Almost at once after the destruction of 1382, the interior of Eurasia was shaken by wars more terrible than the early cycle. A greater than Toctamish gathered together the scattered Turkish forces around the nucleus of Samarkand. Timuri-lang (Tamerlane) passed with his host for a dozen years on a vast orbit from India to the Volga and Egypt, driving Toctamish headlong into the west as a fugitive, paralyzing the Turks in Asia Minor for two generations, and creating the semblance of a military empire around Samarkand. But this vanished, at Tamerlane's death in 1405, into a new kaleidoscope of forces.

Tamerlane's passing left Moscow untouched. But it destroyed Sarai and the unity of the Golden Horde forever.

At the beginning of the fifteenth century, the dispersal of peoples left the Black Sheep Turkomans holding the Caucasus around Tabriz, while in the steppe above the Caucasus the Nogai (Great) Horde had displaced the White Horde. Fragments of the broken Golden Horde held to three points, Bolghar on the upper Volga, Astrakhan at the Volga's mouths, and in the refuge of the Crimea, where they were soon to be known as the Krim Tatars.

So great had been the impact of the two cycles of war that throughout Eurasia the dispersed peoples lived in fear of the reappearance of a Genghis Khan, a Toctamish, or a Tamerlane who might reunite the forces of the nomad interior.

Moscow, in the open plain facing the Volga, was conscious of this fear. For a long time the masters of the Kremlin waited for word from their spies or merchants of a new inroad from the interior. Moscow could continue to exist only if the Volga frontier and the Ukraine remained quiescent, or divided in force. Any alliance of the Tatar-Turkish groups meant danger to this wealthy but almost defenseless city.

Moscow beheld this danger sweep like a storm cloud over the steppe when Vitoft, the "Mad," Duke of Lithuania, led a Christian host that was almost a crusade across the Dnieper, against the allied Tatar khans. The Christian chivalry was shattered in the plains and driven headlong along the "black roads" back to the cities of Poland. Moscow watched, prudently taking no share in this disaster.

The horsemen of Asia were still masters of the open steppe. But a new weapon was appearing, in the small wars that raged from the Volga through the Borderland into eastern Europe. At the Dnieper, Vitoft's Christians had this weapon, clumsy iron tubes from which stones were projected by the explosion of gunpowder.

More than that, the new armies of the west, equipped with such primitive firearms, with crossbows and plate armor, were increasing their discipline and *force*. They were proving superior to the old-style musterings of nobles and peasants, haphazardly armed—such as Dmitri had assembled at the Don.

Moscow had no such army. The sprawling city on the Moskva could claim fifteen thousand square miles of land, yet it had no means of defending the land by the new-style soldiery, or making the new weapons or, indeed, of commanding such an army if mustered and equipped.

This lack was deeply felt by the princes of Moscow.

Isolated from the western powers, they beheld formidable armies taking shape beyond their immediate horizon. New links were entering the chain of forces to the west—disciplined Swedish infantry, impetuous Polish lancers, the *yeni cheri* (Janizaries), the young guards of the Othman sultans. These restless Turks were crossing over into Europe, penetrating the Balkans, pressing toward the Danube.

Facing these forces, Moscow lay at the exposed point of all the lands of Rus. Most of the fifteen thousand miles stretched back of the city like the tail of a comet, to the east and north. Tver, still antagonistic, was only eighty miles from the city; frontier guards of the Lithuanian-Poles camped in the woods some hundred miles to the west, and Tatar patrols rode as near as that, to the south.

To oppose such antagonists, Moscow could count on no ally. Novgorod remained hostile, intent on protecting its trade empire by its bands of pioneer-boatmen, the *ushkuiniki*.

Without a single ally, holding lands in outward subjection but inward turmoil, Moscow had no visible force to rely on. At the middle of the fifteenth century Moscow seemed destined to be drawn after Smolensk into the Lithuanian principality.

That did not happen. In those years two events took place that were to have great effect upon the city's future. The Tatar khanates ceased to have any real alliance. And in 1453 the new Turkish armies captured Constantinople.

After the fall of Constantinople, the leadership of the Eastern Church passed to Moscow, which, in the minds of its people, became the successor to the ancient imperial city. With the Tatar khanates divided by rivalries, Moscow became, if not the successor to the court of Sarai, at least the most coherent entity on the great Russian plain.

There seemed to be little hope at this juncture in the princes of Moscow themselves, who had gained their territory only by money and by wit.

Nor did they hold the loyalty of the people of Great Rus. Complaints against them found many voices, such as: "Why do you bring the Tatars into the Russian land, and give them land and settlements to own? Why do you love the Tatars and talk with them more than is fitting? Why do you oppress the peasants more than is necessary? At the same time you give gold, silver and other good things to the Tatars?"

There was no *ideal* of a nation at that time. The talk was not of a Russian land, as in the day of Kiev and the princes of Vladimir. But something odd was happening. Moscow, the city itself, might not be a Kiev; yet it was the nucleus of a land and people. That land and people formed the most stable force in all Rus. Because of that, they *stood for* all other areas of land and human beings no matter how distant and unruly, or even antagonistic.

Moscow represented something shared by all other cities but not belonging to the others. Foreigners called that something "of Moscow" or "Muscovy," and its people Muscovites. In the same way this was true of the princes. Wealthiest of all the assemblage of incompetent princes, they had been marked out from the others by the empty title of Great Prince. Just as the territory of which the Muscovite state formed the core had been called Great Rus. By surviving themselves the great princes of Moscow had become the defense of a nobility incapable of surviving except through them. By virtue of that, they established for themselves the right to be succeeded by their sons.

All this while the Moscow princes had been following out only their own interest.

They had one aid. Around the new wooden buildings of Moscow, around the Kremlin height and its brick-red square, gathered the memories of Kulikovo. And the Russian people believed that Moscow, which had no visible safeguard, was protected by divine power residing in the miracle-working images of its Usspensy cathedral. In that power they believed.

They believed in it utterly. Knowing nothing of the new sciences, the ordinary folk clung to this old and solitary belief. Other than divine power there was for them no safeguard in this hard land beset by terrifying enemies. No John Huss could walk out here from the library of a university, to change their concept of divine power, because no John Huss existed or could exist here where universities did not exist.

By slow degrees, in a fashion of its own, popular opinion among the Russians began to make a demand upon the princes of Moscow. Since Moscow was a *holy* city, these princes must administer the divine power, the sole aid of the common folk. These princes must be *guardians* of the folk. When the princes succeeded in something, they carried out the divine will; when they failed—as most often happened—they ignored the divine will, and so became faithless guardians.

This was a difficult role to be carried out by men who had confined their energies to financial profit and loss.

During the critical period of isolation and danger in the mid-fifteenth century, the great princes of Moscow made little headway in their new role of monarchs. They kept on gathering land as before.

It was no action on their part that gave Moscow an unexpected change of fortune at this point. It was the action of ordinary folk, who began to cross the upper Volga and settle in the dense forest belt of the far northeast.

III

THE DOMINION

Routes of the Fur and Fish

THEY went in a steady stream. On sledges the families piled their belongings and moved into the forests where the lime trees gave way to the northern spruce. Towing canoes up the streams and floating log rafts down flooded rivers, the emigrants filled the northeast territory beyond the wide Oka-Volga valley.

They had a song: "Where is the land blessed of God? Where is our paradise—our fine paradise? In the desert is our paradise, blessed of God!"

They were moving restlessly toward *something,* these settlers pushing toward the marshy lakes, the brown rushing rivers, the dark forest and the increasing cold of the north. They waited out the spring thaws, cropped the clearings during the brief summer, and went on, among the broad-faced Finnish hunters, the Bulgars with shaven heads, whose girls with white leggings they called "Little Swans." Among timber-wise Karelians and grease-coated Laps, they traded and fought for animal pelts which they sold at the Novgorod trading posts that studded the river routes of the northeast territory. Around such trading posts they sometimes built towns of their own.

For each new thing they invented names of their own. The widest river of the northeast the Finns called Mighty Waters, the Volga. Little Mother Volga, the Russian emigrants christened it. Always they called something *Beyond.* The first towns had been *Zamoskovniy gorody,* the Towns Beyond Moscow. The first forest belt had been the Land Beyond Volga. Now the marshes and pine growth were the Country Beyond the Portages.

Here the rivers ran north. It seemed they emptied into an

unknown ice-coated sea—the Frozen Ocean Sea, these Russians named it immediately.

On these rivers that gave them passage through the forests, they fought and bartered with the *ushkuiniki,* the tough canoemen hired by Novgorod merchants. Those who came out at the mouth of the river emptying into the Frozen Ocean Sea found near it a lake swarming with sea birds that filled the air with clamor.

Not far from the river mouth lay an island, and on that island stood a monastery, wet by the sea spray. The monks of the island fed visitors as if they had been pilgrims.

An educated visitor from the west bears witness to the bleakness of life in Rus at this time. Ambrogio Contarini, ambassador of the Serene Republic of Venice to the court of Persia,[1] made the journey along the Volga shore from the south. "On the twenty-second of September 1475 we entered *Russia,* and discovered a few huts in the middle of a wood. As soon as the people of the huts heard that Mark, a Russian, was in our caravan, they came to see him, to discover if he could protect them from the Tatars. They brought him a present of honey and wax, part of which he gave us. It was most providential, because we were so worn out by fatigue and lack of food that we could hardly sit on horseback.

"The first city we reached in this country was Riazan, in which the castle and houses are all built of wood. Here to our great satisfaction we got bread and meat and honeymead. The next city was Kolomna, across a large bridge over the Moskva, which flows into the Volga.

"On the twenty-sixth of September, we arrived in Moscow . . . where Mark got us a dwelling consisting of a small stoveroom and some sleeping rooms with stables for the horses. Though small and mean, I felt as if it were a palace of security, after the dangers I had been through."

It had taken tired men only four days to travel from the last Tatar outposts in the south to Moscow.

On the northeast frontier of the forests armed bands pa-

[1] Contarini's mission was typical of the time. Sent by the shrewd Venetians to try to influence the Shah of Persia to make war on the Turkish Sultan—and so relieve the pressure of the Turks against Europe and the Venetians—he investigated the markets of Astrakhan on the Caspian where eastern silk, perfumes and "spiceries" were being transshipped. On his way he had ventured into the stronghold of the White Sheep Turkomans, at Tabriz where these military folk held the strategic corridor of Azerbaijan.

trolled the waterways, sometimes pillaging the Novgorod convoys, and sometimes pillaging for them. Even the monasteries that followed the emigrant trails were fortified, with watchtowers and the new cannon.

Still the popular movement went on, and emigrants pressed out of the Oka-Volga valley, to turn into the basin of the Kama, tending eastward, or to the Dvina (Double) River that led to the White Sea.

Land hunger drove the immigrants on, to settle in the unclaimed forest.

These settlers soon learned the value of furs—the price of two black fox skins could buy a cabin, with horses and a small herd of cattle.

Naturally, with such prices in hard money to be had, the settlers did much trapping and killing of the local animals, the dark martens and omnipresent beavers and gray fox. Sable skins were also becoming valuable, and an extraordinary demand was growing for the yellowish-white skins of the hitherto ignored ermine. This fur was sought by the nobility of western Europe. The Novgorod trading posts knew of this demand, and obtained ermine, with the white Arctic fox fur from the hunting grounds far distant under the blaze of the northern lights.

On their part, the Muscovite settlers were pushing farther into the damp forests, seeking a meat supply that vanished as settlements came in. The river fishing did not give an adequate food supply, and the scanty harvests yielded little bread. Food stocks were looted both by traders and settlers, by Novgorod agents and by Muscovites. The river outlaws hired themselves to either side, or plundered both, depending upon who had the balance of strength at the moment.

Through the vast spaces of the northeast frontier this contest went on, with little organized warfare but without truce. The stream of Muscovite emigration had cut across the Novgorod trade routes to the east. The struggle for control of the river routes and portages was soon decided. As the numbers of the settlers increased they destroyed or absorbed the Novgorod fur-trade network. Often the newcomers appeared in towns and posts in such numbers that the towns came under Muscovite control without conflict.

Then, too, the settlements assimilated the native populations—the Finnish villages and the Lap encampments—in a rough intermingling of humans, of mutual barter, and intermarriage. Mentally, the Great Russian settler was little above the Finnish hunter or Lap reindeer keeper.

The settler could not have survived in the bitter northeast

Winter travel by sled and skis. Owing to the lack of roads, land travel went more easily over the "snow road" during the winter months; in the summer journeying became difficult except by the river routes. (from Herberstein)

if he had not been able to get food and to protect his cabin. His attempt at play repeated this struggle—he tamed bears and fought duels with bears, for the sport of a crowd, armed with a knife or club. He named one river the River of the Bears. For other relaxation, he got drunk on stolen beer, and danced or wept when old men sang half-forgotten legends of the heroes of Rus. The wraiths of Boris and Gleb drove their spirit sledges through the flooded forest.

Certainly there is no evidence here of coherent leadership. Only after the settlements were built did *voevodes,* or "governor-commanders," appear from Moscow. The frontier was settled without plan, in the conflict of Muscovites with Novgorod *ushkuiniki* and Volga rivermen. It enriched itself by the furs sent back to Moscow markets, by the discovery of salt pits and silver mines. In doing so, it opened up to Moscow a new dominion stretching from the height of the Kremlin to the monastery of Solovetsky on the Frozen Ocean Sea, beyond the reach of Tatars or western military powers.

What had driven these emigrants from their homeland of

Muscovy, in the mid-fifteenth century, toward the dismal cold of the northeast forest belt? Something had caused them to move thither with their families.

It was not an impulse toward more fertile land. It was more than the perpetual restlessness of the Great Russians. They not only shifted their ground, they penetrated almost into the Arctic Zone, the least desirable of all. This would not have been possible, if the Novgorod network of fur-trading posts had not marked the way. But the popular movement could not have been a *planned* attempt to take over and profit from the northern trading posts. The Solovetsky monastery was not built on the island of the White Sea gulf *because* the cold of the outer sea was tempered at that point by the last current of the Gulf Stream, so the gulf remained free from ice a great part of the year. That fortunate circumstance was discovered later and not by the Great Russians.

Were the monasteries and the people trying to escape from the pressure of the Tatars and the military forces of the west? It is true that there had been a drift of Russian population northward from the Ukraine, away from such pressure, for some time.

Were the monasteries launched forth upon a missionary venture of their own—or what the westerners would call a missionary expansion? But, if so, why did it lead into the almost unpeopled north?

Were both monasteries and people moved by the wayward mysticism of Slavs to seek wastelands? To escape from the bonds of intolerable authority, into lands free from taxes, spies and overlords? True, the *founders* of such monasteries often would leave a cloister to seek the wilderness again and form a new cell in solitude. And the monasteries were called "desert monasteries." One of the emigrant songs repeated, "The desert is our paradise." Yet by such deserts, the medieval Russian meant virgin country, not sandy barrens. In former times soldiers escaping from the Tatars and slaves fleeing from foreign masters had formed cells in some "wilderness" of grassland and untraveled rivers. This phenomenon would be repeated as time went on.

Did the emigrants hold in their minds some memory of an ancient northern frontier, along the seas from which came the first Rus? Were they escaping from intolerable conditions into some irredenta of their imagining? It was a peculiarity of the Russians to cling tenaciously to ancient ideas. And they had the memory of elephants.

This movement was unlike anything in the west—resembling only a little the familiar crusades, explorations, trading ventures and missionary movements of medieval Europe. We cannot look back at it and say, It was due to this force or that. As for written testimony, there remain only a few manuscripts of the monasteries, which perpetuate the sanctity of the lives of their founders in dry Byzantine words. And as for folk legendry, there remain only the sad chants of the rivermen, the merry tale of Sadko, the cunning merchant.

(Kliuchevsky, the wisest of modern historians, says that this popular movement was the discharge of pent-up population in the plain between the Volga and Oka, across the Volga—with missionaries acting as the advance guard.)

Although we cannot identify it clearly, this force was the primary force of Russian expansion. By such emigrants the course of Russian history was to be shaped.

Since Moscow had aided the emigration past the flanking dangers of Novgorod and the Volga khanates, the new settlements in the northeast territory held to Muscovite protection. When governors arrived at long last with armed guards, they were from Moscow. The settlements acknowledged the sovereignty of the Great Prince, because there was no other. And he in turn exacted a toll from the new fur trade, a monopoly of the new salt beds, a tax on silver, and on the cabins of the settlers.

Thus swiftly, within two generations or so, the area of Muscovy increased from the upper Volga-Moskva region— some hundred by a hundred and fifty miles—to a dominion over the northern forest and fur. And that dominion opened up "the long Siberian way."

Lord Novgorod the Great

The migration also brought about the end of Novgorod. It cut across the inland trade routes of that ancient city— "New City, but old as old."

Like Venice, this merchant republic of the north faced toward the sea, the Baltic in this case, the ancient "Sea of the Variags." It was a city of aristocratic burgher families, of flourishing trade guilds—a rude democracy, managed by a penny-counting council, skilled in buying off possible enemies, jealous of its age-old privileges, relying otherwise upon its bands of boatmen-pioneers and marauding "valiant young men" to keep intact its monopoly of the fur and fish in the north—the monopoly that had been broken down by the equally lawless migrants from Moscow.

Straddling the river Volkhov, squarely between two of the great northern lakes, Novgorod barred Moscow from access to the Baltic. Novgorod thrived by conciliating the Lithuanian-Poles, by trading with the Swedes who were occupying the peninsula of Finland, and by channeling its goods westward through the declining Hanseatic city network. While it used its wealth cleverly in this fashion, Novgorod lacked the growing manpower of Moscow, and it was dependent, besides, on the grain and meat of the Moscow area.

In the pressure upon them from all sides during the mid-fifteenth century, it was a question whether Moscow or Novgorod should succumb. And the Kremlin made certain that it should be Novgorod.

Not that the ancient city and the growing metropolis waged a formal war. Like their *ushkuiniki* and settlers, each strained to cripple the other.

Armed bands from Novgorod occupied the strategic portages and rivers, blocking the Muscovites from the Baltic roads. In retaliation, Muscovite guards stopped all grain shipments to the north.

In this process of mutual strangulation, a Great Prince of Moscow made his presence felt. He was (after 1462) the third Ivan (John), a spare and irritable man with a gift for Machiavellian intrigue. Under his guidance the councilors of the Kremlin spread the tidings that the Novgorodians were "pagans" determined to destroy Orthodox Christians.

Secretly, Ivan helped promote disturbance within Novgorod—where guilds and factions rioted during the food shortage. Quietly Ivan aided one of the factions, taking only a moderate payment as his reward. ("The government of Novgorod is democratic," Contarini relates at this point, "and only pays a stipulated yearly tribute to the grand duke.")

Probably the man in the Kremlin respected the Novgorod oligarchs, who were much better managers than the councilors of Moscow. Yet he provoked them deliberately—quibbling once about the manner in which they addressed him in a letter—then accusing them of treachery to him, as their liege lord, which they had never acknowledged him to be. So while one faction held to him, another group deserted to Lithuania, and Novgorod became too weak to withstand even a small army. Still Ivan was kind to them, openly. The small army that Moscow mobilized was sent north to restore order, and punish rebels (and occupy Novgorod).

As Orthodox Christians—and the *krestianin,* the farmers of Moscow, were that indeed—the Muscovites took honest pleasure in punishing these armed marauding pagans, in cutting off their noses, slitting their mouths and killing them. It was even more satisfying to loot the rich warehouses of the northerners, to pursue and possess the northern women, running around squawking like frightened fowls.

This small war had become a popular war because the Great Prince at Moscow egged on his unruly people to fight for their religion. There was no lack of volunteers to serve in an army to defend the holy city of Moscow.

The army that finally decided the fate of Novgorod was gathered together chiefly from the Muscovite river settlements, and from frontier bands who had warred with Tatars. It found its way northward by the river and portage routes. It numbered no more than four to five thousand.[2] But it could use weapons, and it broke up in bloody fashion a mob of some twenty thousand townsmen of Novgorod who had been hastily mounted to give battle in defense of the city. It carried out of Novgorod two hundred cartloads of gold, silver, fine cloths and precious stones.

So Novgorod became a possession of the prince in the Kremlin. Something more significant happened a few years later, when the burghers of the once independent city rioted against the rule of Moscow. This time the rebel city was purged, and the core of its guilds, its church prelates, unruly boyars and wealthy inmates of monasteries removed to other Russian lands. This deportation of fourteen thousand of its citizenry reduced Novgorod to a dependent city, taxed directly by the Great Prince of Moscow. "Its power vanished," the Chronicle relates, "even to the sea itself."

When the Novgorodians appealed to Ivan for terms of a permanent peace, he voiced his anger against them. "Our ruling as Great Prince is of this wise: henceforth there shall be no council and no ringing of the assembly bell in Nov-

---

[2] It is difficult to know the numbers of the armies and the populations of the cities up to this point. Novgorod is said to have had about five thousand houses: the number of people deported by Ivan's command is given variously as seven thousand to fourteen thousand. As to Moscow, we only know that Dmitri Donskoi had paid for burying twenty-four thousand after the capture of the city by Toctamish. Contarini and other foreigners speak of the "uncounted" numbers of Muscovites. In Moscow, people were forever coming and going; there was no clear demarcation between the urban and rural population.

Novgorod and Moscow were by all odds the largest cities in Rus at this time—and while the first was decreasing, the second was increasing rapidly in population. A European visitor estimated that Moscow was twice as large as "Florence, in Tuscany, or Prague, in Bohemia."

gorod, *our land*. There shall be no lieutenant to rule; our rule is to be carried out by ourselves."

The deportations that followed reduced the leading families of the merchant city by a third. The exiles took some property with them, their families were kept together, and they were given lands in more docile cities like Vladimir and Tver and Moscow itself. They were merely transplanted to be directly under Moscow's control, uprooted from their past. (This process of uprooting peoples was to be repeated again and again by Moscow.)

By Ivan's order the great bell of Novgorod, beloved by the folk, was also transplanted and hung in the new Usspensky cathedral of the Kremlin.

This subjection of independent Novgorod (1478) in turn brought Moscow in contact, for better or worse, with the Swedes, Livonians and Esthonians of the Baltic's shores, who held the great ports like Viborg, Revel (Tallinn) and Riga.

It also left Moscow in unchallenged control of the northeast fur dominion, stretching to the very shores of the Arctic. No man knew the extent of the *land* that had become the patrimony of the princes of Moscow. Forest land and frozen land. Ivan III himself sent exploring brigades to survey and take tribute from the new fur and fish dominion.

These small questing armies of pioneers and Muscovite armed men circled cautiously to the north of the Tatar towns along the Volga; they disappeared for years in the dense forest belt.

Several thousand strong, they met no opposition to the northeast; they found the log fortifications of monasteries standing in open valleys along the Dvina. At the Frozen Sea, they found the island of the birds occupied by a stone monastery, Solovetsky, where the monks waited out the long winter night patiently. Passing beyond, to the basin of the Pechora, they came upon settlements that had somehow got around the Tatars of the Volga.

In the broad valley of Perm where the Bashkirs rode herd on their cattle, the Muscovite searchers beheld a log church and school built by a man named Stephen who had ventured out into that "wild land" a century before. Stephen had gone among the tribesmen, searching for the mysterious "Golden Old Woman" who dwelt on a height, holding a child in her arms, unchanging through the years. Was this a Madonna of the wilderness, left by some forgotten people? Was the Woman a pagan image, ruling over superstitition? Many images had been pointed out to Stephen, but none seemed to be of a certainty the Woman. And he found that the pagan tribes feared the power of the reindeer spirit, the spirits of the dark forest itself.

Stephen taught in his school; his converts painted the holy pictures in his frontier church. When he died they proclaimed him to be a saint, and Bishop of Perm.

Beyond, the brigades of Moscow beheld the line of low, forested hills called by the tribes the Earth Girdle—the Urals—and from the tribes they took tribute of furs, claiming the land for the Great Prince of Moscow, and passing on to search and raid, and return with their spoils.

When they crossed the Volga they met Muscovite traders who had ventured far to the east, to a sea called the Aral, and a city called Samarkand, whither came silk by caravan from Cathay. The boyars of the exploring armies confused the two, and reported that the "Lake of Kitai" lay not so far to the east. Still, their reports were welcomed by Ivan.

His new dominion of the northeast, however, stretched haphazardly along rivers to monasteries, away from the Tatar towns—a patchwork of settlements, a crisscross of trading trails, paying tribute only when strong armed bands collected it.

To this vast frontier Ivan and the Muscovites paid little attention.

Meanwhile rumors of "Muscovy" had penetrated to the courts of Europe. Especially in the German courts, it was known that a Rus existed beyond the familiar Rus of Lithuania-Poland.

At last in 1486 an adventurous German, Nicholas Poppel, made his way through the last frontier posts of Europe, to the city lying in the plain beyond and went on, to discover Moscow there. Poppel returned in haste to the court of the Emperor to report that another and vaster Rus lay beyond the known frontier.

Apparently this was startling news at the court of the Roman Emperor, Frederick III. He sent the industrious Poppel back as his envoy to the court of the mysterious monarch of Moscow. Poppel carried with him an offer from the European Emperor to grant the title of king to the barbaric ruler in the unknown east.

(This offer was quite *en règle*. Frederick, as heir of the Roman Caesars, titular head of the Holy Roman Empire, actual leader of a rising Germanic state, merely proposed recognition, with family intermarriage, to the Muscovite, as a king or lesser monarch in his proper country.)

Ivan's response to the German is illuminating:

". . . we have been emperors of our land from the beginning, and from our earliest forefathers, and do hold our commission of God Himself, even as they [did]. . . . May we never need to be commissioned unto that, for no such need do we have now."

Now Ivan III was a realistic man, with a nice sense of values as far as he himself was concerned. He knew that he held no such title as emperor, being merely prince of Moscow, and acknowledged leader of the princes of Rus. (Contarini, the Venetian envoy, phrased it "grand duke of Moscow, and sovereign of this land.") Even after absorbing Novgorod, most of his inchoate dominion was paying tribute in one way or another to the Tatar khans and to the Lithuanian-Polish monarchs.

(Nor had Ivan at this point the actual power of a European king. His land was no natural entity like the great western peninsula ruled by Aragon and Castile, whence ships would presently be sent under navigators like Christopher Columbus to find the way to Cathay across the western ocean; indeed, he had no such trading and war fleet as had the doges of Venice. He had no strong base of industrial cities like the German Hapsburg, Frederick—cities such as wealthy Lübeck, or Mainz, or Nuremberg where talented craftsmen were printing the first books from movable type.[3])

But behind Ivan's claim to empire lay a memory intangible as a dream—of the sons of Rurik who had reigned in the lost paradise of Kiev, of treaties made with Byzantine emperors, of a people roving to unclaimed frontiers, of the sea that had been "Our Sea" and the other that had been the "Sea of the Variags." A kindred memory of the world dominion of the Tatar kha khans had added itself to the first. This visionary heritage had indeed been that of the "first forefathers" and it was truly sanctioned by the patriarchs of the Russian Church, who interpreted it as the divine will.

And this memory was being reinforced by a realization of responsibility. The master of the one city of Moscow was the sole guardian of all the other lands, even in the northeast, even to the Urals. The third Ivan had some trouble expressing this. In a few letters he signed himself Emperor

[3] At Nuremberg within a half-dozen years a huge *World Chronicle* would be published by these pioneer printers. It shows in detail the *German* Empire, and names the Baltic the German Sea, the North Sea the German Ocean. At the edge of the map, marked (in Latin) East, there are scattered names, *Mosovia* and *Nogradium*, with three *Russias* strewn around them.

of All Rus—using the Slavic *Hosudar* for "Emperor." Then, again, he experimented with the ancient title of Caesar—Tsar. His forefathers had addressed missives to Tsar Batu, and to the Byzantines at Tsargrad.

Nothing was definite, even in his mind. Perhaps Tsar of All Rus sounded best to the man who was actually Great Prince of Moscow. But what was Rus?

Designers of the New Kremlin

And then there was Sophie. Sophia Paleologus was the niece of the last Emperor of Constantinople. She had been brought at Ivan's bidding from her refuge in Rome to become his second wife. A Byzantine, born to the imperial purple, she had known the splendid courts of Europe, she had wit. And with her she had brought to Moscow a coterie of Greeks—priests and teachers—and a library of Greek books.

His daughters by her had the blood of Byzantine lineage and of Ivan's forefathers. So they might in a sense be said to be the inheritors of empire. But the boyars of the wooden palaces in and around the Kremlin's walls did not think so. Evil, they thought, came from women to men, and Sophie was an ambitious woman. Marriage with her could not change the stubborn fact that Ivan was not descended from the Byzantine emperors. A cart horse with fine trappings was still a cart horse. The boyars complained that Sophie was suggesting to Ivan all that he did now. She was trying to make Ivan into something not Muscovite—a prop of the fallen Byzantine imperialists. He would fare better if he secluded her in the *terem*, where women should be kept, to pray at their own shrines, and amuse themselves in their own gardens, and to be whiplashed at times for their own good.

Foreign ambassadors sensed the cleverness of the Byzantine woman, and thought she egged on Ivan to free himself from the Tatar tribute.

There is no certainty as to the truth. The Byzantine woman dwelt, partly secluded, in chambers behind the brick walls of the Kremlin. She had a small host of servants, a physician of her own. (Physicians dealing in medicine were unknown in a city where ills came from malignant demons or the anger of God.) Perhaps her windows—which were only narrow embrasures—looked out over the frozen river Moskva where vendors' booths had been erected on the ice, and packed with frozen carcasses of cows, hogs and poultry. Perhaps when her closed sledge drove out the Gate of the Pines, crushing over mud and ice, she watched the workmen climbing down at noon from the wooden church in the market place, crowding among Tatars and fur-clad Cheremiss riders, to get into the taverns wherein each mug of beer paid a tax to her husband.

Certainly after her coming to the Kremlin, the Italian architects had been imported, to draw the plans for every new church. Contarini, the Venetian, boarded with the architect, Alberto Fioraventi, called "Aristotle," near the palace. (Fioraventi also cast cannon for Ivan, aided by Paul Bossio, a metal founder.) And inside the Kremlin, the new Usspensky Sobor was built of stone, instead of the inevitable Russian timber. A new small palace was built by Pietro Antonio, and called by the boyars the Palace of Facets.

The dark cathedral with its faintly gleaming figures of the Last Judgment, obscured by the smoke of candles, must have seemed like a crypt to Sophie, who had known the warm intimacy of the small churches of the exiles in Athens. As for the low-vaulted banquet hall of the terem, with its massive gilt pillars—she must have seen that only when it was empty, because no woman appeared at table in public.

Only from screened galleries could she look down on the gathering of the great boyars, heavily bearded men, their heads shaven like Tatars or monks, their robes heavy with goldwork and fur trailing to the stone floor.

The guards wore more splendid uniforms: those of the imperial guard were clad in white brocade, fur-trimmed, armed with long silvered axes, almost like the ancient Varangian Guard of the Sacred Palace that overlooked the Golden Horn, where Sophie had been born.

As to all that, Sophie left no written testimony. In the Troitsko treasury, a sheet she had woven was kept among the relics. On it she had embroidered her name. And the words her hand embroidered were: *"Tsarevna Tsargrad* [Imperial princess of Tsargrad]."

Contarini was a shrewd observer, and he spent a deal of time in and around the "castle," as he termed the walled Kremlin, because he had no money to pay his debts to the Muscovite merchants, until Ivan paid them and gave the Venetian a gray squirrel-skin coat to wear at court, and a thousand rubles for his journey home. And Contarini invoked a new title for Sophie—*Despoina*, the Byzantine Empress.

"The grand duke," the ambassador relates, "seemed about

thirty-five. He was thin, and handsomely made, had dignified manners, with quite a royal air. By a former wife he had two sons who did not get along with *Despoina,* the reigning grand duchess, and so were not on friendly terms with their father. *Despoina,* being his second wife, had given him two daughters and was rumored to be with child again.

"He invited me to dinner . . . which was quite magnificently served, with every delicacy, and the dishes well dressed . . . before returning to my quarters he presented me to the grand duchess who received me very graciously."

There was a silver service in the banquet hall, and the ceremonial of it pleased even the fastidious Venetian. And, against the custom of Russian nobles, he was presented to the wife of the monarch. To the people as a whole, Contarini was not so well disposed. "Among them are wandering nations and pagans who acknowledge no sovereign. Both men and women of this country have very good faces, but their manners are remarkably bad. . . . They have no wine, and drink instead a beer made of honey which it is not allowed everyone to make. To do so, a license must be had from the grand duke; for if everyone were allowed to make this mead, they would keep on drinking like beasts and so be apt to kill each other. . . . They are by no means warlike."

Yes, Contarini was clever to see this. Other foreigners would merely sneer at "Muscovite drunkenness" or marvel at the little drinking they beheld. Contarini sensed that the "grand duke" kept the mass of his people from intoxication, while adding rubles to his personal credit, in the great ledgers that were as close to his heart as the Scriptures themselves.

If Niccolò Machiavelli had been the involuntary guest of the master of the Kremlin instead of his countryman Contarini, he could not have described so easily the powers and prerogatives of this prince. For here was no occupant of a throne, dictator of a city, patron of arts, using proper, merciless intrigue, and the deft operation of small wars to gain his ends. Here was a man of property, adding up accounts by candlelight, sleeping little because he sweated with fear in the darkness, oppressed by dangers he could not understand or defend himself against—the peril of plague and sloth among the people, of pestilence among the cattle, of attacks from Europe, and inroads by the dark clouds of Tatar horsemen.

How could even Sophie, who had known the arrogance of armed Turks riding into holy Constantinople—how could she understand the effect of two centuries of subjection to the will of the Tatars? Sophie, perhaps driven by her own fear, had contrived to have torn down the wooden building within the Kremlin that had been the guest house of the visitors from the Hordes—because she said she wanted a new stone church on the site. But there was a spot marked—Ivan had built a shrine there—on the road out of Moscow where his ancestors had stood, with a goblet of mare's milk, to greet thus humbly on foot an emissary from the Hordes, or to kiss the stirrup of a visiting khan. Ivan had refused to go out to this spot, or to kiss the stirrups.

Probably Sophie had not nagged him into that. For Ivan, it seemed, would cheat others and debase himself when necessary to gain an end. Like his ancestors, he knew nothing of the Anglo-Saxon and German code of chivalry, or of the festering, inbred Byzantine pride. When he departed from the custom of his ancestors—"the candle to be kept alight" —he did so reluctantly, distrusting himself.

He let "Aristotle" Fioraventi, the Italian architect, design new defense walls to rise around the Kremlin.[4] The like of these battlements had not been seen in elder Rus. He instructed the new Italian metal founders to cast large brass and iron cannon as well as the great bronze bells for the cathedrals. The people loved to hear the bells as far off as possible, and as loud as possible. In a time of trouble like this, the people told Ivan, those bells might sound at night of their own accord, and that would be a warning.

Ivan needed no warning. Nothing is more certain than that this thin man, silent and suspicious, expected catastrophes to come upon Moscow. The priests of the now wealthy Troitsko monastery assured him that the year was near at hand which would be the seven thousandth year from the creation of the world (1492 in the calendar of western Europe), and that would be the end of the world.

Sitting in his chair in the *duma*, the council room, he listened to the angry tirades and shouts of the other great princes and boyars, who accused him truthfully of cheating them. (And Sophie wept, asking him what kind of a ruler he was to let his nobles howl at him.) Yet if Ivan should bring out the holy images from the Usspensky cathedral, these same sons of Rurik, princes and boyars alike, would follow him with blind obedience. Swindling them out of taxes, he lent them money.

---

[4] The picturesque towers of the Kremlin were designed and built later, from time to time. They often assumed the shape of Italian campaniles. The most famous of them, rising over the Borovitsky gate, was copied from the Tatar tower, the Sumbeka, in Kazan.

Even the bearded *krestianin* who guarded his gate might tramp into his presence when drunk and weep for his sins; madmen might chant old songs at his gate; hermits from the desert might stand in his way in the mud of the streets and revile him for departing from the word of God. Was he not their guardian, the servant of the Lord?

"God's Steward and Gentleman of the Bed Chamber," some of the boyars called him. At least one foreigner said so.

Bu what *power* did he have? True, he could influence the council of the boyars. Yet he could not take decisive action without the acquiescence of this large and tumultuous family of nobles. He could persuade the mass of the people to serve him at need; otherwise he had little control over such a restless mass. And the mass was propagating itself, increasing the numbers of its sons and daughters. Even the natural wealth of the land was unconvertible, lacking trade outlets—the horses, oxen, cattle, sheep, poultry, the hides, furs, wax and honey, timber, flax, furs and silver could avail to do no more than feed and clothe isolated Moscow. Coined money was scanty. (The foreigners were all struck by the superabundance of food, even in winter, and the cheapness of prices.)

The very monasteries were expanding along the frontiers, absorbing tilled fields and forests, increasing the numbers of peasants employed by them. Over churches and monasteries, Ivan had no control.

Yet the conviction was growing everywhere that there must be *one* land and people of Rus, to be cared for by Ivan.

Patiently and very slowly the people were fashioning things for themselves, in a style of their own. In the cottages the ikon stands were brightened with silverwork. The painting of the beloved saints, done by peasants as well as monks, became deft and beautiful—often copying the transcendent work of the monk from the Troitsko, Andrew Rublev, whose figures lived in strange fashion, like those of Fra Angelico which Rublev had never seen.

So the great monasteries and small churches began to take on shapes that fitted into the villages and forests, with gate towers and burnished domes that owed nothing to the ideas of foreign artists in Moscow.

The Bloodless Battle on the Oka

For nearly eighteen years Ivan had made sacrifices to avoid a decisive war. To the Tatar khanates he paid bribes, while he endeavored to stir up conflict between the remnant of the Golden Horde on the Volga and the stronger Nogai and Krim (Crimea) Tatars. In this he followed out his expedient of the Novgorod affair, working under cover for dissension, openly befriending the Tatars. Actually, he dreaded most a combination of the Hordes, knowing that Moscow could not resist a powerful army.

Meanwhile the European powers had been approaching the Krim khans—the omnipresent Venetians endeavoring to secure the aid of the Tatars against the advancing Turks. And what Ivan dreaded most came to pass, a combination against Moscow. In this case it was the Polish King and the Volga Tatars.

In 1480, just a century after Dmitri of Moscow had won the glorious and costly victory at the Don, the Khan with a large field army advanced across the Don to the Oka, menacing Moscow.

Ivan's agents worked among the Krim Tatars to persuade those ready pillagers to raid the half-deserted cities of the Volga and so compel the invaders to return to protect their homeland. But time lacked for that.

In spite of all his efforts, Ivan was compelled to take command of an army and to march out to a defensive battle that he dreaded. He sent Sophie and his children away to safety, then journeyed out to where his armed forces were mustering along the Oka. There, in sudden hopelessness, he abandoned the camp and raced back to Moscow, where he found the citizenry moving into the walled enclosure of the Kremlin to stand a siege.

Before his gates, a panicky crowd blocked his way, shouting at him: "You, the Tsar who rule over us—you have milked us of money in peacetime. Now, because you have paid him no tribute, the Khan is angered, and you fly away from him, betraying us!"

Accustomed to appeasing such mobs, Ivan protested that he had come back to consult the high boyars and clergy. But the nobles present and the clerics added their voices to the crowd's, clamoring at sight of their prince leaving the battle-front. A patriarch cried at Ivan: "Why do you try to avoid your fate? I am wearied with years, yet I will not turn away. I will go to face the Tatar lances."

Confronted by the panic of his people, Ivan controlled himself and said briefly that he was going back. He busied himself with some attempt to order the defense of the Kremlin, while the Metropolitan of the cathedral came out in robes to bless him, calling him a soldier of Christ, a shepherd of his flock—until the people were calmed and Ivan had no recourse but to return to the camp.

As he rode back the bells of the Kremlin tolled, and the great bell of Novgorod pealed its warning. Ivan went back to the camp because he was helpless to do otherwise. Afraid, clearly aware of his own incompetence, he kept to the ornate pavilion, which in Tatar fashion had been prepared to house the prince who was now commander of a great army.

To that pavilion came impatient *voevodes*, and officers of newly arrived contingents, which had marched in from far frontiers. They all seemed to have one thought—to advance across the river, and "go against the Tatars."

That was the one thing Ivan would not do. He knew himself to be a coward; this turbulent camp, noisy with altercation, was a torment to him. Across the river waited terror. Ivan's imagination peopled the far bank with dark masses of charging horsemen.

Actually the far bank looked peaceful enough after the first few days. For the Tatars withdrew their encampment, to let their horses graze and to offer the Russian host every opportunity to cross the small river on rafts or makeshift bridges. Some detachments rode down to the water's edge to taunt the Russians—"If your prince would escape harm, let him stand no more in the way of our Tsar!"

The Tatars fired cannon that blazed and smoked, without doing much damage. They sent exploring columns across distant fords, only to be turned back by bands of experienced Muscovite frontiersmen. Still, Ivan would not give his word to cross the river.

Priests sat with him, telling him how David had gone against the Philistines, and Constantine, the Emperor, had carried a cross into battle with his own hands. Ivan made no reply.

When some of his councilors asked why, then, he would not beg for peace from the Khan, Ivan agreed to do that. He sent envoys with gifts, asking for terms. They came back with the demand of the Tatars, that Ivan should come in person to kiss the stirrup of the Khan and pay the tribute he had not paid for nine years. This, however, he would not do. Nor would he send a son, to make submission for him.

A letter was brought him, from Troitsko, urging him to give battle to the pagans and not to humble himself before one who had shed Christian blood. "The shepherd must not desert his flock. You, our prince, must not bear the name of traitor and coward. Take courage, for there is no God like our God. His strength he gives to warriors, like your ancestors, Igor and Vladimir."

Always Ivan found himself reproached by the name of Dmitri of the Don, and the glory of Kulikovo. "How he fought! He did not say, I have a wife and children and wealth—if my country is lost to me I will go elsewhere."

And boyars came to kneel at his tent entrance, to remind him that the river could be crossed safely. Did not the waters of the Red Sea allow a Christian host to pass? But Ivan's imagination recalled the slaughter of that great citizen army of Novgorod, the dead on the field of Kulikovo; he could not feel any *power* in this camp with its wrangling officers, and he knew himself to be inept and powerless. Now that all these men waited upon his command to give battle, he refused.

Weeks passed in this strange inertia; autumn cold set in. Whether Ivan was wearied past endurance, or whether the first freezing of the rivers made him fear a sudden attack by the Tatars, he gave a command at last. It was to retreat closer to Moscow.

To his surprise the mass of the army, that had been so unmanageable in camp, showed itself satisfied to be moving, in whatever direction. The withdrawal of the undisciplined mass was disorderly, and Ivan must have felt anew that its numbers did not make of it an army.

His action, however, preserved the army, and probably saved Moscow from another devastation.

Immediately the Tatars retreated from their side of the river, and swept back to the Volga. They may have turned back to protect their own cities from the raid of the Krim horsemen; they may have been disturbed by the unaccountable maneuver of the Muscovites. More probably they had watched the Russian host grow in size, and when it refused to risk the river crossing, they gave up the campaign as useless.

The folk in Moscow beheld the strange spectacle of its armed host returning home without a battle. Long afterward that same folk would speak of this nameless campaign along the line of the Oka and of this year of 1480 as the one that ended the Tatar yoke.

In a truer sense than the monks of Troitsko realized, Ivan had found himself to be the shepherd of a weak, leaderless flock. As when he had found himself in a position to dictate to the burghers of Novgorod, he lashed out now to enforce his will while he could do so. After that winter he paid no tribute whatever to the Tatar khans. He intensified his alliance with the Krim khans, even sending his own boyars with contingents of fighting men to aid those friendly Tatars. Very soon thereafter the Krim raided Lithuania and sacked Kiev in the Ukraine.

Within Moscow, he hastened the rebuilding of the Kremlin citadel, and the outer city walls. And those walls were to stand. The outer face of the Kremlin remains today as it was rebuilt then.

No man could have brought order at this time into the disordered lands of Rus, but Ivan III, in his lashing out against opposition, managed to weaken the authority of any cities distant and strong enough to head a rebellion against Moscow. He had done so with Novgorod by operating on the recalcitrant burghers, removing part of them elsewhere. He operated more gently against other northern cities, Tver and Viatka, by making them subject to the command of Moscow.

Inexorably but without open war, Moscow was gathering in the surrounding cities; having bought one half of Rostov in 1474 and forced Viatka to surrender in 1489, she stretched out farther to Chernigov (1500), to Pskov (1511) and Smolensk (1514)—the last three being gateways to the west. Riazan, the uncertain neighbor, was incorporated in 1517. During this time the lands of Muscovy expanded from fifteen thousand to forty thousand square miles.

So, while his own city was strengthened somewhat by the new fortifications, it was actually *protected* even more by the reduction of possible rivals.

In doing so, Ivan was not carrying out a definite policy. But he was gaining ideas, and putting them into effect after a fashion.

Something odd was happening within Moscow. As it had become the largest city of Rus in numbers, and the greatest in military force, it was becoming the only international center. Foreigners were arriving there constantly. Besides the

Italians like "Aristotle" Fioraventi and Ambrogio Contarini, there were the engineers; some of the heads of the Usspensky cathedral were Armenians; merchants inhabiting the quarter by the market place and river were Tatars, Persians, as well as Armenians. Ivan kept sons of Tatar princes, as guests and hostages, to serve at the state banquets. Contarini says: "Every winter great numbers of merchants come to Moscow from German lands and Poland, to purchase furs of all kinds, which are exceedingly beautiful."

About this time Ivan (and the Duma) closed the trading house of the Germans in vitiated Novgorod, thus ending the tie-up of that city with Baltic commerce and making Moscow the main center of commerce. This move had unexpected consequences, not all favorable.

It always happened that the most intelligent foreigners were summoned to talk with Ivan, who gained in this way some knowledge of what was going on in both the west and east.

Within his own citadel, Ivan staged a demonstration. In reality, it was staged for effect upon the onlookers.

In the Usspensky cathedral, under the great bell of Novgorod, a grandson was crowned with the jeweled crown of a Byzantine emperor as Ivan's successor.

In full robes the priests performed the ritual—because it was to the interest of the Church to enhance the personal authority of the prince of Moscow. The Metropolitan intoned words over the boy's head: "Great Tsar and Autocrat." [5]

Witnesses to the ceremony testify that the man most impressed by it was Ivan himself.

Ivan's parade out to the Oka and back had happened at a point in time when the great balance of human forces was shifting throughout the plain of Eurasia. It had been shifting for generations—before Donskoi's time. By slow degrees the settlements were becoming stronger in manpower and experience than the nomad camps. In weapons, the balance perhaps was equal now. Soon, with the new firearms, ships and military discipline, it would incline toward the settlers,

[5] From the Byzantine *Autokrator*. But this did not mean an autocrat in the modern sense of the word; it was more a self-sufficient prince—one who was independent of other authority. In the same way *Tsar* did not then convey the meaning we attach to the title today. It was no more than the vaguely remembered title of the first emperors, the Roman Caesars, which had been given by the Muscovites to the Tatar khans like Batu.

the westerners. The Muscovite pioneer in his cabin was now the equal of the steppe horseman.

The rulers of the horsemen, the khans of the Krim, Nogai and Volga peoples, were becoming heads of settled nations; in the Crimea they lived in the garden palaces of Bagche Serai, under a benevolent sun; on the Volga, in the rich trading centers of Kazan and Astrakhan, they thrived more by merchandise than by war. Their control of the silk, carpet and perfume imports from Asia had become more profitable than the slave raiding of the century before. Even the Venetian merchants had ceased buying young slaves because they could no longer be sold publicly to Europeans.

In this generation, when powers balanced, the half circle of nations around the city of Moscow fell into a live-and-let-live rhythm which was not disturbed by a fresh explosion in the east. The Muscovites appeased the military forces so near them, making gifts with open hands, especially to the Krim khans who held the open steppe below them.

Gradually these Krim khans were scattering the Volga armies, driving the last remnants of the Golden Horde into the towns at the mouth and along the upper reaches of the mighty Volga.

In this expedient of bribing and conspiring, the Muscovites were imitating the Tatars themselves. And they were aided by an increasing pressure from the victorious Turks, who threatened the rear of the surrounding nations—the Krim, Moldavians, Hungarians and the Poles themselves. The Turks of Constantinople were not buying slaves so much as they were taking them, and training them to arms.

The generation of troubled truce from Ivan's accession gave Moscow an opportunity to gather not only land, and the subjection of other cities, but some means of defending itself.

How an Army Came to Be

The best defense was, obviously, a strong army.

Having only one model for a new-style military force, the Tatar, the Muscovites imitated that, without great success. They experimented with mounted divisions that could maneuver together, keeping a flying column concealed to strike a decisive blow. With Tatar weapons, the bow, the curved saber, small shield and light lance, they could at least oppose the warriors of the steppe. But their most reliant human force remained on foot—the rivermen, hunters and frontier settlers who could fight over any kind of ground with cunning and endurance. These were not so easily drilled into disciplined regiments. They persisted in acting like partisans.

Under Ivan, military service became compulsory. It was rewarded by grants of land, to those who had served, and those who were now obliged to serve. Much of the new land in the east was parceled out to the soldier-servants, who had to report for mobilization at command.

This in turn created, by degrees, a new military class of both landowners and peasants. It added a heavy expense of upkeep to be paid by the Moscow treasury, and a new *prikaz*, a bureau to be administered. In time it had a peculiar effect on the new soldier homesteaders. They could not very well leave the land allotted to them. In particular, they could not go off as before when the mood came on them, to serve the Swedes in Viborg, or the Lithuanians in Vilna. To do that now would make them deserters and traitors.

And especially on the frontiers, at a distance from Moscow, the homesteaders were bound to labor to maintain their land, each man on his lot, unless serving in the armies. Those in debt had to work out the debt or be imprisoned and cudgeled for failure to pay. In these isolated frontier holdings appeared the first trace of serfdom.

Something else was happening along the frontiers. Here stood fortified monasteries, and blockhouses that served to defend settlers and traders when attacked. These forts along rivers and the network of portages were called *ostrogs*. Clumsily at first, and then carefully, the planners in Moscow tried to link up these scattered frontier strongpoints in a kind of defense cordon. Ostrogs were garrisoned by trained troops, and outposts extended, to give notice of the approach of an enemy.

This rough defense line, manned for the most part by the settlers of the vicinity—especially by the new soldier-homesteader class—served to protect the lands inside and by slow degrees to create a connected frontier of Rus, in the west. It had grown out of the necessity of the frontier lands, chiefly to check the swift and devastating raids of Tatar horsemen, but it became a people's frontier.

Another idea had been growing more and more clear to the men who pored over maps and accounts in the workrooms of the Kremlin. It was about the rivers.

In the century before, Muscovite territory had grown

haphazard outward from the Moskva—down the Kliazma along the Oka to the Volga. And in the same way, it had stretched northerly along the upper Volga, taking in at first the plain of the two rivers. It happened that by controlling the territory around cities like Vladimir, Moscow had brought Vladimir into its fold, with the rest of them. Now, in turn, by holding a city like Nizhni (Lowland) Novgorod, where the Oka flowed into the Volga, the *trade* of the upper Volga became subject to Moscow control.

The taking over, as it were, of all that other Novgorod's network of trade and transport routes, from river to portage in the north and east, linked up the Moscow-held river routes to the new fur empire.

It was evident that in the unsettled condition of the frontiers, control of the rivers in the central plain meant control of the land. For those great rivers flowed like immense canals, almost free from rapids, through the plain which was almost without mountains. And between them there remained the old Tatar post roads.

If more of those river routes could be linked to the Oka-Volga valley terminal, more of the plain could be won for the new Muscovite state.

And now a new move was being made by some of the settlers in the northeast. They started to drift down through the forest belt, out of the extreme northern cold toward the line of the Kama River, once held by Tatar outposts, and opened up by the weakening of the Volga peoples. The hunters, homesteaders and land seekers were migrating south, through the wooded steppe toward more fertile ground. Curiously enough, they were now the roving and looting bands, while the Tatars had gathered into settlements. They were aided in this southward move by Muscovite troops in the lowlands around Nizhni Novgorod, and by the new defense cordons of blockhouses.

This drift of people, leaving huddles of cabins deserted in the dense forest, could not be checked or diverted to a planned destination. It tended directly south, toward warmer lands, beyond which lay the open prairies of the Ukraine.

It was the first advance to conquer the steppe.

Exactly at the beginning of a new century, in the year 1500, under Ivan III, Moscow began slowly and cautiously to use the internal forces, stored up for defense, in an attack on the great half circle of powers around her new frontiers.

It was not war, or invasion by a great field army. It was a

series of moves so slight as to remain almost unrecorded in history. But it manifested a change from the long retreat before the outer forces, to an expansion of Moscow as a nation.

Ivan had broken off trade relations with the outer sea, the Baltic, by liquidating the Hanse terminal in Novgorod. As a result, Moscow had been cut off from active contact with that sea. Now the Muscovite forces pushed slowly toward the Baltic, from stream to lake, almost following the ancient road of the Variags—building settlements and forts opposite the German-Livonian key center on the Baltic, the town of Narva.

The Muscovite fort built opposite Narva, at the outlet of the river Narova, was christened Ivangorod (City of Ivan). This cautious thrust toward the sea resulted in a succession of small combats, of forts against trading posts, of river barges against encampments—the method of attack of the newly strengthened Muscovite army.

At first it succeeded.

A second military move was made outward, this time to the south, following the new drift of the settlers. Here it followed the curve of the upper Oka. It advanced from the dense forest zone down into open woodlands. It moved very slowly toward the ancient city of Kiev. It encircled and then took over the old Slavic town of Chernigov where Vladimir had once hunted bears.

As the settlers advanced with the troops, a new chain of forts were built behind them. These forts were armed with the few available cannon.

A third military move was made, this time in the east. Here it marched with the rapid drift of settlers down the plains along the Volga—across the river Kama and the valley of Perm. It extended outward from the base at Nizhni Novgorod. It was backed by groups of populace transferred from the west to these prairies, and carried out largely by soldiers who had been given lands in the Perm depression. And it moved toward the juncture of the Oka with the great Volga, where the old Tatar center of Bolghar had stood and where the new Tatar city of Kazan had been built.

These three moves, carried out so slowly and tenaciously, made a curious pattern. Two of them worked to free the whole line of the Oka. The same two either followed or were supported by the drift of the settlements toward the south. The third, toward Narva on the Baltic, was aimed at a port on the sea, at a river mouth.

Slight though these gains might be, they evidenced a new

strategy on the part of Moscow. Cautious though they were in operation, they had consequences felt by Moscow.

In Moscow there was a new feeling that out toward the horizon *empire* might lie.

The clumsy little expedition to Narva was followed by a succession of nine wars against Swedes and Germans—wars that grew in intensity.

In the eighty years from 1500–80 there were forty wars.

The thrust to Chernigov was followed by war with Lithuania in 1507, and 1512.

The move to possess the middle Volga, in the east, had no such immediate consequences. But in 1521 two defenders of the steppe, the Tatars of Kazan and the Krim, launched a counteroffensive, penetrating the Muscovite defenses and besieging Moscow itself. But by then the Kremlin was able to defend itself from such attack.

It nearly succeeded, however. At the advance of the allied Tatars, the Muscovite field army fled from the Oka. In a panic the people of the countryside pressed into Moscow, which was deserted by its Great Prince (Vasily, the son of Ivan). Surrounding the city, the Tatars burned and ransacked, and drove off multitudes of captives. German engineers helped in the defense of the city, which had been left by its prince to the command of a Tatar half brother. "Gifts of gold" were made to the besiegers, and an agreement signed that the ancient tribute would be paid.

So the raiding Tatars profited heavily, selling their throngs of captives down the Volga at Astrakhan, and auctioning off the rich spoils at Kazan.

Meanwhile Ivan III had died. His people called him Ivan the Great, and historians were not long in pronouncing him the founder of the new Muscovite state.

Before his death the husband of Sophie, imperial princess of Byzantium, had taken for the insignia of Moscow the archaic black two-headed eagle that had been the symbol of the Byzantine emperors—and a symbol of ancient Persia before them. At long last Ivan and his advisers in the Kremlin had devised a proper style for him.

It was *"Johannes* (Ivan) *by the mercy of God, Emperor of All Rus and Great Prince of Vladimir and Moscow and Novgorod and Pskov and Tver and Perm and Ugra and Bolghar, and the rest."* In Ivan's new style he is no longer merely ruler of Moscow or *Hosudar* (Slavic), King. He is Emperor, of no ancient realm, truly, but of "All of Rus." To that has been added the frontier zones of the east traveled by his investigating armies, along with the old Tatar town of Bolghar.

And the rest. He is careful to leave unspecified the title to new regions or cities. They were to be numerous.

Testimony of Herberstein

By all odds the best reporter to reach Moscow at this time was Sigismund von Herberstein.

Herberstein, occupant of a castle in Austria, had an eye for details. At an age when most youths were attending universities, he had served in wars as standard-bearer, and had been sent on diplomatic missions across the small checkerboard of Europe. He had a German Catholic's sense of cleanliness and order. He knew war as it was fought by disciplined (and hired) *landzknechts*. He was sent to Moscow as ambassador, to try to make peace between the Great Prince and Lithuania-Poland. In that task he failed, but he impressed the Muscovites by his own stubbornness and boldness.

From the moment Sigismund von Herberstein crossed the unmarked line of Muscovite territory in 1516 he made the discovery that, at least in the spring thaw, roads hardly existed, whereas waterways did. "The further you go, the more marshes, rivers and woods you meet," he complains. "They are hard to travel unless bridged over by ice."

Along the upper Dnieper, the German ambassador found the countryside flooded by "so great an inundation that a monk transported Count Nugaroli and me across the woods a great way in a fishing boat, and the horses on their part came most of the way by swimming."

During the winter he found the cold so intense near Moscow that "water cast into the air freezes before falling to the ground . . . bears, driven by hunger, wandered into the villages, and dashed into the houses, while the throngs of peasants, terrified at the behavior of the animals, fled out of their doors and then died miserably in the cold."

He was received on his first approach to Moscow with amazing hospitality, and some suspicion. First a courier met him on the road with a gift of two horses, then an interpreter appeared, who warned Herberstein that he should dismount first at the meeting with a courtier of the Great Prince—advice which the experienced Austrian took by dismounting so slowly that the Muscovite noble was first on the ground. (Since Herberstein represented in his person the honor of his German master, he was careful not to make himself subservient to anyone.)

He was escorted into the Moscow gate by fifteen nobles and thirty grooms, who cleared a way through the staring crowd. But when he asked questions about the Kremlin and its people out of frank curiosity, he aroused the suspicion of his guides; thereafter he got information in roundabout ways, without asking questions.

Lodged splendidly, in the house of a prince fitted out for his visit, he was brought more food than he could use, every day, yet when he tried to buy some fresh fish with his own money, he was told that would be an insult to his host—and fresh fish was added to his daily rations. Courtiers shared the house with him and allowed no one to talk with him unless at least two of them were present.

Vasily (Basil), Great Prince of Moscow, 1505–30, son of Ivan III (the Great) and father of Ivan IV (the Terrible). (From Herberstein)

His audience with the prince of the Kremlin took him

through more ceremonial than any such reception in Europe. Three mounted courtiers called for him at his house. When they passed through the Red Place, he found the shops closed, and the way crowded by spectators.

Inside the Kremlin gate the groom leading his horse wanted him to stop and dismount before reaching the steps of the Palace of Facets. Herberstein however spurred his horse up to the steps, thus claiming, as it were, the right of a German envoy to dismount only at the last moment. On the steps counselors shook hands with him, and within the door other courtiers closed in behind him.

In the anteroom boyars were waiting who took no notice of him. In the first reception room he encountered nobles who wore only silk or brocade—in the second young princes and ministers wearing jeweled and pearl-sewn headgear over shaven skulls. He was led in to the chamber of the Great Prince (Vasily, the son of Ivan III), who sat in a chair raised above the others, with his Tatar brother-in-law beside him (the same who defended Moscow against the Tatar attack four years later).

Here the ceremonial was rigid. Complete silence was kept until Vasily spoke, requesting the German to stand by his footstool. At mention of the name of Maximilian, Herberstein's lord, Vasily rose and uttered a routine question. "How is the health of our brother Maximilian, high and noble King, and Roman Emperor-elect?"

So by question and response the audience went on, with the interpreter stopping Herberstein, to explain every three or four words.[6]

[6] Herberstein claims that Vasily was "tenacious" about having every word of his title pronounced correctly. He adds that interpreters rendered *Tsar* as *Imperator*, Emperor. Vasily, prompted by his counselors, had been most careful to concede Maximilian every possible degree of rank by his *"high and noble* King." That is, a king superior to others (and so almost but not quite the equal of the Muscovite "emperor").

Herberstein noticed something very interesting—that many Muscovites spoke of their prince as *"Tse-Tsar."* Now in the Turko-Tatar western dialects then, that would be a repetitive emphasis— signifying a most great tsar and not a simple tsar like Batu. The Mongols used the emphasis in their *kha khan,* for the great khans of the house of Genghis. The Mongols also spoke of them as the "White Khan"—white being a color of distinction, as with nobles of the "white bones." Often in Russia thereafter the rulers were called the White Tsar.

Much of the ceremonial at this palace of the Kremlin resembled that of the Tatar khans. The wearing of headgear, the silence of all others in the room, the presence, seated, of brothers of the Tsar, and even the form of interrogation was typical of the Tatar courts with which the Muscovites had had long experience.

The Great Prince in the end offered his hand to the ambassador. Immediately after he stepped to the side, where courtiers held a silver basin of water, and washed his hands, to remove from them the taint of the foreigner, who was no Orthodox Christian.

At the state dinners, which the foreign ambassadors attended in a group, Vasily would summon his favorites, Herberstein among them, to his own table, and offer a goblet of wine that he had tasted, saying, "Thou hast come a great way from a great master to a great master—to behold the light of my eyes. Drink, then, drain thy glass, that thou mayest be in health."

Brandy, malmsey, Greek wines and honey mead made up the drinks at the dinner. But Herberstein was escorted back to his quarters by gentlemen of the court, who fetched along one cart loaded with silver vessels and two others with liquors, "for the purpose of making the ambassador merry and full."

These gentlemen offered toasts first to the health of the Great Prince, then to the Emperor of Europe, then to the health of all those present. "When such a toast is drunk," Herberstein explains, "the person drains the glass and holds it upside down over his head. I had no wish to drink so much, but I had no alternative, except to say I was drunk, or too sleepy."

Herberstein's mission failed and his peace proposal was categorically declined. On his departure Vasily gave him sable and ermine furs, several fine wolfhounds, an oversize horse and a traveling sled fitted with furs.

Nine years later, in a new European political crisis (just after Charles V had become the head of the Holy Roman Empire, which now extended to Spain, and Suleiman called the Magnificent had become Sultan of the Turkish Empire), he was sent back to Moscow on a mission as thankless as the first, and with no greater success.

Yet he brought back with him this time the result of nearly two years of painstaking observation. Now the baron had grown up within the mountains of southern Austria, across from Salzburg and an obscure village named Berchtesgaden; he had been close to Slavic communities in the margraviate of Moravia, and down the Dalmatian coast, and scattered through his own mountains of Styria. He knew these varied Slavs and could talk with them; he could talk with those in Muscovy.

So the picture he formed of Muscovy was pieced together

carefully out of what he drew from the Slavic minds as well as from what he saw. The constant warfare between the rulers in Moscow and Vilna-Kracow he looked upon as a kind of civil strife, to decide which prince should hold which fort or town. Smolensk, a former ostrog, was the most bitter bone of contention at the moment.

Rus, or Russia as the name appeared in Greek or Latin, was little more than a name to him, attached somehow to this vast plain. "Many are the opinions about the origin of the name of Russia. Some maintain that it came from one Rus, a prince of the Poles. . . . The Muscovites, however, contradict those who hold these varied opinions, and they say what was called Rus anciently was a nation, scattered since and dispersed. . . . And the mixture of races now blended with the inhabitants, within the regions of Rus, all inter-mixed, manifestly prove that this was the case." Whatever the origin of the world, "all races using the Slavonic language, and holding to the faith and forms of Christianity in accord with Greek ritual . . . have increased into such a great multitude that they have driven out all intervening *nations*, or have absorbed them into their own way of living so that all together may be characterized by the one word, Russians."

He realized, too, that the Russians held to the concept of a dominion they once possessed but which was not yet cleared of other peoples. "A certain jester paraded the streets in Moscow carrying a broom and when asked what he meant by doing so, replied that the prince's dominion was not yet cleansed, and now the time had come to sweep the filth out of the dominion."

He is aware of the new policy of deporting outlying people from one region to another, to intermix the populations—"by dispersing the citizens [of cities] through the colonies, and sending Muscovites to fill their places." Of this happening in Novgorod, he says, "The people used to be very coura-geous and honorable; but now, doubtless from contagion from the Russian people who emigrated here out of Moscow, they have become degraded."

Here Herberstein expresses himself as a German and a Catholic. Yet he is clear that the people of Moscow differ from the others. "The people of Moscow are more cunning and deceitful than all others. Their honor is particularly slack in business agreements—of which fact they are by no means ignorant, for whenever they have dealings with for-eigners, they pretend they are not men of Moscow but strangers there, to appear more creditable." Herberstein adds frankly that the western merchants would demand two or three times a fair price of the Muscovites, if they could.

Like most foreigners, he complains that the Muscovites delay interminably and fail to get things ready in time; but adds shrewdly that when they are ready to act, they want to get it over with immediately.

Moscow he describes as by far the greatest city in Rus, having 41,500 dwellings, including the quarter beyond the river and the suburbs stretching into the plain. The other "cities" he finds almost alike, usually dominating a navigable river, built of wood on a bluff, defended only by a wooden wall. "For whatever is hemmed in by a wall, or oak stakes or in any way enclosed, they call a gorod (town)."

Always he is struck by the miracle of the rivers that interconnect with each other throughout the vast plain. Here is something startling to a European. These rivers are the artery of trade. "This convenience of navigation upon the rivers is the cause of the great wealth of the merchants of the country, who are able to transport goods by them, as from the Caspian up the Volga into different regions, and even up as far as Moscow."

His description of the country is almost a tracing out of the design of the rivers, whence each rises, whither it leads, and where it is navigable.

He hears that St. Andrew brought a small boat overland by this river route, all the way to Novgorod. "The Russians openly boast in their legends that before the time of Vladimir and Olha [Oleg?] the land of Russia was baptized and blessed by Andrew, the apostle of Christ, who came—as they assert—from the Greeks to the mouth of the Dnieper. And that he sailed up the river, against the current as far as the mountains where Kiev now stands, where he planted his cross. . . . Thence he went to the source of the Dnieper, to the great lake Volokh and descended by the river Lovat to lake Ilmen. Thence by the river Volkhov which flows out of the lake, to Novgorod. Thence by the same river to lake Ladoga and then by the river Neva to the sea which they call 'of the Variags' but we call the German sea."

Skeptical about Andrew's journey and Russian legends, the baron is very clear about the river route from Constantinople to the "German sea." He knows that a boat must go up against the current to the point at the lakes whence it "descends" to his German sea. Almost every town he locates in its proper position on this amazing map of river courses.

And the baron is aware of something more momentous. Somewhere back in the small lakes and flooded forest through which he entered Muscovy in a skiff rowed by a monk, there is a central point where many of the great rivers of a continent connect. This strategic center at the headwaters of the rivers gives access, even if by portage, to almost all of them.

"There is a wooded region . . . from which four rivers take their rise. In this wood is a marsh [land] named Fronov out of which flows a river of no great size which after two miles falls into a lake named Volgo. From this lake it emerges again, swelled by a multitude of streams, and is called Volga after the name of the lake. And after receiving many rivers it empties itself by five and twenty mouths into the Caspian sea.

"In the same wood about ten miles from the marsh named Fronov is the village of Dniepersko near which rises the Dnieper. Not far from there is a monastery of the Holy Trinity where rises another river, smaller than the first, called Little Dnieper. Both meet, however, between the source of the Dnieper and the marsh of Fronov. And the merchandise of the Russians is shipped at this place and carried into Lithuania, the merchants usually putting up at the monastery or at the inn.

"The lake of Dvina is nearly ten miles distant from the source of the Dnieper, and as many from the marsh of Fronov. A river also named Dvina flows westward out of the lake passing by Vilna at a distance of twenty [German] miles. It turns north after this and falls into the German sea—called by the Russians the Vareczkoi Morie [Varagian Sea]—near Riga, the capital city of Livonia. The Livonians call this river, which is navigable for the most part, the Duna.

"The Lovat, the fourth river, is not to be at all compared with the other three. It rises either between the lake of Dwina and the marsh of Fronov or out of the marsh itself—for I could not explore its source entirely, although it is not far from the source of the Dnieper. This is the river to which, according to their accounts, the Apostle St. Andrew brought a little boat by dry land from the Dnieper. It has a course of nearly forty miles [i.e., German miles] it flows by Velikiluki, and falls into the lake Ilmen."

Here, quite accurately described, is the birthplace of the rivers of a continent. Herberstein puts it at 140 German miles west of Moscow (actually west by northwest). The rivers he names so carefully do connect with the Baltic, the Caspian and the Black seas.[7]

Toward these three outer seas the Muscovites were then pushing their way purposefully—at Narva on the Baltic, past Chernigov toward the lower Dnieper and Black Sea, and past Nizhni Novgorod to the Volga, and Caspian.

Unknown to Herberstein, his four rivers interconnected with the other Dvina, leading to the White Sea, and hence to the icebound Arctic waters. And by portages, they connected with the "long Siberian way."

His amazing knowledge of this system of waterways came from some personal exploration in the west, as he makes clear. But he did not venture in other directions from Moscow, being occupied there, and his description of the further river system must have come from the Muscovites themselves, who explained to him this plan of the river network so carefully that he was able to set it down afterward as a coherent whole.

He gives at least one such conversation, with an elderly prince of the great Kurbsky family—"an old man and very much reduced in body by fasting. . . . The grand duke used to send him with an armed force through Perm into Ugria . . . to subdue distant nations. He accomplished a great part of this journey on foot, because of the heavy snow . . . when the snow melted, after crossing the mountains beyond the Pechora, he made the rest of the journey in boats. These lofty mountains slope down to its banks. Their summits are swept bare of grass or any other vegetation by exposure to the constant winds. Although they bear different names, they are commonly called the Earth Girdle [the Urals] . . . Kurbsky was still alive at the time I was in Moscow, and he told me that it took him seventeen days to ascend the mountains, and that in the end he could not reach the summit."

Beyond the Urals, Herberstein was told, stretched the dominion of "the great emperor"—that is, the dominion of the surviving Mongols, descended from Genghis Khan. Beyond the Urals lay the lands of fable—"scarcely believable" —of people with the heads of dogs, of the Golden Old

[7] Herberstein is not alone in realizing the command of the Eurasian rivers by this strategic portage system. Both Matthew of Michov and Paulus Jovius, who visited Muscovy, explain that "near to Moscow" rise the Dvina, Dnieper and Volga—Jovius adds the Moskva and the Oka. To western Europeans, this means of sailing, or at least being towed, across a continent was something of a marvel. To Hollanders, accustomed to miniature canals, it was a miracle.

Woman, of the Tatars who traveled without roads, "picking their course by the stars, especially by the pole star . . . in battle they keep a wonderful order, both in advancing and retreating—they call this in their language, dancing."

Here, in Zavolosky or Beyond-Volga, the Muscovites told of a wealth of dark sables, of sulphur, and salt mines, and even iron—the minerals they craved and had to buy at high prices from other peoples.

Already, they had made a long stride of nearly five hundred miles to cross the Volga. They assured the baron that the fables were reality. "So every man swears, yet I have not met one who beheld the wonders himself."

The Volga Artery

"The church of Slavetown stands two miles from the river, and here the *fairs* are more frequent than elsewhere in the Russian dominions. For the Tatars and many other nations from the east and north journey to this place to barter with the Swedes, Livonians and Russians. There is scarcely any use made of gold or silver [coin] among all these nations—they exchange homespun garments, needles, knives, spoons and hatchets and so forth, mostly for furs."

These fairs were the recreation of the common folk, and almost their only trading place. On the rivers the boats would be lined up in such a mass that you could walk from bank to bank over the shipping—on log rafts and luggers. Within circles of tavern sheds, hastily nailed up, families could get drunk—safely beyond the watchful eyes of the priests, who might be drinking out of sight themselves—while watching dogs tear bears in pens, or listening to the wailing of old blind singers. Finnish hunters could barter skins for the carpets of bearded Turks from the Volga, rivermen had sturgeon's roe to offer for Tatar boots, Swedes from beyond Ladoga could trade iron plows for the honey of Russian farmers.

Here the folk could bathe and drink and forget, in gambling, shouting, dancing. . . . A woman well drunk came naked and sweating out of a wooden bathhouse, and fell on her back among the people in the outer air. A peasant threw himself on her, while the crowd pressed close about the two, shouting with laughter. . . . A settler from the Kama, having paid silver coins to the tax collectors, gambled away his furs, and drank up his clothes in the tavern, and, when he sobered enough to stand, crossed himself and spat three times and started to walk back to the Kama naked. He would not starve.

Herberstein felt without analyzing this abundant force in the barbaric people, and the fertility of the land. ". . . between the Oka and the Volga, in a spot so fertile that from one bushel of wheat twenty, or even thirty may be produced . . . a lake from which salt comes by evaporation . . . sulphur of which they know not the method of use as yet."

Yet he saw no printed books, and no coined money except in the hands of the treasurers of that mighty hoarder the Great Prince—and some of the wealthiest merchants. Even there, the gold coins are foreign, ducats, florins, byzants. There is no printed paper in Moscow; there is no printing.

Nor does Sigismund von Herberstein describe here what we would expect him to be most interested in—coming as he does from the hivelike authorities of Europe, the margraviates, bishoprics, counties and dukedoms of Austria—and that is any government of Moscow, with its laws. But in Rus he is aware only of areas that are provinces, or regions, and of inhabitants who are nations or peoples. Of laws he hears little, except how debtors who cannot pay are beaten by a number of strokes varying with the size of their debt.

True, there are military guards at road intersections. These posts of the Watch and Post service are called *karauls,* a Tatar (or rather Turkish) word. Such a road control was in fact instituted by the Tatars. The word for postrider is *yamchik,* Tatar also. "When I was making a rapid journey from Great Novgorod to Moscow, the post-master who is called *jamschnick* would have from thirty to fifty horses brought out for me the first thing in the morning. When the horses tired, we changed them on reaching another inn along the road, but kept the same saddles and bridles. They are small ponies and far less cared for than ours, yet they endure greatly. One of my servants rode from Novgorod to Moscow, a distance of six hundred versts—that is, a hundred and twenty German miles—in seventy-two hours."

Herberstein's trip had been in winter; if he had come through the post stations in summer he might have found no horses at all—they would have been grazing or hired out on the sly to peasants. There was, however, an alternate way to travel, on the river craft belonging to the Great Prince. The watch on the roads and the relay post service had been put into execution by the Tatars. The river transport, however, was Russian.

Yet even this was a hit-and-miss affair. Sometimes there would be boats available to serve as ferries; sometimes Herberstein and the other travelers would have to bind branches of trees or logs together to float them across.

There is the same rough-and-ready attempt to fight plague. The dread Black Death (bubonic plague) did not penetrate Rus as it did western Europe. When it did appear, it came unmistakably from the west, passing from Pskov to Novgorod and from Polotsk to Smolensk. The Muscovites isolated these western frontier towns; the guards of the road watch turned back all wayfarers from the west; in Novgorod, newcomers from Pskov were ordered to leave, and those who refused were burned alive. Herberstein remarks that the sickness prevalent in Rus caused "pain in the head and running of the bowels," which might mean typhus or cholera or dysentery.

In the same way, rude measures were taken to control drunkenness. At Moscow, "across the river Prince Vasily built a new city called Nali for his courtiers to drink in, because other Russians were forbidden to drink mead or beer, except on a few days of the year."

No orderly police patrolled the rambling streets of Moscow. Instead, the semblance of a night watch was kept. "In some places the streets are blocked by beams thrown across them, where watchmen take their stand at early nightfall, so that no one is allowed to pass after a certain hour." Moscow, it seems, had its curfew.

All such controls over the populace—rude and barbaric as they may have been—stemmed from Moscow. The one rigid control, enforced more and more as time went on, was over money. Tithes and road tax took constant toll of the coins in the hands of the peasantry. True, anyone could make coinage of a sort by stamping oblongs of gold or silver. But in the course of time most of this makeshift money took its way into the treasury of the Kremlin, where it was stored.

Yet in spite of the growing wealth of the Kremlin, and in spite of the fertility of the soil along the frontiers, most of Muscovy suffered from a famine in 1525. The vast stocks of furs, flax, hides and hemp, accumulated in centers like Moscow, lacked an outlet to the western markets.

The largest outlet for trade led along the Volga to the cities of mid-Eurasia, to Tabriz, Isfahan, Samarkand. The "through" Eurasian trade, as in silk, spices, was now detouring around Rus, and going by sea. Yet internal trade went on between what Herberstein calls the "nations" of Rus, by barter, by exchange at the fairs, by the use of squirrel skins for token money.

It is a strange picture that the baron draws, of a timid prince sheltered behind the walls of the Kremlin—walls built by foreign architects—taking tribute from the wealth of a growing nation with all a merchant's skill, while he experimented clumsily with governing that nation through his lieutenants.

Punishment, whether by law or princely decree, also stemmed from Moscow. A man killing a thief caught in the act of robbery went unpunished, "provided he brought the man he had killed to the prince's palace and explained how it had happened." As with the post service, punishment of criminals depended much on the weather. "Few justices, [lieutenants] have authority to order death as punishment. No subject dares put another to the torture. Most criminals are brought to Moscow, or to other large cities, but convicts are generally punished in winter, for in the summer the demands of military service prevent attending to other matters."

The demands of that military service were growing. And Sigismund von Herberstein was skeptical of the results. "Rest is seldom given them, for either they are waging war against the Lithuanians, or the Livonians, or the Swedes or the Tatars of Kazan. Or, if no war is going on, the prince usually details twenty thousand men every year to posts along the Don and Oka to guard against inroads of the Tatars of Crimea."

The German's description of the Russian horsemen shows their very close imitation of Tatar tactics and equipment. The horses are geldings, the stirrups are "drawn up" so the riders can use a bow in any direction; they carry rations in a bag—some ground millet, pork and salt—and endure "severe fasts" for a pittance of pay.

"They do everything suddenly and rapidly, whether advancing or fleeing. They make the first charge with great impetuosity; but their courage does not hold out, and they seem to be hinting to the enemy, 'If you do not flee, we must.'

"When he once takes to flight, the Russian thinks there is no safety but in flight; if then he be taken by the enemy he neither defends himself nor asks for quarter. On the other hand the Tatar, thrown from his horse, stripped of his weapons and even severely wounded, will usually fight with hands, feet and teeth as long as he can breathe. The Turk, when he has no hope of escape, throws down his weapons and holds out his hands clasped ready for binding, hoping to preserve his life."

Shrewd in this appraisal, the German who has come from a world of tournaments and small ranged battles does not understand the strength of the Slav as an individual fighter. He sees only novice soldiers who "load themselves rather than protect themselves with a number of different weapons." In Moscow in 1526, he discussed with the German and Italian cannon founders and artillerists the near capture of the city by the Tatars five years before. The foreign experts told him much of the "terror and despair of the Russians." They said: "Johann Jordan, an artilleryman from the Innthal, judged the extent of the danger more clearly than the Russians. Of his own accord he discharged the guns which had been ranged in order against the Tatars and Lithuanians, so that they fled from the fortress."

And Herberstein relates with jest the irresolute attempt of the timid Vasily to retaliate on his enemies after their withdrawal. "Afterward, as summer came on, Vasily resolved to avenge the slaughter by the Tatars and to wipe out the shame that had come to him from his flight. He levied a large army and provided it with a great number of guns and other contrivances, and marched out of Moscow with his army as far as the river Oka."

Vasily pushed his ill-assorted army eastward to Nizhni Novgorod. As it advanced, the shipping of this army nearly blocked the Volga. "On the river Sura near Kazan he built a fortress which he named after himself . . . and retired."

But he kept sending men, guns and boats down the Oka and the Volga, and extending the line of ostrogs along the rivers. Ambushed and outmaneuvered to such an extent that Herberstein almost jeers in relating it, the Muscovite frontier posts held to the Volga valley. Bribed and vacillating and afraid, the Muscovite officers of this inept new army, stiffened by hired Lithuanians and German mercenaries, learned to defend themselves in forts and on boats.

Vasily struck an indirect blow at Kazan itself by stopping the annual fairs on the Island of Merchants near that city of Tatar merchants. He stopped the sale of salt to the Tatars. "The Russians suffered as much hardship as the people of Kazan, for it brought about a scarcity of many things that had been imported through the Caspian Sea from Persia and Armenia, by way of the Volga and the emporium of Astrakhan."

Under protection of the forts, the settlers, drifting down

from the north, occupied the west bank of the Volga. In this strange but inexorable warfare, as the years went by, the balance of force shifted, and Kazan became the city besieged instead of Moscow.

Helpless to encounter the Tatar horsemen in battle, Vasily had used the rivers and the river-borne trade to fight his battle for him. "Which undertaking was made less difficult by the lie of the rivers, that flow from Moscow to the Volga, and by the dependence of the Tatars upon trade. For those in Kazan are more civilized than the others, cultivating the ground, living in houses, and branching out into different kinds of merchandising."

Herberstein had been contemptuous of the failure of the Muscovites to capture a hostile city. When he took his last adieu from Vasily, whom he called at the end "Prince of Muscovy," Vasily gave him his farewell presents and a warning that may have been touched by malice: "Be careful how you return to your homeland, for news has just reached me that the Turks have captured Buda-Pesth."

The Women of the Terem

The great princes had been heads of a family also. For some generations they had toiled to uplift their family's fortune. In doing so they had raised the family itself above others in Muscovy.

That family was making its presence felt. Uncles rode in from their personally owned towns, and argued as to what should be done to improve Moscow; elderly aunts in the seclusion of their chambers conspired to appoint a new archimandrite to rule in the Church; young cousins had to be given suitable commands in the nebulous army of Moscow; daughters had to be married off and their families-in-law compensated in some way, to maintain their new dignity.

To rule in Moscow, the Great Prince had first of all, and very firmly, to rule his own family.

Ivan III had been bedeviled by a family quarrel as to who should succeed him on the throne. In a fit of temper he had ordered Dmitri, the son of a daughter of his Byzantine wife Sophia, crowned as Tsar-to-be. Then in his last years he had changed his mind and announced publicly that Vasily, a son of his first wife, should reign after him.

But the family quarrel was not pacified by this ukase. Such jealousies and striving for power did not result in open rebellion. Moscow differed from the European courts in this as in other respects; it carried on its feuds more silently yet not the less inexorably. Recalcitrant uncles were imprisoned, young cousins who happened to win military glory—which always appealed to the people—might find themselves transferred to a desk in the bureau of war, out of the public eye. Antagonistic boyars might be visited by an envoy from the Kremlin who would pour out the wine with which the boyar was obliged to drink the health of the Great Prince, even if he died of the poison in the wine.

So conspiracy went underground, confined in the arena of the Kremlin.

It remained, however, a family affair. The family as well as the Great Prince had the responsibility of the well-being of Rus; rebellion against the man on the throne would be rebellion against Rus. Underneath the personal bickering lay mute fidelity to tradition. This loyalty was stronger, perhaps, than in the more culturally advanced European nations.

Then, too, Moscow had become something of a national shrine, over which the Church laid its outwardly rigid discipline. At the worst, unruly spirits in the family might flee across the borderland to the Lithuanian court. The powerful Lithuanians were kindred Slavs, their court more up to date.

Another reason for the outward silence of the reigning family was the seclusion of its women. Instead of relaxing, this seclusion had grown more rigid since Byzantine times.[8] Only the wealthy classes, of course, could afford it. Peasant women labored like animals within the sight of all.

The brides of wealthy men entered the terem or women's quarters after their marriage night, and seldom left it except to ride forth in closed vehicles until they were old enough to be unattractive to amorous men. In the terem they had a shrine of their own; there they were visited by priests, beggars and mountebanks; there they directed the women slave-servants of the household, and painted and dressed and fed themselves. Few of them had been taught to read; they

[8] Contrary to general belief, this internment of upper-class Russian women was not due to the influence of Islam, through contact with the Tatars. The Tatars of the Golden Horde did not mingle with Russian communities, except in war, and they did not seclude their women. As late as the mid-fourteenth century their conversion to Islam had been only partial. In 1526 Herberstein, speaking of the Kazan Tatars, states that the upper-class women veiled only when they appeared in public gatherings.

Seclusion within Rus was due to reactionary Byzantine and religious influences, fostered in some strange way by the Russians themselves.

depended on talk for their knowledge, and—as always happens in *harim* life—they made their presence felt in conspiracy.

The wife of a boyar might be summoned to appear before guests, to offer the drink of hospitality. Clad resplendently in satin, silver tissue and pearls, the *boyarina* would descend to the foot of the stairs, holding the goblet of wine, which she sipped and offered in turn to the guests, who kissed her in greeting. Always the boyarina must have a rosary on her wrist, as if doing eternal penance for sin. To inflict punishment on her, the husband touched her lightly with a whip during the wedding festivity, and he might use the whip not so lightly afterward. He was the *grodzniy*, the dread master of the family, his wish the law of the house.

"There is at Moscow," Herberstein explains, "a certain German metal-worker named Jordan, who married a Russian woman. After she had lived with him some time, she thus lovingly addressed him: 'Why is it, my dearest husband, that you do not love me?' The husband replied: 'I do love you, passionately.' 'You have given me no proof of that, yet.' The husband asked what proof she wanted. 'You have never beaten me,' she explained.

"The husband answered that he did not know that love had to be proved by blows, but if so he would not fail her. So not long after that he beat her cruelly, and confessed to me that afterwards his wife grew much more affectionate. So he repeated the exercise often; and finally, while I was still in Moscow, cut off her head and her legs."

As might be expected, Herberstein is critical of the terem —although semiseclusion of women prevailed in Spanish and Italian courts, and in Venice the class of public prostitutes had great influence. "The condition of women is most miserable, for they think no woman virtuous unless she stay shut up and closely guarded. To be thought modest, she may not be seen by strangers or people outside the house. Shut up at home, she does nothing but spin and sew, as the housework is done by the servants."

There was a taint of homosexuality arising from this separation of women, in ordinary life. Men would not shave their beards willingly, for fear that it might be whispered they were unsexed.

"Love between those who are married," Herberstein relates, "is usually lukewarm, especially among the nobles and princes, who marry girls they have never seen before. Then, too, being engaged in the service of the Great Prince the nobles are obliged to desert their wives for long intervals, when they become corrupted by connections with other women. . . .

"The women are seldom let go to church, and still less frequently to friendly gatherings unless they be very old and so free from suspicion. On rare holidays, however, men allow their wives and daughters a special gratification—to meet with other women on a meadow-ground, where they all sit in a sort of wheel of fortune, and are moved in turn up and down, or they sit in a rope seat and swing back and forth. Otherwise they make merry by clapping their hands and singing, for they have no dances whatever."

For a woman of the "western lands" to enter the area of seclusion in Moscow was to challenge the jealousy of the women of the great families, especially if she should be a pagan, that is, not an Orthodox Christian. For a foreigner to become the bride of the Great Prince was to intensify the challenge, for two reasons.

Old custom—the fetish of the reigning family—demanded that the Great Prince give over the highest offices nearest his person to kinsmen of his wife. (This was a measure of protection, because his family-in-law would have every reason to support his authority, and to safeguard the interests of the children; whereas his own relatives would work to increase their own prerogatives and power.) Also, the family of the Great Prince was still a newcomer among the princely stock of Vladimir and the elder families of Kiev. These, surrounded by *dvors* or courtly establishments of their own —with armies of servants and dependents—but without the huge estates of bygone days, hugged close to them their glory. Moscow was packed with boyars who had been princes themselves, even if their ancestors had been Lithuanians, Germans, or Tatars or Finns. The position of the Great Prince was like that of the Capet Louis XI, among the great peers of Burgundy, Orléans and Berry in France. He was monarch in name rather than by title.

Among these jealous and exacting families Sophia Paleologus, the second wife of Ivan the Great, had come as by right, being herself a descendant of emperors, and Orthodox.

Such was not the case with Vasily's second wife.

The affair of Vasily's divorce and remarriage created a feud within the Kremlin that spread to the outer circle of the great boyar families, and finally out to the frontiers themselves.

Ivan III, that thin, worried man, had been *grodzniy*— dread, or great—in fact as well as in fame, within the fam-

ily circle. He had held the whip firmly, and used it sparingly.
Irresolute as he might have been when confronted with
Lithuanian or Tatar antagonists, he had ruled within the
Kremlin. The baton he carried in public, the *kisten* or staff
of wood tipped with a sharp steel point, had been more
than symbolical. Not even the brilliant Sophia Paleologus
could influence him to go contrary to his own mind—although the leading boyar families claimed she did. Sophia
had needed to trick Ivan into doing what she wanted.
Vasily, a man of less force, although more benevolent in
intention, did not hold the *kisten* so firmly.

He had the best of all possible reasons for a divorce. His
first wife had not borne him a child in twenty-one years,
and he was growing old, without an heir. Divorce was common enough in Moscow at that time, although not counte-
nanced outwardly by the clergy (who made great objection
to a third divorce, and would not marry a man to a fourth
wife). The feud here raged over the successor to Vasily, son
of Ivan the Great.

As might be expected, all accounts of this internal strife
vary greatly, according to the teller. The most exciting interesting story is that of a certain George, called the Little, a
wily boyar of old family who served Vasily as treasurer
and counselor when he was not in disgrace. As it happened
George the Little was appointed to carry on the person-to-
person talks with the Baron von Herberstein—those quiet
talks in which the views of the master of the Kremlin were
passed on privately to foreign envoys, or the ideas of the
foreigners tested out. Probably George the Little was more
than a match for Herberstein at this. (Herberstein was persuaded to have his master, the Roman Emperor, sign a pact
of mutual assistance against Poland—a pact not disclosed
at the time.)

At any rate, here is George the Little's story about the first
bride of Ivan, his master, as he told it to Herberstein. Not
at all did George the Little approve of Vasily wedding one
of the attractive foreign girls, because such a wife would be
expensive, and quite different in her way of living, and a
pagan to boot. No, George the Little thought definitely
that Vasily should marry at home, and among the daughters of the boyars. In fact what daughter of a boyar would
be more inexpensive, docile and religious than the daughter of George the Little?

But Vasily chose another girl. When the procedure of
selection had been gone through—the formality of having fifteen hundred candidate brides picked out of the whole

of Rus, and the fifteen hundred narrowed down to five and then to two hundred, and these carefully scrutinized by the Great Prince (very much as the Great Khan of the Tatars in Kambalu had selected his girls aforetime)—and the final group of ten daughters of boyars presented for Vasily's choice, what should the Great Prince do but point out one named Salome.[9]

This choice was certainly ill-fated, George the Little pointed out, because Vasily had had no child from Salome in twenty and one years. When she was divorced finally and sent against her will to a convent in the Suzdal district, she wept when they cut off her hair—she threw to the floor the hood they tried to put on her. A prelate was called in who threatened sternly to beat her. "By whose will?" demanded Salome. When she was told it was by the will of her master, Vasily, she only wept more, and invoked God to avenge her.

Then, at the first report of Vasily's new marriage, this Salome gave out word that she was with child, and near her time for the birth. When the wife of George the Little and another boyar's wife were sent to investigate this situation, they told in the Kremlin how the discarded wife had sworn to the truth of it. Whereupon Vasily had the wife of George the Little beaten for not telling him of the truth sooner, and two other male ministers were sent to Suzdal for evidence. Various stories went the rounds of the Kremlin as to whether or not a child had been born. Salome could show no child, yet she swore she had had one who would avenge her when he came of age.

Into such a troubled family circle Vasily brought his new bride. She was young, she was striking to see, she was a foreigner, being a Lithuanian Ukrainian, daughter of the Glinsky who—by report—had sold Smolensk to Vasily's inept army and was now in disgrace in Poland.

So the new bride, Elena (Helen) Glinskaya, was not only a Lithuanian, an exile accused of plotting against the other king, Sigismund, of Poland—she was a pagan.

George the Little, seeing his own career go up in smoke, assured Herberstein in one of their quiet talks that the Lithuanian family had tricked his master, and intrigued their way

[9] Although this ceremonial selection of a bride from the daughters of all the land resembles unmistakably the procedure in the China of Kubilai Khan, as related by Marco Polo, the choice in Rus was usually decided beforehand and for political rather than personal reasons. In the Kha Khan's selection, the final ten girls were kept in attendance on him and enjoyed as he liked; in Moscow the unsuccessful nine were dismissed with gifts from the Great Prince.

to seats around the throne of Rurik. Herberstein, however, found her young and fascinating. He noted that Vasily had even cut off his beard to please her.

The truth seems to be that the aging master of the Kremlin had fallen wholeheartedly in love with the blond, vivacious girl from the west, who could read and talk with him of his troubles, and who cared not a jot for the dumb seclusion of the Muscovites.

More than that, the careful Austrian records, "Besides the hope he had of having children by her . . . he had a second hope that the children would have for their uncle Michael Glinsky, a man of rare ability and distinguished valor —for the prince had two brothers-in-law yet living, George and Andrew. Therefore he thought that any children by his new wife Helen would not be safe within the government while those two brothers were alive. But he doubted not that if Michael Glinsky were released from prison, Helen's children would enjoy greater peace."

Vasily lived only a short while, to appreciate the impetuous spirit of his young wife and to have two sons by her. Nothing more was heard of the invisible child of the convent. "Some constantly denied Salome had had a child," Herberstein points out.

Yet the feud rankled. After Vasily's death, Helen reigned as guardian of the prince-to-be. Around this dynamic young widow centered a twofold conflict: that of the supremacy of the Lithuanian Slavs over the Slavs of Rus, and of the concept of autocracy over the old feudal oligarchy of the land.[10]

Helen acted with more force than Vasily had ever shown, and with less pity. One of the former brothers-in-law, George, was imprisoned, and died promptly; the other, Andrew, was caught trying to escape to the Polish court, and imprisoned. He also died in his cell, of the food he ate.

The military commanders of Moscow were lashed into action against the Tatars, and Helen ordered a new wall built around the boyars' quarter of the city, called—perhaps after the eastern merchants, perhaps after her old home— the Kitaigorod, or Walled-city. When she took for her lover Telepniev Obolensky, her master of the horse, even Michael

[10] Succession caused conflict in western Europe even more than in Rus in this age of the growing monarchies. In England, the child Elizabeth, pronounced successor by Parliament, was to be set aside twice before reaching the throne. In Spain the conflict of the Comuneros was being fought out. As for executions, the reigns of Henry VIII and "Bloody" Mary would be studded with them; and within a generation, that of Philip II in Spain.

Glinsky remonstrated with her. "He admonished her to live a more religious life . . . and was arraigned for the crime of treason, and again thrown into prison, where he died."

Deprived of her one protector, and handicapped by her lover, a nitwit, Helen Glinsky did not survive the anger of the great families, who had found her to be an inward as well as outward enemy. She died five years after her husband, apparently of poison.

Her younger son was feeble-minded; the elder, the prince-to-be, bore the old family name of Ivan and he was to be called the Terrible.

IV

IVAN THE TERRIBLE
1533–84

Boyhood of Ivan

IT WAS a strange circumstance, with which he had nothing to do, that the eleven-year-old Ivan became master of the Kremlin in name without a single friend to support him. The leading boyars had the master of the horse assasinated, and his sister, who had been Ivan's wet nurse, imprisoned. Ivan's own brother was like a mindless shadow at his side.

The two children had to dwell in the palace, waited on by the army of servants who carried out the duties of bygone generations. They had religious manuscripts to read, and a monk, Sylvester, to tutor Ivan. He played with dogs and with the boys who were keepers of the dogs, and he fought with them. On state occasions, holy days and even audiences of foreign ambassadors, the servants unearthed him, as it were, and robed him magnificently, while for an hour the boyars, who ruled Moscow between them, beat their foreheads before him and held out the silver basin for him to rinse his hands. Yet he had no friends.

The boy Ivan IV, ignored the greater part of the time, was no more than the concept of the tsar-prince, the personification of the past, wandering among the shrines, the graves and the cathedrals that made Moscow a holy city. There were no women except a Glinsky grandmother, and servants in the terem.

Years later, and all through his life, he was to remember how one of the boyars, watching the boys in the bedroom of the dead prince, had put his feet up on Vasily's bed. "We and our brother George," he wrote in after life, "were treated like foreigners, like the children of beggars; we were badly clothed, we were cold, and hungry."

He was terrified when, during a savage clash of rival

107

nobles, a man was pursued to the palace, and killed near the boys and thrown out of a window. Ivan seemed to find the summer residence in the forest less hostile than the brick buildings and ill-kept gardens of the Kremlin enclosure. Yet here also a fugitive was pursued and caught. Ivan apparently learned to observe the conflict around him, to hide his fear, and hold his tongue. Certainly he drew no attention to himself.

The two orphans rested in this strange counterpoise, kept alive in the semblance of rule by the antagonisms of the nobler houses, the great families that could not agree upon a head to the government, or even upon a head to the Church —the Kurbskys, Bielskys, Shuiskys, and the other "sons of Rurik." "They wandered everywhere," Ivan wrote later, "from palaces to the different villages, exacting fines from the people there, making slaves of dignitaries, raising their own slaves to be dignitaries."

He wrote of the "terrible deaths" that he saw inflicted. His watchfulness increased, until he became suspicious of any strange faces, and unexpected actions near him. Since he himself was watched continually by servant-spies, he learned to conceal his own rage. When hysteria seized on him, he broke out into weeping.

Ivan had inherited a predisposition to fear. He had no one to confide in. The monk Sylvester impressed on his mind that life must be spent in penance, in fasting and righteous living, in fear of God's anger. The manuscripts of the library, written out in church Slavonic and put in order by Maximus the Greek, told him indeed of the grandeur of ancient tsars—Tsar David of Judea, Tsar Nebuchadnezzar, and of the war chariots of Tsar Solomon. Avidly he read about them. But in those manuscripts—no printed books were to be had nearer than Vilna—the boy Ivan read also of prophecies of doom, of the coming of the dragon of the Apocalypse, when fire would descend from heaven to destroy man-made cities. All these concepts entered his thoughts, to abide there and come out long afterward in his labored, brilliant writings and frenzied speeches that held listeners spellbound, hardly understanding, but feeling his emotion.

Any person who showed him attention, except Sylvester, aroused the suspicion of the watchers. He had two friends of a sort among the boyars' sons of his own age—the brilliant Andrew Kurbsky, who seemed to like military life, and one of the Vorontzevs. Ivan was warned against Vorontzev, and he seemed to feel relief later when that youthful scion of nobility was seized and beaten by the servants of other boyars.

As time went on, he developed a firmer friendship with a certain Adashev, who served as maker of the beds, who belonged to no great family, who had common sense. Like the dog keepers, Adashev treated the adolescent and moody Ivan as a fellow human being.

Ivan owed his life to the circumstance that no one family of boyars could oust the others and so gain firm control of the Kremlin. When the Shuiskys prevailed over the Bielskys, the treasury would be emptied, and new taxes levied haphazard, to enrich the Shuiskys' following. The head of the Shuiskys, also named Ivan—the same who propped his legs on the bed of the dead Vasily—was perhaps the most powerful among the heads of families. At least he squeezed out more gold than the others. But the Shuisky clan was overbearing, and Lithuanian to boot. The Bielskys and Vorontzevs and Kurbskys grouped together to oppose them, without being able to exercise authority themselves.

This was not even a regime of robber barons. It was no regime at all, but anarchy.

Yet anarchy in Rus of that day, especially in Moscow, was not like misrule in western Europe. No eve of St. Bartholomew occurred, no Inquisition summoned heretics to a tribunal, no civil war divided the people. Rus simply lay inert, plundered by its best families, who held to "ancient usage." These blamed the catastrophe of chaos on the foreign women, especially on Sophia Paleologus—"Since her coming hither with the Greeks, there has arisen among us such strife as was formerly in her city of Tsargrad; she came hither to our undoing."

The folk around Moscow simply went hungrier; the upriver trade dwindled; outlying cities like intelligent Novgorod proceeded to manage their own affairs while waiting for the collapse of Moscow.

Apparently the only authority capable of bringing order out of the chaos in Moscow was that of Sigismund, who ruled Poland through a modern Diet and feudal class of the nobility.

Like an animal organism deprived of its head, the great body of Rus lived on, by automatic reflex. Such life could not endure long even in a food-producing country, with more settlements than cities.

As Ivan grew a beard and came to marrying age, his

strange double life became intolerable. Even in their dissensions the boyar families must have realized that the inmate of the Kremlin palace had grown into a man who might strike back at them. But he was still ignored. Apparently Ivan dissimulated perfectly the emotions he felt.

He fought successfully his insatiable craving to escape. He led his dual existence without attempting to change it.

Under the mask of the boyars' creature, he signed decrees, and read what he signed. Few of his masters could read as well as he. On the throne seat he made no attempt to gain help from foreigners. To the Archimandrite (Metropolitan), who blessed him as Great Prince of All Rus, he made no protest.

In his self as a seventeen-year-old youth, he roamed the empty terem apartments, listening to the gossip of the serving-women, who heard bells ringing mysteriously at night, and sighted radiant figures of the dead weeping among the gravestones in the cathedral. When this human Ivan—tall, fierce-eyed, red-bearded—walked from the Gate of the Saviour, beyond the surviving pines, the guards with their halberds shaped like ancient Variag axes bowed to him clumsily.

Descending to the gray river, he could lose his identity among the fishmongers and butchers, who cast the filth of their shops into the water of the Moskva, where the boats of traders' convoys no longer rowed around the bends. Unnoticed except by the spies who followed lazily, he could drink with the grandfathers and thieves of the taverns, and amuse himself afterward searching for a girl among those who waited in the darkness outside the windows where men well drunk stretched out as if in their beds.

He could watch the trading across the Red Place near the whitewashed wall of the Kitaigorod, built by his mother's order, where hunters of the plains brought their skins to the stalls of Manchu and Persian merchants. Here sun-blackened fighters wrapped in silk shirts and furs, with their heads shaved except for a hanging scalplock, spent their money on wine and singing girls, and looted the stalls to get more money. They were from the frontier lines, some of them from the brotherhood of the Don, some from the Dnieper, and they were called, after the Tatar word *Kazaks*—masterless riders—Cossacks.

Like the Polovtsi riders of the steppe, these frontiersmen had contempt for the city folk who labored on benches and delved in the ground. "The Tsar rules in Moscow," they proclaimed, "the Cossack on the Don."

This life of the distant lands beat strongly against Moscow—which, to the outlanders, was Holy Mother Moscow—and thronged about the Kremlin height where the gold and blue and gray cupolas of churches showed over the walls. Pilgrims passed under the house windows, sheltering the flame of oil lanthorns which, they said, had been lighted at the Sepulchre in Jerusalem, and from which they lit the candles of devout housewives for a kopeck. Actors from Poland performed miracle plays between curtains rigged at street corners; marriage processions passed, singing behind lighted candles; minstrels from the northern seas chanted of Solovei Budomirovitch and *Potuik*, his falcon ship that sailed to all the lands of the earth; blind *bandura* players from the steppe sang of Maria the White Girl-Swan.

To the old favorites like "Baba Yaga," new songs had been added—"Helen the Fair," and "Ivan the Son of the Prince." And in one way or another, Ivan himself must have heard this unwritten literature of a people.

Yet the monk Sylvester, Ivan's tutor, wrote laboriously in his book of rules to be obeyed—the *Domostroi*—"When the *bandura* is played, when folk dance or jump and clap their hands, then like bees driven by smoke, God's angels fly away from that place, and demons come hastening in."

To these varied influences Ivan was exposed in the enforced solitude of those early years. Nor could he have escaped the influence of foreign skill. The great cannon inside the Gate of the Saviour, the cannon called Tsarpushka, had been cast by Germans; the clock in the gate tower of the Kremlin was also German—the tower itself designed by an Italian. Most of the manuscripts he read had been copied out by Greek hands. The one master scholar of the Kremlin had been a foreigner, Maximus the Greek, a pupil of Savonarola, who had gone from Mount Athos and Florence to the cities of Europe, who knew the thought of the Renaissance and the talk of Aldus Manutius. Maximus the Greek had been exiled to a monastery by Vasily because he objected to the divorce of Salome.

More than that, Ivan, whose mother had been Lithuanian, found German engineers building bridges over the Moskva, and when cavalry of the small Muscovite army appeared in the Red Place, it was often commanded by Hungarian or Swedish or Brandenburger officers, who talked familiarly of new firearms called wheel-lock pistols or matchlock shoulder guns.

Ivan made his attempt to assert his authority as prince

only cautiously. Robed and seated, before an assembly of the heads of the boyar families, he accused them suddenly of guilt. The words meant little, except a formality of scolding for their sins—quite in ancient usage. But he ordered the arrest of the head of the Shuiskys—"Only one among you will be punished this time"—and when Andrew Shuisky fled from the palace he was caught by the dog keepers and killed. This had been an accident; yet when he learned of it, Ivan did not deny responsibility.

"If you threaten it not with terror," he was told, "you will not bring law into this land."

Quickly then, in 1547, he demanded his cornation. And in it he had his title repeated as "Tsar and Autocrat of All Rus," not as "Great Prince." Again, this was no more than a new word. Ivan's marriage meant more, because it would decide the succession. Counselors and boyars had planned a marriage with the royal family of Poland. Ivan selected instead—after the customary parade—a girl who was not of a great family but of an obscure one, Anastasia Kochkin, a Romanov. He could then summon her relatives to posts close to him.

By this, at the age of seventeen, he had gained a wife and a following, but little actual power. An accident nearly ended his rule at the start, when one of the periodic conflagrations destroyed most of Moscow. In the excitement, the families who feared Ivan's marriage spread the rumor among the superstitious population that the fire had been caused by sorcery. The Glinsky brood had burned the city by infernal means, by sprinkling the wooden houses with water in which human hearts had been soaked. The panic in the city changed to a riot, and Ivan waited in terror in the shelter of his summer home while his relatives were hunted even to the portal of the great cathedral. But he refused to give up those who had taken shelter with him.

And afterward he ordered the execution of only the few leaders of the riot. Shaken himself by the catastrophe and by the rumor that the figure of an unknown priest had appeared during the fire to proclaim that the anger of God had visited the city, Ivan seemed to be unable to assert himself. Very much in love with his bride, as his father Vasily had been with Helen, he left the active administration in the hands of a council headed by the Metropolitan. In this Chosen Council, as it was called, the monk Sylvester and the former bedmaker Adashev acted for the youthful Ivan.

So great had been the disorder of the time of trouble, ending with the conflagration in Moscow, that the ensuing calm in Rus seemed almost beneficial. Even the impressionable and suspicion-ridden Ivan seemed to find hope in this calm. As his marriage had ended for a time his moody craving for women, so the companionship of his new counselors ended his period of mental solitude.

Perhaps with Anastasia, his "little heifer," in the near escape of his summer house of Alexandrov on the height not far from Moscow, he might have spent a tranquil life. Certainly for him these first years of authority were a good time, and chroniclers were to write that then Ivan "had a good heart" toward his people.

But there were forces exerted upon the man who called himself Tsar that were almost if not entirely beyond human capacity to meet. Ivan opposed them. And therein lies at once the achievement and the failure of his life.

The Forces within the Kremlin

In accepting the tsarate at that time, he had inherited the spiritual responsibility of the dead emperors of Byzantium. At his coronation he had worn the *shapka,* the gold cap with carnelian brim, and the imperial collar of solid pearls—the regalia of the Byzantines.

From the time of Ivan III, his grandfather, and Sophie, his grandmother, the princes of Moscow had been besieged by demands to aid the exiled imperial family of Constantinople—those shadowy heirs of a Byzantium now lost forever to the military power of the Turks. To such pleas for material aid his grandfather and father had paid little attention for the practical reason that nothing whatever could be done about it.

But Ivan was also heritor of the Orthodox Church that had had its primacy in Constantinople, and was now scattered throughout the indifferent cities of renascent Italy, and the faithful towns of Greece, as well as the Balkans. By now the Turkish power had engulfed both the peninsula of Greece and the Balkans. They were lost. Yet pressure was maintained by the Church itself, to recover the lost heritage. Moscow, so said the spokesmen of the Church, had become the third Rome (the lamented Constantinople having been the second).

More than that. By divine preordination, the spokesmen argued, Moscow would also become the second Jerusalem (the first Jerusalem having been lost to the Moslems for more than three centuries). The Byzantine clergy were very skilled at such argumentation. Ivan, quite clearly, had become the sole defender of the Orthodox Church, as well as ruler of the new holy city that would succeed, by divine will, Jerusalem. Had not his grandmother Sophie Paleologus been an instrument of the divine will?

This argument propagated some fantastic proofs. The legendary voyage of St. Andrew gained new meaning, and merged somehow into a second Noah's Ark survival, destined to save humanity from engulfing paganism. This responsibility, also, now lay upon Ivan.

More practically, the message of greeting as Tsar from the heads of the Church outside Rus summoned him to fulfill his responsibility and end the calamity of Orthodox Christendom. Almost all the signatures to this petition turned out to be forgeries.

It was also discovered, suddenly, at this critical time, that Ivan's family had descended from no less a person than Augustus Caesar, the first Emperor of the world.

So tremendous pressure was brought upon Ivan to play a superhuman role—to transform him into a potentate combining the duties of a European pope and emperor, over much of the world.

At first Ivan reacted only partially to this pressure. He believed that his ancestors in the great days of Kiev had shared the authority of the Byzantines, who were then under full power. He liked to think that St. Andrew had carried a torch to Rus. But he pointed out that the Byzantines failed, because their autocracy had been fettered by conspiracy. The brooding practical part of his mind beheld in this a warning against the machinations of the boyars and great families of Moscow.

He was always quick to imagine dangers. Yet the arguments of the clergy had a double hold upon him. They fitted into his dream world of the ancient Tsar David and Tsar Nebuchadnezzar. They ministered to his self-absorption, and his deep religious feeling at the same time. Moreover Moscow, whether or not it had inherited the task and power of Rome, had in reality become the holy city of the inchoate people of Rus. Even the Tsar bared his head before the Gate of the Saviour, designed by the architect "Aristotle" Fioraventi.

Another pressure came from the dead past. Every human being within sight of Ivan was subservient to him. Around him the concept of an Asiatic potentate merged with the memory of the great khans of the Tatars. Seated in majesty higher than his fellows, surrounded by guards of his body

Ivan IV, the Terrible, in early middle age. (From contemporary German wood engraving. Hakluyt Society)

clad in gleaming white, Ivan was addressed by men who made the Asiatic gesture of prostration, and spoke of themselves not by name but as "Little George," or "the slave Peter" and before speaking at all mouthed the plea, "May it be allowed to speak without harm."

Under this servility of "those who served" Ivan too often suspected antagonism. His imagination beheld in the bowed heads and outstretched hands hidden *forces*. His own person being sacrosanct, he could—and often did—strike a man with the *kisten* in his hand. No one could strike him, or oppose him.

As time went on, inevitably, he fancied that anyone who opposed his will was an instrument of the intangible forces of evil. And, just as inevitably, he clung more and more to the concept of himself as an instrument of divine power.

When Ivan strode among other men, there was no mistaking the high robed frame, the lifted shoulders, the uncombed reddish beard beneath the thin tense head with its beaked nose, and the eyes close-set that wandered and glared as if probing the thoughts of those near him. Instinctively boyars and servitors bowed to the girdle to hide from the "fiery eyes" that seemed to seek out and understand everything. Perhaps they were strained by constant reading under candlelight; perhaps they were hooded by the concentration of thought that never released him.

Certainly Ivan appeared to his people as one possessed by saintly or demoniac impulse, ready to flash out in a second in benevolence or malignancy. Naturally the common folk felt the benevolence in him because he stopped invariably to read their petitions or to listen to their shouted prayers. Opposition, during his middle age, could throw him into a frenzy; this, after a moment's quiet, he could control; but he never seemed to forget the opposition.

Self-educated, Ivan—so some foreigners say—was the best-educated man of his generation.

Past middle age, he was to write to his most dangerous foreign enemy, as "We, the humble Johannes, by the will of God and not by any *false dispensation of man,* Tsar and Great Prince of All Rus."

Ivan had an intuitive intelligence, and a most active imagination. Like other unloved orphans, he was shrewd beyond his years. Even as a boy wandering the Kremlin grounds, he had been angered by the financial crimes of his enemies the boyars—by the unlawful taxation and looting of the treasury —as much as by their ill-treatment of himself.

And in his early attempts to improve conditions around him, Ivan showed shrewd common sense. He accepted counsel avoiding executions whenever possible. He tried to bring some order into the confusion of taxation, to call together a sort of general assembly of all classes of people, and to make literacy a requirement for holding government office.[1]

He made such attempts. In the moribund Moscow of 1547 –53, the will of one man could accomplish little. The

[1] No attempt can be made here to touch upon internal reforms, or changes in administration, which belong to the social history of Rus.

semblance of government was no more than a vast roster of servants, a honeycomb of bureaus—the inevitable *prikaz'* ranging from Bureau of Hawk Tenders, to Bureau of Entertainment of Ambassadors and of Secret Affairs. There was also the Razriad, the Bureau of War.

When a new bureau incurred new expenses the time-honored method of paying them was to levy a new tax.

Outside Moscow, no good roads existed, no shipping, little coined money, less printed matter. The law of the land, except for the Tsar's decrees, was still "ancient usage." One historian sums it up: "The State was too old, the people too young."

Nor did there exist in the cities elsewhere the vital culture of city centers in western Europe, where Milan became noted for its architecture, Venice for its handicrafts, Paris for its universities. The Germanic culture of Novgorod had been lowered since Muscovite occupation. Other marginal city centers like Pskov, Smolensk and Chernigov had been brought down to the Muscovite level.

Into Moscow, meanwhile, a heterogeneous population was swarming. Perhaps two hundred thousand human beings surrounded the Kremlin.

Ivan, who held the title to almost unlimited authority, had almost no means of carrying out that authority, beyond range of his sight and hearing as a human being.

Was it then his own unbalanced imagination or force of the circumstances in which he found himself placed that made Ivan—the first among the Muscovites to do so—visualize himself as not only Great Prince but Tsar, and not only Tsar but Lord's Anointed?

Nor had Ivan statesmen who knew the outer world, to guide him. The best minds around him, or at least the most educated, were apt to be Lithuanian, Polish or foreign, and therefore "pagan." At this point—until Ivan himself provided a stimulus—the sharpest stimulus to stagnating Moscow had been the impact of those foreign minds.

Beyond the western lands in a small island of the outer sea Henry Tudor, the eighth Henry, administered England brilliantly, emotionally and brutally. Yet Henry Tudor had at least the instruments of that administration, a Parliament to pass an Act of Supremacy to separate his kingdom from the political tutoring of Rome; however he disposed of Wolsey, Thomas More and Cranmer, he at least had the benefit of their counsel before ridding himself of them. And men like Sir Thomas More had the scholarship of Oxford and Cambridge to inform them. They could read the international language, Latin, if not Greek, as well as English. A generation before Ivan became Tsar, Sir Thomas More had published in Latin his Utopia, an account of an ideal government somewhere in the new world beyond the western ocean. Burly Henry had been fond of reading cosmographies and voyages into the outer world, as well as the geography of Ptolemy.

In his chambers overlooking the Moskva, Ivan pored over holy writ by the gleam of tallow candles—the more precious wax was exported, when opportunity came, by the port of Narva. His only manuscript of travel seems to have been the *Aeneid*, his nearest approach to philosophy the occult dogma of John Chrysostom; and these were mixed inextricably with hagiology, miracles and martyrdoms of the Byzantine Church. What he liked best he memorized. A devout chronicler speaks of his "shrewd memory of holy writ."

Many such passages—as they were repeated by him later —seem to have been articulation of divine authority, and the sin of withstanding it. He pondered much over the epistles of Paul, especially that to the Romans, which contains: "Lord, they have killed thy prophets, and digged down thine altars; and I am left alone, and they seek my life."

It was something of a miracle that Ivan, so fanatically self-taught, could evidence keen judgment in dealing with the outer world; he tried to control his paroxysms of rage when faced by obstacles; but he gained a persecution complex, from which he never freed himself. By degrees he fancied himself entirely friendless, and in every opposition he came to see the machination of a nameless "they." Nothing could have fitted his case, as he saw it, so well as those words of Paul. *They* did not exist.

When Anastasia died a dozen years after his coronation he wrote—perhaps brooding over the death of his mother— "They have taken my little heifer away from me."

In vain he tried to oppose the force of his spirit and body to the overmastering forces exerted against him.

How the Line of the Volga Was Freed

Look for a moment at the frontier.

Now, while Moscow lies moribund, the frontier is alive. It is most alive toward the east, and it struggles for life in the south. Eastward lies the vast interior of Asia; southward lies the fertile paradise of the Ukraine.

Along these borderlands, far distant from Moscow, human beings formed *brotherhoods;* settlements developed a strange communal life; the life lines of the rivers became pregnant with new activity; monasteries grew into frontier colonies.

Look at the far northeast. The settlements here have pushed back the stubborn Finnish and Lap tribal groups— the hunters, and keepers of reindeer. They have sustained themselves on meager gleanings of fish and salt and the poorer furs, and their way of living is a little like that of the Finns, but they are now settled communities with churches and even some schools. For the monks here are still of the missionary type, and can teach a little, as did the revered Stephen, Bishop of Perm.

The taxgatherer and the conscript officer collect little from them in the way of men or money; to that extent they are free people.

And the communities of the monks have grown. Beyond the reach of plague, war and taxation, they have waxed too fat and comfortable. Monastic life has ceased to be a quest for seclusion and sanctity. It has taken to farming, wood-cutting, salt mining. "The holy men of yesterday," the villagers say, "have become the black-robed landowners of today."

That is a surprising circumstance, but true. The monasteries now own perhaps one third of the land of Rus. Their agriculture is planned for large areas, and on the whole the brotherhood of monks get in better crops than the free peasant farmers. Like the settlements, they are self-sustaining and have even stored up an unsaintly amount of money. Solovetsky monastery, on its island in the White Sea, has developed a massive salt industry; Troitsko, near Moscow, has one hundred thousand workers employed.

Even along the frozen northern seas there are small communities now gleaning blubber from seals, oil from (stranded?) whales, and ivory of sorts from walrus and narwhal.

Those outlying settlements differ from the villages around Moscow. The restless folk in the fir forests can still leave their land and go elsewhere; the folk in the central villages are often so deep in debt they cannot leave, without becoming defaulters and having the men bound and beaten, or the women and children taken to work out the debt as slave-servants.

Something has been happening to the monasteries, which might have been anticipated. This religious brotherhood divided internally. One portion held to the rightness of things

as they were, the ownership of land and the wealth that
came out of it. Did not the *abundance* of the monasteries
help out the people in time of trouble and famine, as in
1525? How could the monasteries prevent pious boyars
and even tsars from making donations of land and money
for the eternal good of their souls? For "finding quarters
for their souls?"

The other portion believed that wealth had become a
curse, not a blessing and that, to save their own souls, the
dwellers in monasteries must give away their worldly goods
and go forth into desert or wilderness as servants of the
Lord. This movement of the to-have-nots owed something
to the impulse of reform that had swept European churches.
Its particular preacher was one Nils Sorgsky, who had been
educated at Mount Athos in Europe.

This internal strife between the to-haves and to-have-nots
was bitter and long drawn out, as always with Slavs when
their faith was concerned. It did, however, send a new mass
of seceding monks eastward and northward, into the forest
and across the Volga. We hear of the "Beyond the Volga"
monks as a new brotherhood, remonstrating with Prince
Vasily about his divorce from Salome.

At the same time the roving fur hunters and traders, building their ostrogs along the old trails and portages of the
Novgorod "companies," were far past the Volga, and exploring the Urals.

They were searching for new land on their own accord,
without the consent of Moscow.

Moscow had been sending occasional expeditions out to
this borderland to raid and trade, but the settlers occupied
the land, and stayed, where the sables were darker and the
black or white fox could still be hunted.

In fact a small land empire was forming in the basin of
the river Kama, where the Stroganov family had been given a
grant of land by the Kremlin. Their family estate, called
Chusavaya, centered in a giant blockhouse with its own
shrine and priest, and its army of servants and guards armed
with the new matchlocks.

Here, beyond the Volga, the Stroganovs tapped the rich
fur trade and ruled the river traffic as the powerful Hud-
son's Bay Company was to rule the traffic of a portion of
the New World in the following centuries.

Not the Stroganovs nor the mission-bent monks, nor the
border settlers could have obtained a foothold so far within
Asia except for the aid of a weapon. They had matchlocks

and pistols, which the native Tatars did not have. With matchlocks they could fight off the warlike Mordvas, Bashkirs, and the Cheremiss—"who never left the bows from their hands"—who had not yielded to the authority of Moscow.

The unmapped frontier was moving eastward spontaneously, while Moscow remained inert.

Down Mother Volga to the sea, the *burlaki* floated their rafts from the Tatar market at Kazan. On the mile-wide stretch of water that bisected the steppe like a gigantic canal, the rivermen in their skiffs and the traders in their sailing barges occupied a corridor safe from molestation by land dwellers. Certainly these pioneers founded no great city, or trading monopoly. It was always a kind of *brotherhood* or host, unknown to western Europe.

And here, seemingly, is a paradox not easy to understand. The Slav under our eyes is an individualist, yet he is forever grouping up in communal life. It has always been like that—since the Slavs began their incredibly slow movement eastward from the Pripet marshlands.

Of course the Slavs held firmly to family ties, and their *mir* or commune became simply a group of families which combined their activities. Yet they tended just as readily to leave the group and go off as families or individuals.

When a village migrated, the *mir* often broke up on the journey into groups of two or three families, but these groups attached themselves in time to new communal settlements.

There is a simple answer to this apparent riddle. These Slavs were individualists and collectivists at the same time because they had been shaped by frontier life. They passed their lives, as it were, between the one-man cabin and the community blockhouse, as would the settlers in the New World who first ventured into dark lands like Kentucky.

Certainly the pioneers who lived beyond the southern frontier of Rus did that. They were the *stiepniks*, the steppe-born. They clung to the rich grasslands in spite of raid and war and the changing of the political kaleidoscope. So they formed a brotherhood or host of their kind, known as the Cossack.[2]

[2] These were the ancestors of the Cossacks who became the unique cavalry force of the tsarist armies, recruited from the Dnieper, Don, Kuban, Terek and Ural regions. In their origin they were a people distinct from the Great Russian, speaking Ukrainian. Not until late in the seventeenth century did the more independent Cossack "hosts" acknowledge the sovereignty of Moscow, and after that they rebelled more than once against such sovereignty.

Perhaps no other people were so definitely a product of frontier life as the Cossacks. In part the original settlers who did not join in the early migration north, in part those of them who intermarried with Polovtsi and Tatars, in part refugees from the northern cities—even escaped debtors and criminals—they had become welded together by the hard conditions of the frontier. Some of them held out in clumps of cottages along streams in the sunken ravines, where tree growth hid the cabins. Some of them survived in amphibious fashion along the riverbanks. But always they grouped together in such regions, beyond political authority.

In the "wild lands" along the Dnieper where forests of reeds often grew to the height of a man, Cossack settlements held fast to the banks, sustaining themselves by hunting, by the easy agriculture of the black-earth belt, by cattle raising and raiding "foreign" towns which might be Polish, Tatar or even Turkish. Such raids were often carried out in the longboats like the earlier craft of the Variags—large enough to carry rowers with an armed force, and small enough to hide along the banks. On land the Dnieper Cossacks made use of the universal safeguard of the hostile frontier, the wagon train which they called the *tabor*. When attacked, these hunters of the plains drew the wagons into a square and defended it. The men themselves practiced all trades, being their own carpenters, blacksmiths, shipbuilders and tanners; but all had to use arms at need.

Below the rapids, in a chain of islands the war brotherhood of the Dnieper Cossacks had its encampment—the Siech—which shifted from island to island to keep in hiding. These restless warriors of the river, the Zaporogians, or Those Below the Rapids, made that waterway an inland Spanish Main. Under their *koshevoi ataman*, a military leader who held little authority over them in peacetime, the Zaporogians formed a rudimentary army, the outgrowth of continued conflict with the Tatars. Cossacks assembled by barracks (*kurens*) elected their own commanders, who were usually those with the longest experience and the hardest heads.

Discipline they hardly knew, except in battle. Impulse governed them, spoil served for pay, and their loyalty lay only with the brotherhood and the Orthodox Church. Around them grew up legends.

These legends of the Don and the Dnieper took many forms—ballads of Cossack wanderers, chants of slaves chained to the Turkish galleys, and the hero tales of the Cossack Hosts sung by *bandura* players who went like the

minstrels of feudal Europe from village to village. This unwritten literature of the southland merged with the songs
of the Volga *burlaki,* the plaintive drum and pipe music
of the Tatar tribes.

The unruly Siech of the Dnieper had its legends of laughter and tears as well as battles, like that of *Our Lady of the
Siech* told by the *bandura* minstrels:

"Brother falcons, it was long ago in the time when the
Cossacks had gone together to the battle on the Dark Sea
where the souls of the slain flickered in spirit light along the
salt shallows and the dry marshes.

"It was a time of mourning in the cottages after the battle, and the weeping of women was heard like the rush of the
water in the shallows.

"Listen to what happened. At that time, Our Lady of the
Siech came down from the night sky, seeking the water of
the river. With St. Nicholas guiding her, she walked over
the Cossack land, wearing her splendid *kokoshynk,* her
headdress sewn with pearls.

"It was very hot in the land, and when day came Our
Lady felt thirsty. So, when they passed a cottage they
knocked on the door. The doors were closed, and behind
them the two wanderers heard the sound of weeping. No
one came to the doors.

"Then St. Nicholas took Our Lady into a wood where
ran a stream, and she knelt down, bending to reach the water.
Her pearl headdress fell from her head into the water, and
was lost. 'Oh,' said Our Lady, 'how sorry I feel. They were
such beautiful pearls, I will never have the like again!'

"St. Nicholas said nothing to that. When the two reached
their heavenly home, Our Lady found, lying on her throne,
a headdress as beautiful as the one she had lost. 'They
must be my pearls,' she said. 'The Cossacks found them,
and returned them to me.'

"'No, Mother,' said her Son. 'They are new ones. They are
not pearls but the tears of the Cossack mothers, shed for
their dead. The angels,' said he, 'have brought them, every
one a tear.'

"And that is why to this day pearls are called tears, in
the Cossack land."

Between them the Cossack brotherhoods held much of the
Ukraine south of the wooded steppe, and naturally enough
they held in contempt the Muscovites, town dwellers, traders and hirers of foreign soldiery. Although they ranged the
river courses freely, often sailing down to the Black Sea

coast, they had little cohesion; the Dnieper Cossacks came under Polish influence and often enlisted under Polish command, while the Don brotherhood allied itself more with Moscow.

At this time the southern defense line of Moscow itself—and the limit of raids by the Krim Tatars—was from Tula, along the portage to the Don headwaters, and to Pronsk. This line of blockhouses and barricades lay no more than two days' fast ride from the city itself. The Zaporogian Siech and the Don Cossack encampments lay ten to twelve days south of Moscow.

From the Siech below the Dnieper rapids to Solovetsky monastery and the hamlets on the northern ice sea there was a vast stretch of fourteen to fifteen hundred miles. Very little of that stretch lay under the authority of Moscow.

In the beginning of Ivan's reign Moscow could do little to defend its own territory beyond Nizhni Novgorod, the frontier town at the junction of the Oka with the upper Volga. Tatar raids came through the southern defense line at headlong pace, over the ice and snow of midwinter, or during the early summer when Muscovite manpower was tilling the fields. They came along the half-hidden *shliakhi* or horse trails known to the Tatars.

Some attempt was made by the Kremlin to mobilize a field army during the summer months by calling in the "men who served" and the "sons of boyars." But the permanent defense was the fortified line of blockhouses, palisaded towns garrisoned by recruits—towns placed about the distance of a fast day's ride apart, so that aid could be given quickly to a menaced point.

Far out from these blockhouses and towns, observation posts watched the roads—small detachments of adventurous boyars' sons, hunters of the plains and Cossacks, kept in concealment, with their horses saddled, ready to send a rider speeding back at the first sign of dust along a Tatar trail.

These outpost riders, the *storozha*, became famous in the service that shielded Moscow—"that fighting men come not unaware with war into the out-borders of the State."

Kazan

So great was the tension along this frontier between the steppe and woodland, between Muscovite power and Tatar-

Turkish power, that it became inevitable for the Muscovites to annihilate Kazan, the last Tatar stronghold on the middle Volga.

By Ivan's time, Kazan flanked the Tula-Nizhni Novgorod defense line; Kazan, at the juncture of the Kama and Volga rivers, stood astride the river traffic; Kazan held together the remnants of Tatar dominion, and knit together the Moslem peoples like the Chuvashes and Mordvas. Worse, Kazan, weak though it might be beside expanding Moscow, defied the Muscovites and their tsars. Ivan's grandfather and father had failed to capture Kazan. The Bielskys and the Shuiskys had bargained and negotiated for the submission of Kazan in vain.

From the wooden walls of Kazan on the height between the river and the small Kazansky stream and the lake, the ghost of Batu Khan mocked the man who called himself Tsar of All Rus. The very weakness of Kazan made its defiance more intolerable to the men in the Kremlin.

Kazan was virtually surrounded by the Muscovites, whose frontier posts had crept out to the Volga itself; once the Khan of Kazan became no better than a tool of Moscow, and the gates had been opened to Muscovite troops. All that Moscow demanded, outwardly, was that the people of Kazan leave their wooden walls and settle elsewhere. But then a sudden wave of religious feeling swept over the inhabitants; the gates were closed to the Muscovite soldiery. A certain Idiger, Khan of the Nogais, arrived to take command, and the *imams* of the city whipped up the courage of their people to die instead of surrendering.

And it seemed for a while as if this spirit of a few thousand Tatars might withstand all the force that Moscow under Ivan might bring against it.

Twice before armies under Ivan had bogged down in the swamps, or had been caught by the first winter storms or had simply disintegrated, owing to lack of discipline, on the way down the Oka to attack Kazan. Ivan had refused to flee from Moscow itself at the approach of Krim raiding armies. He could not turn back from a third attempt to destroy Kazan.

All the power that the Razriadni Prikaz, the War Bureau, could mobilize was started down the Oka this time. Against the counsel of a friendly Tatar officer—who advised that the siege be laid in midwinter when the rivers and swamps were frozen hard—the army started in summer again and moved from city to city, accompanied by a flotilla of boats "like a fair," and feeding off the country.

After interminable delays it passed the last outpost town and reached the Island of Traders where the minarets of the Kazan mosques could be sighted above the mist. Terms were offered the Kazan folk and refused—"We ask for no pardon from you." The walled height was surrounded, trenches were dug, a battery of twelve huge guns installed by foreign artillerists on a raised earthwork opposite the main gate. These works the Tatars attacked and attacked again.

Russian chroniclers of the time say that Ivan led a hundred and fifty thousand men with a hundred and fifty guns against the walls of Kazan. Actually, the roster of the Muscovite "men who serve" came to no more than sixty-five thousand in those years, and nearly half of these were required to man the frontier posts. Probably no more than fifty thousand were in the lines around Kazan, and perhaps half of these were the Muscovite horsemen. The infantry, which had to storm the city, were Cossacks, hunters, and the nucleus of a new army, the *Streltsi*, the "firers" or harquebus men, enlisted for a lifetime and given this European weapon. There were many commanders—*voevodes*—and also the *goulai gorod*, the "city that walks"—a mobile palisade with double parapet to protect the infantry that did not function well unless barricaded in front and back.

Although Ivan appeared as commander in chief, the men who led the assault of this makeshift army were two princes, Andrew Kurbsky and Vorotinsky. The Muscovites, enduring and uncomplaining behind their own fortifications, seemed incapable of penetrating the weak defenses of Kazan. Continuous rains set in, weakening the bombardment. These rains, the Muscovites believed, had been summoned by Tatar sorcerers who showed themselves on the walls at sunrise and let down their trousers, to perform incantations against the Christian cannon.

A miraculous cross, sent for from Moscow and carried in procession around the walls of Kazan by priests, overcame the sorcery, and the rains ended. Foreign engineers sank a mine under the gate, against the dugouts in which the Tatar garrison took shelter during the bombardment. When the great mine was exploded, the Cossacks and infantry attacked across the crater, and were driven out by the Tatar counterattack—all but a detachment commanded by Vorotinsky, which held fast to a captured tower and called to the fugitives, "Come back soon, you'll find us still here."

Even Ivan, to whom warfare was strange, understood the necessity to press the attack. That night smaller mines were sunk under the facing of the wall (a wooden palisade supporting a massive earthwork) and before dawn Ivan appeared at prayer in the small church erected in the camp.

While he knelt there the mines were exploded, and the infantry attacked the smoke-filled breaches, to be driven out by a blast of fire and arrows from the surviving Tatars. Kneeling in the makeshift wooden church, Ivan must have heard the reverberations of the assault over the voice of the priest intoning, "Thy will be done." But he continued to kneel in prayer.

At length officers entered the church to beg Ivan to show himself in his robes to the troops. Afraid, or paralyzed by indecision, Ivan would not interrupt his prayer. When he did mount his horse and ride up the hill, he saw the black banner of Dmitri Donskoi already raised on the outer wall of the city. This man, the leader of an army, became weak at the sight of blood and torn bodies.

Within the walls, the ill-trained Streltsi and unruly Cossacks broke formation to plunder, and they were driven back by a counterattack led by Idiger. Ivan then ordered half his horsemen to go in to the aid of the battered storm troops, yet he did not accompany them.

Ivan forced himself to play the part of commander; the real courage was shown by the ill-armed Tatars, and by Idiger, who had answered Ivan's offer of terms with a fatalistic "When will the banquet begin? We are ready to drink the cup of blood." By the mullahs who had ordered arrows discharged into the captured Tatars staked up outside the Muscovite lines—"A clean death is better than torment at the hands of infidels." By the women of the palace who faced the incoming soldiers clad in their finest garments before being stripped and violated.

Even after losing the palace, the Tatars feigned flight and made a savage attack from the mosque, in which imams, mullahs and women shared. The survivors who broke out on the far side numbered no more than four to five thousand. These were driven off by the Muscovite artillery, and a charge of horsemen led by Kurbsky. That impetuous prince wrote afterward: "No prisoners were captured who were not so crippled by wounds as to be unable to struggle." And the chroniclers of Moscow wrote that the costly attack had been made glorious by the valor of the Tatars.

Ivan made the final gesture of the part he was playing. With his own hand he placed a banner on the spot where the Tatar standard had been seen, and ordered a church built there. All men found within the walls were killed, and the women and children removed. Kazan was to be re-populated by Muscovites.

As in the loss of the Alhambra, the loss of Kazan marked the end of a nomad supremacy. The defenders had yielded not so much to the fighting qualities of the Muscovites as to the supremacy of the fire weapons, the mines, serpentines, falconets and great mortars—called *haufnizi* by the Muscovites after the *Haufnitz* of the Germans who had designed them. The Tatar defenders had been wraithlike guardians of an empire that no longer existed, of a religion that was slowly forsaking the sword for the merchant's rug and book of philosophy.

Now the tribal peoples of the upper Volga and Kama basins—the Cheremiss, Mordvas, Chuvashes and Viatkas—understood that the greater force lay with Moscow. They no longer had a religious center to hold them together. For several years they inflicted savage defeats on the Cossacks and Streltsi garrisons around Kazan; then they accepted fate in the form of the Muscovites, to whom taxes must be paid.

After the capture of Kazan, the chief officers of the army had urged Ivan to remain for a while in his new stronghold, to lend his presence and advice to the resettlement of the area. But this Ivan would not do. More than the growing cold and the miasma of the swamps, the stale stench of the siege lines and the sight of the scantily dug graves affected him physically. Apparently he did not trust his army commanders, the leading boyars, and he worried about Anastasia, whom he had left pregnant in Moscow. At all events, he returned to that city, leaving a portion of the army to guard his conquest on the Volga.

Along that huge winding river something unexpected happened. Down from the north, from the Kama basin and the dense spruce forests, came a migration that was like a human flood. Now that the river was freed, the human tide followed it south, through the watered feather grass and the green grass steppes, seeking virgin soil rich enough for wheat and cattle.

Down Little Mother Volga the migrants poured, on timber rafts, in cart caravans. River *burlaki* and fishermen of the north came down to claim land of their own. From the hamlets in the west, too, along the Oka, immigration set in to the new Volga territory.

Unknown to themselves, these *krestianin* were taking a

tremendous step outward. In seeking the Volga, they were
passing beyond the ancient lands of Rus to the eastward.

The river pirates followed south, to cluster and ply their
trade around the sharp bend in the Volga where the log
walls of Samara were being raised.

No ukase from the Kremlin could stop this migration, no
regiments of town-trained Streltsi could head these settlers
another way. They were following an unmarked road, where
the rivers led to the sea.

The settlers penetrated as far south as the brown or dry
steppe where the Nogai Tatars had their yurt villages. In
1556, four years after the capture of Kazan, a Muscovite ex-
peditionary force, transported by Volga boatmen and living
off the country, was able to move down the length of the
river to the strategic bend where it almost touches the easterly bend of the Don. There a blockhouse was built and
called Saritsyn (Gold Point) on the bluff where Stalingrad
now stands. From that base they moved on to take over
Astrakhan, which controlled the mouths of the Volga. Astrakhan opened up the great inland Caspian Sea, which
they called the Sea of Baku.

The popular movement did not confine itself to the Volga.
Back in the west, the Cossack communities and the ever
restless frontier settlements stirred and drifted south along
the channels of the Dnieper and the Don. The explorers here
pushed past the ruins of ancient Kiev. While the *military*
frontier of Moscow remained static and guarded at the
Nizhni Novgorod-Tula line, the *popular* advance penetrated
to the Ukraine here. Some adventurous Cossacks actually
reached the mouths of the Dnieper and Don and began to
loot along the shores of the Black Sea.

Here Adashev, that man of common sense—Ivan's personal lieutenant—appeared as adviser to one of the exploring
divisions, which ran into the resistance of Turkish troops
and Krim Tatars. But when Adashev returned to Moscow, he
urged that these rivers be freed like the Volga. Here, he believed, was an empire to be occupied, by reclaiming the
Ukraine, and the shores of the Black Sea.

This was not done. Instead of following out the capture
of Kazan and extending with the popular migration into Asia
itself, Moscow faced the other way. The next military move
was made not toward the southeast, but to the northwest and
the Baltic Sea, then closed to the Muscovites.

This abrupt change in direction of the armed force of Moscow came about apparently by decision of the planners in

the Kremlin, and of Ivan himself. Actually, no one *planned* it; it happened because of developments beyond the control of the men in the Kremlin.

For one thing the monasteries had become huge land enterprises in the northern regions. They could no longer move with the population, and in any case there had not been time for the churches to follow the new drift to the south. So the interest of the Church itself lay imbedded, as it were, in the north, from Smolensk to Solovetsky.

Along the "great north road" from Moscow to Novgorod, many hamlets were losing their people.

For another thing, trade had found a new inlet. During the time of decision in the years 1553–57, there was a great influx of oriental wares from the Caspian zone and Persia. The trade axis of Moscow now lay from the Caspian to the Baltic, by way of Astrakhan, Kazan and Moscow, through Novgorod and on toward Narva and Pskov, toward the old end of "the road from the Variags to the Greeks."

But this end of the ancient trade route was now sealed off, by the Swedish merchants and military posts around Lake Ladoga, by the Livonians (and the Knights of the Sword), around Riga and Pskov, by the ancient antagonists the Lithuanian-Poles, and even by the German traders of the Baltic itself—all of whom might compete and fight among themselves, but joined together in an effort to keep the Muscovites from the Baltic.

So the immense raw products of the expanding Russian lands could not be marketed in the west, and the new influx of eastern goods from the Caspian piled up in Moscow itself. The great merchant families—that of the Tsar being the greatest—felt this economic pinch.

Then there was the new army, so slowly and painfully welded into a combat force. Despite the orders of the Razriadni Prikaz the numbers of men required in the yearly musters fell short, or the most powerful boyars brought in only ill-mounted peasants. The lesson of Kazan had not been lost upon Ivan. The victory over the Tatars had been won by artillery and gunners, not by an army.

To stiffen the Muscovite ranks, the War Bureau enlisted many foreigners, wandering Turks and Brandenburgers, and Swedish soldiers of fortune—signing them on as *ritters*, riders. Cossacks and friendly Mordvas were hired as light cavalry. The new Streltsi were put on outright pay. By degrees, government grants to boyars became contingent on the numbers of servicemen they brought in. This in turn bound the home-keeping peasants more closely to their tillage, as more men were drafted, and higher taxes were levied to pay the new army. So, as time went on, the old feudal order, or disorder, was replaced by a military class and a peasant working class, tied to the soil.

For the present Ivan exerted himself to get guns, the new matchlocks and pistols, the brass and lead, sulphur, saltpeter and powder. For the most part, these had to come from the west, and it was precisely from the west they could not come owing to the trade barricade around the Baltic.

So Adashev and a few other leaders like the eastern-minded Michael Vorotinsky argued in vain for a campaign to the east. The verdict of Moscow was that a campaign must be fought for control of the Baltic's end, where the Muscovites held only the thin line of the river Neva. A way must be opened through the barricade in the west.

To this Ivan agreed. No soldier himself, he had his grand-father's bitter realism where war was concerned, and he feared to risk his sluggish Muscovite forces against the experienced Turks or the formidable horsemen of the Krim khans in the open steppes. On the other hand Muscovite numbers and artillery must, in all reason, break through the small Livonian towns, and win the Baltic shore from the Neva and Narva to Riga.

So the decision was made. Probably no one then in Moscow, and certainly not the youthful Ivan, realized how momentous the consequences would be—of endeavoring to return to the west, instead of continuing on into the east. True, Moscow had a shadowy claim to the Baltic shore. Long before, the "men of Rus" had held a trading post on the Baltic, and the Livonians had paid since then a yearly token tax to Moscow of ten pounds of honey or six crowns of money. And now suddenly the ambassador from Moscow demanded arrears of taxes of fifty thousand crowns from the Livonian authorities. When the Bishop of Derpat handed the ambassador instead a letter of protest and evasion, the envoy from Moscow weighed the letter in his hand and laughed. "Why don't you say yes, or no?" And he nodded at the letter. "Here is a little thing that will grow great."

The Muscovite forces moved against the Livonian coast in 1557, and at first they moved onward almost unchecked. But the campaign begun so easily that spring resulted in a war that flared up and died for nineteen years, and involved Sweden, Denmark and Lithuania-Poland.

The first advance of the Muscovites had been spearheaded by Tatar horsemen.

The Sickness and the Terror

Ivan had not been responsible for the wars. Faced from boyhood with the necessity of putting an end to Kazan, he had managed to do so. Faced by the demands of the merchants, the northern boyars and churchmen, he had given consent as Tsar to the beginning of the Baltic war.

At the same time a change occurred within himself; the young Ivan began to fight against pressure exerted upon him, and to enforce his own will. In doing so, he became more solitary and malignant—"terrible," the chronicles say, "to his own people as well as to his enemies."

What caused this change? It is important to trace out what happened to this master of the Kremlin, because after the change, after a dozen short years, his new personality influenced not only the frontiers of Muscovy but events in distant England, and the further regions of Eurasia.

Ivan had been only twenty-two years of age when Kazan fell, and he had left the army with his companion officers to ride home to his wife in Moscow. Winter was setting in. His triumphal return became quite a pilgrimage, when he visited the ancient church of St. Dmitri in the old capital of Vladi-

Muscovite envoys at makeshift altar for prayer, in German city of Regensburg, 1576. (From contemporary wood engraving)

mir. He was hailed and blessed by the clergy at Troitsko. And at the gate of Moscow he was greeted by the Metropolitan, who gave thanks in prayer for victory of the true faith over the pagans, and liberation from the Tatar yoke.

When he dismounted at his own door, Anastasia bowed to him and led him in to his first child, a son christened Dmitri.

That other boy, the wraithlike Ivan who had wandered the Kremlin gardens, could order a new church to be built within the Kremlin, with nine cupolas.

Outside in the streets a new song was heard: "The Tsar Captures Kazan!" It was repeated through the hamlets. For the siege of Kazan had seized upon the fancy of the people, and had become, like the field of Kulikovo or the lake of Alexander Nevsky, the glory of the cottages. It was a good omen, the *krestianin* held, that Ivan's son should be named Dmitri. Great was the young Tsar's power, the folk said, and dread his name. So they began to call him *Ivan Grodzniy,* Ivan the Dread, or Terrible.

Before he could escape from the general rejoicing, he came down with a fever caught in the swamps and mud of Kazan, and grew worse rapidly. Attended only by priests, he read in the books they gave him how Tsar David had been afflicted by the Lord and how Tsar Nebuchadnezzar had wandered from his palace to live with beasts and sleep in the fields wet with night dew. When it seemed as if he would die, he heard the bells tolling at night from the cupolas of the Kremlin.

Shaking with fever, he became afraid. Calling in his nearest advisers, and the heads of the great families, he tried to make them swear on the Scriptures that each one of them would protect his wife Anastasia and safeguard the succession for the infant Dmitri.

It was known that Ivan might die, and his demand that they take oath precipitated discussion among the chief families, descendants of Rurik. There was the ancient custom, disregarded by the last great princes of Moscow, that the uncle rather than the son should succeed. There was also the stubborn fact that an infant and a young woman could not give leadership to Moscow.

Ivan heard no violent argument against his wish. But only boyars related to Anastasia, and Vladimir Vorotinsky, came forward to take the oath and kiss the Scriptures in pledge. Accustomed to his people, even in his weakness Ivan could sense the general antagonism against the man who had named himself Tsar, who demanded that his will be carried out after

his death. Among those who refused to obey were his two
intimates, Sylvester and Adashev.

The next day Ivan began to recover. As soon as he was
able to do so, he took Anastasia and Dmitri away with him,
to his recreation spot in the *sloboda* of Alexandrov on the
hill within sight of the Troitsko monastery. He never forgot
that Adashev and Sylvester had turned away from him in his
crisis.

Instead of striking at those who had revealed themselves
as the enemies of his dynasty—who would have been
doomed by like circumstances in any country other than
Muscovy—Ivan dissembled. Perhaps Anastasia's influence
checked his ungovernable temper. Some of the boyars most
suspect fled to safety across the frontier in Poland. Those
who were caught and brought back, Ivan reproved and pardoned. Only a few of his silent antagonists were executed;
but with them the other members of their families were
killed.

So strongly did the family tie bind the princely Muscovites that if a head of a family were condemned, those closest
to him shared the guilt. And in Ivan's own written record,
calling for prayers for the culprits, this often appears:
". . . with wife and son . . . with two daughters . . . with
twenty-two who served him."

Moderate as this retribution might be, the great families
felt that Ivan meant to put an end to their caste. His friend,
the brilliant Andrew Kurbsky, wrote: "You are turning
against those who have been the sole support of the State."

After the crisis of his sickness Ivan would not be guided
by Sylvester and Adashev—nor by the advice of the Chosen
Council he had first formed around them. When Adashev
argued against the Baltic war, Ivan approved it. He would
not listen to "That man I raised from a dunghill."

Adashev had not changed in the last dozen years. Nor had
Sylvester changed, unless he had become more importunate
as Ivan's confessor in admonishing the Tsar. The change had
taken place in Ivan.

The new Ivan beheld his former companions as men who
had tried to restrain him, who had forsaken the infant Dmitri,
and who now opposed his wish for the Baltic war—Sylvester
had even threatened his master with God's wrath for warring against the Christians of the north instead of the in-
fidel Tatars of the south.

Upon the pair of them Ivan poured out the vials of his

capacious memory—"They would not let me sleep or dress as I chose—they commanded me to listen to counselors, saying nothing myself, like another Aaron."

Having judged them so in his new-found omniscience, Ivan punished them mildly enough by sending Sylvester to Solovetsky and Adashev to a command in the Baltic, where he died.

At this time and often thereafter Ivan had to struggle first and foremost with his own restless conscience.

There was no Eve of St. Bartholomew in Moscow, and no street fighting, no open assassination, or clashes in the Duma. But the conflict between the self-styled Tsar and his feudal lords went on to a decisive end under the appearance of benevolence on one side, and loyalty on the other. In fact, so complex was the Muscovite character that Ivan actually appeared patient and mild at this stage. ("When have I ever ordered an assassination?" he asked in one of his letters to Andrew Kurbsky later.) And the most antagonistic boyars had a core of fidelity to the man who, by God's will, governed their families. (One who fell sick remarked, "My sickness matters nothing if the Tsar is well"; another told a Polish noble, "We do not lose our love for our princes, if they be cruel as well as kind.")

Even Ivan's imagination and genius for expedients could not avoid the conflict. If Moscow was to have actual authority, ancient customs must go; he refused to occupy the throne as the boy the boyars had tolerated. ("I could not speak my will; no command of mine was obeyed.") Since the boyars, as a class, held stubbornly to their old rights, they must go, as a class. To kill a few only roused more antagonism among the others.

Early in the long-drawn-out duel between the monarch and his great vassals, Anastasia sickened and died, after an illness of more than a year. The son, Dmitri, did not survive. There was no hint of poisoning, but Ivan grieved excessively. Like his grandfather and Vasily his father, he seems to have loved only one woman—although he craved many.

We do not know what Anastasia's influence upon Ivan had been. But the change in him after her death is clear enough. His temper became ungoverned, his self-will unbridled. It was as if in losing Anastasia and her child, he had been struck down by his impalpable enemies. Still, this towering man with the beak nose and reddish beard—now in the fullness of his strength—kept restraint on himself, to outward appearance. He was merry with others, inciting them to talk, while he listened in friendly fashion; only rarely did he fall into one of his black rages and foam at the mouth, striking out with his steel-tipped *kisten*.

Almost at once he married a second time, a Circassian girl of fierce instincts, who was baptized as Maria. He had other children and other favorites—the chief of them shrewd Maliuka Skuratov and some of the Basmanovs, folk who could spy for him and serve him without question, a lower breed than the priest Sylvester and the outspoken Adashev.

The brilliant soldier Andrew Kurbsky, who with Michael Vorotinsky had captured Kazan for the Tsar, fled suddenly to the sanctuary of Poland, after suffering a disastrous defeat on the Baltic. From the Polish court, he lashed out at Ivan's new personality in bitter letters. "How have these things come from the throne of a Tsar once kind and gracious, who neglected his health in toils for his country and the Cross of Christ . . . aforetime . . . if I were to relate all such things . . . I should be forced to write how the Devil has sown evil in that goodly house, especially through the wives taken from strange people."

Kurbsky's desertion and reproaches stabbed into Ivan's hidden pride, and the master of the Kremlin answered in even longer, more embittered letters, harping upon one theme —"Every soul is subject to the ruling power" and "There is no authority except in God." For the first time a ruler in Moscow put aside all old tradition and proclaimed that he acted upon divine authority.

Michael Vorotinsky followed Kurbsky out of favor, into exile at the White Lake monastery where Ivan, moved by one of this strange impulses, sent him French wines and servants to wait upon him—and summoned the experienced Vorotinsky back to Moscow at times for his advice.

There could be only *one* authority at Moscow. As Ivan's intimates tended to become servitors, so all his officialdom tended to become "men of trust" and "those who served." Outside of this growing army, Ivan ruled no coherent state. In a sense—and Ivan's clairvoyant brain grasped this clearly —the army *was* Moscow. By a really brilliant expedient, he combined the impoverishment of the boyar class with the improvement of the army. The higher privileges given to "those who served" were bestowed upon those boyars who devoted themselves to military duty. Then, by slow degrees, the great families who had held estates around Moscow were removed bodily from their holdings and exiled to the now distant frontiers where they had to make the best of things. Ivan applied his grandfather's concept of transplanting people to his own boyars.

His overpowering imagination dealt too much with abstractions. He conceived of himself as the enemy of all that was old, and as the fabricator, divinely inspired, of a new state. He became, as Kliuchevsky puts it, his own priest.

As Ivan had educated himself secretly in his boyhood, to conceal his knowledge from the all-powerful boyars, so now he studied western inventions at night, with the aid of astrolabes, globes of the sky, and the maps which only men of the west could draw. These he found, too, printed in the new books, from Polish, German and Italian presses. Marveling at the delicate woodcuts, and the clear black letters—few of which he could read—he fashioned for himself a new cosmic dream, of luxurious courts, and men engaged in industry, of shops that stood upon bridges, and great ships that navigated rivers. This craving for what was new and fine led him to recall his ambassadors from these same western lands, to hear them describe the wonders he had seen pictured.

Before long, he dared import two German typesetters, to fashion a font of Russian letters and print the letters of St. Paul. These foreign masters of an unblessed art were driven out by the superstitious people of Moscow, and not until years later was the first Russian printed book circulated among churchmen. And that book dealt with the national saint, Basil.[3]

Not only did his own people object to foreign instructors. At the Livonian frontier such foreigners were stopped more than once from entering Muscovite territory—at one time some thirty artisans and scholars recruited in the west for service with Ivan were turned back by order of the Emperor.

Before then Ivan had conceived of a church of his own, to rise not in the Kremlin enclosure but in the corner of the Red Place near the bridge over the Moskva—to be dedicated to St. Basil and to be designed by Muscovites who would not merely copy the Italian campaniles and the Byzantine cupolas so characteristic of the older structures in the Kremlin.

It seemed as if Ivan had intended this church in the public square of Moscow to be purely Russian in design and significance. (Perhaps he wanted to improve upon the Russian-

[3] One printing press had been operating since 1549, but not in Moscow. In Ostrov, down in Volhynia, a nobleman, Constantine, had collected Slavic manuscripts and published St. Basil's *The Book of Fasting*. At this time the obscure press in Volhynia was preparing the first Slavic Bible.

Byzantine Dyakovo church built near Moscow the generation before.)

Now as he rode into the main gate of the Kremlin, he passed the unfinished edifice, his new church of Basil the Blessed. It stood at the brink of the slope to the river like a dragon in torment. Nine bulbed domes twisted and rose against the central spire. The whole was savage, oriental, without symmetry. What Ivan thought of it has escaped the record; but the two Muscovite architects of Basil the Blessed do not seem to have built another church in the land.

Victories had ceased in the Baltic war, when the clumsy Muscovite armies encountered the well-drilled and equipped Swedes: internally the stress of heavier taxation, and rising prices—during Ivan's attempt to remake his people by uprooting men bodily from their past and transplanting them elsewhere—brought suffering and even hunger to the Moscow area. The administration by the new bureaus somehow creaked, and drained away money poured into it. Faced with these increasing difficulties, Ivan resorted to one of his extraordinary expedients.

Instead of trying to relieve the stress, he increased it. Instead of laboring further with the tottering Moscow government, he deserted it. He withdrew bodily and set up an administration of his own.

One story has it that he packed his family, treasures and accounts in a caravan of carts and fled the city, to his sanctuary at Alexandrov. Another account claims that his disappearance was merely a usual inspection trip, wherein he visited outlying monasteries. In either event, he notified the religious heads of Moscow that he was withdrawing from them, since they had become intolerant of his orders. And he wrote, separately, to the populace that their Tsar had not ceased to love them and had not deserted them.

Back of this bit of play acting—however it was played —lay a daring stratagem. Ivan separated himself from his council, from the boyars, and the bureaus. He left them, ostensibly, the responsibility of "All of Rus," of Holy Mother Moscow, and the far frontiers, and the war. He kept, outwardly, only the responsibility for certain lands, his own property, in the north. And around him he kept only the now famous "thousand men," the true servitors of the flesh-and-blood Ivan.

They were his new entourage, the *oprichniki* ("the surrounders"), garbed in black, carrying whips shaped like brooms—to sweep filth out of the empire—and a dog's head —to bite the enemies of Ivan.

They formed a brotherhood, young and eager to serve the new state, skilled at spying out enemies, riotous in their revelry at night, mysterious and omnipresent by day. If they were questioned as to who the *oprichniki* might be, they answered that there were no such persons. Over this brotherhood, obedient to his least word, Ivan presided as master, often putting on the garb of a monk during the stress of the day's work and discarding it at night to relax in drink or watching obscene jugglers, and women dancers of the modern strip-tease variety.

Endless tales are told of orgies at Alexandrov, of the tasting of new species of vice by a half-mad Ivan. But perhaps the truth is that a great actor was playing an extraordinary part. Sometimes he appeared in the raids of the black-garbed crew, as when they descended on the foreign village in Moscow—the German quarter—in the middle of a winter night, and looted all the houses, stripping the inmates and driving them out naked into the icy cold, while collecting their goods. There was much method in such madness. A boyar proclaimed guilty by the brotherhood could be made to vanish without appeal to the lawful Tsar. The lands of exiled boyars he gave to his new followers.

Ivan took his elder son with him on the raids of the Alexandrov crew, loosing bears on frightened burghers, galloping through the night on black horses, or sitting in judgment, silent, in black monk's hoods, upon a boyar who had been pointed out by spies. Very soon Skuratov and his henchmen improvised new refinements in mental torture for the victims. Jerome Horsey, an Englishman, declares that an Italian told him how his own brother was killed slowly "by exquisite tortures, his wife stripped and set naked to the eyes of all, and then drawn by a rider on horseback, at a rope's end through a river and drowned."

Ivan himself appears in Horsey's recital. "John, son of Peter, a chief commander, was accused of treason, and without being allowed to clear himself, was clad in royal accoutrements, and set on a throne. The Emperor stood bare-headed before him, bowing, but soon after thrusting him to the heart with a knife. The Attendants added other furies 'till his bowels fell out. His servants were slain, with three hundred others in his Castle."

Victims were not allowed to justify themselves, it seems. "His Chancellor, Dubrowsky, sitting at table with his two sons were all three, upon accusation and without answer, cut to pieces." Men were tormented through their women. "Miessoidovsky, his supreme notary, displeasing him, his wife was taken and after being detained some weeks was hanged over her husband's door and so kept a fortnight, he being driven to go in and out under her all that time." Always, even in these envenomed tales, the *oprichniki* henchmen appear with Ivan. "In travelling if he met any woman whose husband he disliked, he caused her to stand with her nakedness exposed till all his retinue had passed."

Dignitaries of the Church were made ridiculous in public. "The Archbishop, set upon a mare with his feet tied under him, was made to play the bag-pipes through the city."

Horsey did not see these things. He quotes after ten years the stories of foreigners, Dutch, German and Italian, who claimed to have seen them. In those years the stories had grown, and we read also of women violated in a mass by the Streltsi, at command, in Moscow's streets—"their screams were heard across the river all the afternoon"— of other women stripped and hunted through a forest with bows, of people penned up and starved until they were seen eating the flesh of the dead, whereupon the survivors were slain.

Newcomers like Horsey were ready to believe that anything could happen in Muscovy. "I will not depose for their truth," Horsey says of the stories, "though I cannot disprove it. . . . I found a universal report against him. I honor his other good parts, his wit, his learning (perhaps better than almost any other Russe in his time). . . . Yea, his memory is savory still to the Russians. . . . His love to our Nation is so magnified by our countrymen whose gains there, being begun by him, have made them also in some sort to turn Russe (in I know not what loves or fears, as if they were still shut up in Russia and concealing what they know of Russian happenings)."

Throughout this triumph of misrule, Ivan was careful to see that foreign negotiations came into no hands but his. Apparently his purpose was to make it impossible for the Moscow council to administer the country, and if so he succeeded. Naturally, in such a turmoil, the people of Moscow soon paraded out to Alexandrov to petition Ivan to resume his throne, as Tsar.

The Dead, and the Prayers for the Dead, of Novgorod

Ivan, however, would not resume publicly his former honors, and obligations. He was playing what is now discernible as one of his favorite tricks—gaining a real objective by a pretense in another direction. (Remember that he could not yet force popular obedience to a new law; the lawmaking machinery resided in the *Zemsky* and Duma councils, both in a state of sad chaos; you might say he was still engaged in wrecking the old laws to replace them with the new.)

At the moment, several of the leading boyars, Vorotinskys and Trubetskoy, joined the *oprichnina* to serve it voluntarily as individuals. Yet this very *oprichnina*, this *imperium in imperio*, had taken over their great estates along the Oka basin. Similarly, Ivan profited from the seizure of the wealth of German traders in the Moscow *sloboda*, at a time when he could carry on no trade with the Baltic owing to the wars that dragged on stubbornly.

In the same way his black-garbed hands seized strategic trading towns along the "great north road" to the Baltic, under pretense of stamping out rebellion.

Of all these towns, ancient Novgorod suffered the worst dismantling. Novgorod, on the vital river route, was still Germanic in customs, still alien from Moscow.

The only charge against Novgorod was laid by one informer who declared the citizens meditated treachery.

Streltsi matchlock-men entered the old northern city on a bitter midwinter morning, and the *oprichniki* bands followed. Ivan came last in what seemed to be a mood of benevolence. At the banquet of greeting that was tended him perforce, he dropped pretense abruptly, his raiding bands surged in; the leading personages of the city were stripped, and the castle plundered expertly.

For five or six weeks the Novgorodians were subjected to terrorism, purge and thorough plundering. Ecclesiastics were held to ransom and in some cases scourged to death. New instruments of torture were laid out in the public squares, and used—notably a new grill for roasting to death. Methodically, each day batches of captives were taken from the prison pens (into which they had been driven while their houses were gone through) and flogged with weighted whips, or forced into sleds that slid down the snow of the bank into a bend of the river clear of ice. These condemned souls disappeared under the ice.

The executions did not happen during spasmodic violence. They were carried out by order—so many each day. When the goods, furniture and money had been removed from the houses of a street, the buildings were burned.

Reports vary as to the actual number of deaths in Novgorod. The best evidence is furnished by Ivan himself, who wrote down the total of fifteen hundred put to death, in his memorandum that their souls be prayed for in perpetuity— "For fifteen hundred souls, Novgorodians——"

It was inevitable that the man who had begun to act as his own priest should come into conflict with the chief priest of Moscow. That is, with the Metropolitan, the head of the Orthodox Church.

With his usual cunning, Ivan had foreseen the likelihood of such a clash, and had put himself to some pains to prevent it. The metropolitans of his boyhood days had been partial to the—then—ruling caste, the boyars. But at the height of the *oprichnina's* activity, just before the mass executions in Novgorod, the Metropolitan happened to be one Philip, former abbot of Solovetsky monastery, an uncompromising soul. Through his emissaries Ivan had urged Philip not to concern himself with politics but to think only of Ivan's feelings as an individual. And Ivan tried to avoid meeting Philip on public occasions.

One spring morning they met, perforce, at the opening of a service in the Usspensky Sobor. Old custom prescribed that at such a meeting the Metropolitan should bless the prince at the door and at the same time intercede with him for any persons unjustly punished by the prince. This morning Ivan seems to have had his new bodyguards with him, clad as monks. Philip confronted him in silence.

When the Metropolitan refused to speak, Ivan had to ask for his blessing. Then before boyars and people, Philip accused Ivan bluntly of misconduct. How could he give the blessing to such a prince?

Ivan listened for a while, then broke in fiercely: "Be silent! All I ask is—be silent!"

"Silence brings sin," cried Philip. "Silence leads to thy death."

Ivan's restraint broke down and he lashed out in angry words. Philip reminded him, "I did not ask to be appointed. Why did you call me from my hermitage?"

Apparently, Ivan calmed himself after that. When Philip attempted to resign his office, however, Ivan forced him to undergo trial before prelates who feared the Tsar—some from Philip's monastery. Again, Ivan seemed to reconcile himself to Philip, who was allowed to conduct services again as Metropolitan—until the day when *oprichniki* agents entered the church to stage a mockery—to remove Philip's robes, and put a worn monk's habit on him and, laughing, to lead him out the church, sweeping the stones before him and behind him with their brooms, and to carry him off to a monastery that was not his own.

In so doing, Ivan had staged a spectacle that did much to divert the people's attention from Philip's integrity. As usual in such cases, different stories are told as to how Philip died. Perhaps Maliuka Skuratov (Ivan's Tristan l'Hermite) visited him to request that Philip's blessing be sent Ivan, and then strangled him, leaving no mark visible on him.

After that, however, a rumor went through the lands that a saint had been slain, and Philip's body was brought back to his own monastery after Ivan's death.

Rumor was in fact the only voice of that disordered time. With no books printed, with no machinery existing for public debate, with only the clergy—and not all of them—able to read ordinary letters in the ancient Greek script, the Muscovite *krestianin* had news only by word of mouth—told by pilgrims and wayfarers at the hamlets, taverns and monasteries. The grandfathers of families salted news with superstition, women prayed to be freed from the curse of ancient evil. Bells, the bells of churches in villages and monasteries, served as public criers of calamity or blessing.

Wonders and portents loomed large in the active imagination of the workers in the fields, who looked for miracles to preserve them from misfortunes. And to the imagination of the folk of Rus, Ivan had become a wonder-worker, a true guardian of his people. Had he not driven the Tatar from Kazan? Did he not dismount from his horse at crossroads to speak to crowds with a fiery tongue, of the majesty of Tsar David and the glory of Mother Moscow, which had become a new Jerusalem? He did, because he had been seen to do it.

This terrible master of Moscow, surrounded at times by white satin-robed guardsmen, marching with silvered axes, at times prostrate in prayer, beating his forehead against the stones of an altar until his blood flowed on the stones, at times attended by black-garbed servants, like monks—this man did not act like an autocrat. Inner conviction fired him, he spoke words of power, and if he was possessed, as some said, it must be by a holy spirit and not by an evil demon. His wrath turned only against princes, prelates and boyars. Them he bit like a dog. Poets sang:

> ". . . when he's done praying
> He'll go and cut their little nobs
> Off princes and great boyars . . ."

Not only that. Ivan suddenly launched his anger against the monasteries. To his thinking, and in reality, they had waxed rich in wealth and lands. (Now that the embryo Moscow state had taken over most of the strategic lands—and all of the terrain of the expanding eastern frontier—it found itself in competition with the fairly well-managed monastic enterprises.) As usual, the new Tsar made his complaint a personal matter.

On the pretext that some of the boyar "exiles" to the monasteries were living in filthy luxury, he penned one of the fiery epistles that intrigue and puzzle modern psychologists. It began mildly by confessing that he was himself "a stinking dog," given to "murder, adultery and thievery."

Yet even a humble sinner (so says Ivan) like himself is aware how these boyar exiles are contaminating the monastic orders. And the consequences! Ah, the consequences. Why, the monks themselves are beginning to live like licentious boyars, in uproar and rebellion against order, in drink and meat gorging, and unmentionable amusements. They harbor Pilates under their roofs, and they are nailing Christ himself to the cross. "Why? For whom? For sons of dogs, for offspring of devils, and idiots."

(Later on, the monastic landholdings were taxed and the newer acquisitions confiscated.)

By ridicule, by concealing his liquidation of the boyars under the appearance of something very much resembling a popular crusade, Ivan managed to cripple permanently the boyar class in the ten years from 1564–75.

In so doing he added greatly to the potential wealth of the Kremlin treasury. But he was not able to create in that time a substitute for the old government. What he destroyed was done—in whatever fantastic manner—realistically; what he planned was too often an effort of the imagination, left half finished because he could devise no way to finish it.

While material wealth accumulated in the treasury, the purchasing power of money went down steadily. The police power of the new Moscow, so ironlike in the Moscow area, hardly extended to the new frontier zones in the east and south. Settlements along the Volga and in the Ukraine grew because the land was rich, and populace was drifting out to them. The lords of the Kama basin, the great Stroganov family, joined the *oprichnina* officially but paid little attention to it otherwise. Contingents of Cossacks and Tatars, Mordvas and Bashkirs made up a good third of Ivan's new European-model army.

But slowly the popular devotion to the hero of Kazan seemed to change. When Ivan arranged an amusement for the masses in the Red Place after the destruction of Novgorod, by announcing that rebels and criminals would be tortured for all to see, the expected crowd failed to appear. Even when Ivan himself went out to the Red Place, few spectators came forward.

Up on the Baltic, the siege of one town dragged on so long that Ivan had to take command of the operation himself and to order an attack. By now the *krestianin* had no heart in the Baltic wars.

Then Ivan suffered a shocking humiliation. For too long he had neglected the south for the civil conflict within Moscow and the military ordeal of the north. He paid the penalty of his neglect to the full, in the year 1571.

Last Raid of the Tatars

Egged on, if not supported, by Turkish power and Polish intrigue, the Krim Khan struck at Moscow itself and gained a complete surprise. Twenty thousand Tatars wound their way northward by the almost invisible *szlak,* the old Tatar raid routes of the steppes. How they kept themselves hidden remains one of the mysteries of Muscovite history.

Traitors or captives guided the attack column through the strong points of the Tula-Nizhni Novgorod line. Winding between the watch posts, the Tatars crossed the Oka at night, and were plundering and burning in the Moscow suburbs the next day. Ivan fled to safety in the north, by way of Alexandrov.

There was no army to hold the Tatar horsemen off. The fire spread from the rambling suburbs into the flimsy wooden structures of the streets. Most of Moscow burned to the ground. The Kremlin escaped injury. The Tatars made no attempt to storm it, but they captured a large part of the populace—perhaps fifty thousand souls—and drove it south without hindrance.

Worse, the Krim Khan, Davlat Ghirei, dispatched a vale-
dictory letter to Ivan.[4] . . . "I would have taken also your
crown and your head, but you did not show yourself . . .
yet you call yourself a Tsar of Moscow. . . . I have seen
the roads that lead into your *empire* and I know them.
. . . If you wish to live in peace henceforth, yield me up
Kazan and Astrakhan."

The next year the Krim horsemen raided again. They were
met and driven off by a Muscovite army at the river-block-
house defense line, commanded by a Vorotinsky.

It was not only the dread of new Tatar inroads that
started the mass migration out of the Moscow area. Early
in the seventies, at the height of the operations of the
oprichnina, of the stagnation of transcontinental trade, and
the uprooting of the old landed estates, the peasantry and
common folk began a drift to the south and east, away
from the authority of Moscow.

Apparently this movement had no leaders, and certainly
it had no spokesmen. Silent and inexorable, the migration
pressed toward the Volga and the Ukraine. Somehow overnight a hamlet would become half deserted. Carts multiplied
on the roads leading east. The people had a saying about it:
"Heaven lies beyond, in the far land."

Beekeepers, salt miners, fisherfolk, carpenters and most of
all the still independent farmers wandered eastward, getting
their food as they went. This march of thousands became a
rebellion because it fought its way at times through the
cordon of the guard troops.

The moving masses broke through, because many among

---

[4] Ivan had not failed to anticipate such an attack; his network
of spies beyond the frontier extended through the Nogai encampments, the Crimea and Istanbul itself, as well as the Balkans. The defense line from Nizhni Novgorod to Tula was manned as usual that
summer. But that defense line still lay dangerously close to Moscow, and evidence is clear that Muscovite refugees guided the Tatar
attack column through the defenses.

Yet Ivan was preoccupied with his manifold conflicts elsewhere; he
had got rid of his best field commanders. The Tatar operation,
carefully planned and timed and carried out by a small mobile force
of veteran cavalry, broke through the sluggish frontier defense. Ivan
of course blamed the treachery of the boyars for the catastrophe.

Immediately afterward he did what could have been accomplished
fifteen years before—ordered the southern defense line to be moved
farther down into the steppe, and began to cultivate seriously the
Don and Dnieper Cossacks.

It took Moscow generations to recover from this devastation.
Some of the city was never rebuilt. Von Herberstein had estimated
the dwellings of Moscow at 41,500. A century later the count of
buildings came to 40,000.

them were veterans of the Baltic campaigns, and many were prisoners of war—Germans, Swedes, Finns and Livonians who had been put to labor in the Moscow area. There was nothing Ivan could do about it.

Defeat in the North

By now, during the seventies, the mysterious Muscovite was making his personality felt throughout the courts of Europe. Even the courts farthest from Moscow heard tales of the power and wealth of this Great Prince of the east, this obscure lord of Muscovia and Tartary who moved about —so they were told—with a vast horde in tents, or hibernated like a bear in the far fastness of ice and snow, within walls of gold set with jewels. Even the young redhead in Windsor Castle, Elizabeth, heard of him, and so did the somber Philip II, administering a tottering world empire from the halls of the Escorial.

"No other Prince," said the ambassadors, "is so obeyed by his subjects . . . we do not know whether his people have brutalised him, or whether he has made his people brutal."

It is clear that these highly educated monarchs of the farther west like Philip of Spain did not know that the Great Prince of Muscovy had just seen his city burned by Tatars, or that when he could not sleep at night, he called in blind *bylini* singers—tellers of the folk tales—to chant their epics in the darkness, or that when his nerves were tortured by fatigue he descended a private stair in his house to watch the tortures of fugitives who had been captured and brought back.

There was no law that did not rest on force emanating from Moscow; there was no *nation* beyond the periphery of that force which Ivan was obliged to maintain if he would rule at all.[5]

In a way he had brought this situation upon himself. In his youth he had been obsessed by the fear that the boyars

[5] Unlike the English Parliament, the lawmaking assembly, the Moscow Duma, had no means of limiting Ivan's authority. While Elizabeth had to wring money out of her Parliament by expedients, Ivan was incomparably the greatest merchant and wealthiest individual of Muscovy. There has been much discussion of the measures effected by the new Zemsky Sobor, which resembled an embryo Estates-General (". . . his State gathered together from towns of every rank . . ."). But the Zemsky council of Ivan's time consisted of representatives *named by himself*.

and officials who bowed the forehead to him might be in reality his enemies. Now, twenty-five years after his coronation, he had enemies who were only too real. (Boyars *had* guided the Tatars to the Oka, and lieutenants like Kurbsky *had* served foreign princes in open war against Moscow. Ivan was the last man on earth to be mistaken on that point.)

Meanwhile during the campaigns in the north, he had made himself a master of European diplomacy. As he had contrived to cope with the great families around him in his boyhood, he learned the art of negotiation among western nations very swiftly—even for one accustomed to Tatar duplicity. Alliances, threats. bribes, trade privileges and concessions, control of districts by puppet lords, bargaining for towns, river mouths, powder, metal, the skill of engineers, the knowledge of astronomers and physicians, rights secured by state marriages—all these stakes at wager upon the great European chessboard, Ivan manipulated with consummate skill. He almost managed to compensate for failure to obtain final military victory in the north by his genius in such negotiation.

The combat, both military and diplomatic, ebbed and flowed over the strategic strip of Baltic coast, with the adjoining lakes, and connecting rivers—from Ladoga down to the vital outlet of Narva, on to Lake Peipus and to the goal of Riga at the end of the western Dvina. This was the ancient battle ground of Alexander of the Neva, as it would be that of Gustavus Adolphus, and the Russian Peter, of Hindenburg and others far into the twentieth century. And as usual with Ivan, the dazzling virtuosity of his negotiation had a concealed and realistic objective—in this case control of the rivers and ports at the Baltic's end. But what virtuosity! To a churchman he could write, "I am the defender of the Christian faith." To an exile in Poland he could make himself humble with words: "I am still alive, yet how ugly I am—one huge sore, like a corpse in a grave."

Once he became obsessed with an idea of a political marriage for himself, and to that idea he clung with all his savage tenacity. The girl in question was Catherine, younger daughter of Sigismund of Poland, who had been described to Ivan as a beauty. Even when Catherine was given in marriage to the Duke of Finland, Ivan's ambassadors continued to negotiate for her. Perhaps Ivan craved a talented girl from the west; perhaps his obsession came from memory of his mother Helen, the Lithuanian; perhaps he fancied that the marriage would yield a claim to the throne of

Lithuania; perhaps the refusal of the westerners roused his stubborn anger. At least, he explained finally that he wanted her as a hostage.

Ivan craved women insatiably. When Maria the Circassian died, he stormed at his church for objecting to a third marriage, arguing that he only desired it "to keep from sin." His third bride, the daughter of a highborn family, died within a few days. Ivan contented himself with two mistresses, utterly unlike.

Then came the offer from Poland. That troubled kingdom had united itself to Lithuania, and after the death of the politic Sigismund, the council of the dual kingdom disagreed as to who should be elected to the throne.

During the dispute one faction sent a proposal to Moscow. Very discreetly the envoys from Warsaw, now the capital, put a question to Ivan. Would the great Tsar consider the advisability of having one of his sons crowned king at Warsaw?

Faced with the possibility of a union between the three Slav states, Ivan's clairvoyant mind probed the consequences. At the moment his armies were pressing to the Dvina, menacing Vilna itself. To unite Polish culture and Lithuanian hardihood with the power of the nebulous Moscow state—and only Ivan realized how nebulous it was—would secure for the new alliance all that portion of the Baltic, would press the Finns back farther from Lake Ladoga, and would erect a barrier against the most dangerous enemies, the Germanic peoples. Ivan's *concept* of a great Slav state was modern enough. The only enduring cleavage lay in religion—the schism between the Orthodox and Catholic churches—and Ivan had ceased to weigh religion against political gains.

He replied that he thought well of the proposed crown of Poland, not for his son but for himself.

Displaying every courtesy at his command, he gave the Polish envoys sagacious arguments on his own behalf, knowing that he needed to offset the accusations of cruelty made against him by fugitives from Muscovy.

"If your lords who seek a king desire me to be that to them," he explained, "they will find in me a protector, and an understanding superior . . . not only to respect the franchises of the Polish lords, but to increase them . . . Where you come from, many have said I am cruel. It is true. I am both cruel and impatient. But I ask you, to whom am I cruel? I am cruel to the ones who are cruel to me.

"But not to those who are kind. Ah, to *them* I would give

the gold chain and the robe from my shoulders. It is not
strange at all that your princes have loved their people, if
the people loved them. But what have mine brought to me?
Mine have delivered me to the Krim Tatars. My military lords
became silent when the Tatars arrived. They did not send me
warning. If they had sent even a word, or one Tatar whip, I
should have bowed to them and thanked them. And if some
of them were chastised for that silence of theirs, it was for
treachery. Tell me—do you not chastise traitors?"

Ivan beheld a great stake almost within his grasp. At that
moment his prestige was at its highest in the west. After
long dissension, the throne of Poland-Lithuania was awarded
to Stephen Batory, a young Transylvanian who vowed that
all Ivan's captures should be wrested from him. And Batory
was to prove a brilliant military leader.

At that point Ivan seemed to have no one he could trust
to lead his own armies. His captures in the west had stirred
no such enthusiasm in Muscovy as had the taking of Kazan.
His peasantry was migrating away from the "great north
road," leaving ghost towns between Moscow and the Baltic's
shore.

Moreover Ivan found a new force opposed to him. It had
appeared among the Baltic folk, who followed the teaching
of evangelists, and called themselves Protestants. They had
pastors and they invoked the words of a man named Luther.
In a Livonian village Ivan struck down with his whip a pastor
who argued that Luther was doing such work as St. Paul had
done.

With his astonishing tenacity, he summoned spokesmen of
the new faith, to explain it to him, and when they had done
so, he wrote out a careful rebuttal to their arguments. For
each point of the evangelists, he had a brilliant if irrational
answer. "You summon up the sayings of the prophets: then I
will confront you with Moses." To his own intimates he con-
fided that "Judged by their actions, these evangelists are
nothing but pigs."

The pigs, however, helped make matters difficult for Ivan
in the mists of the Baltic. Many of the Protestants appeared
in the ranks of the fine Swedish infantry with which the Muscovites now had to contend. And the spirit of Protestantism
itself proved troublesome, because it led individuals to
search the pages of printed Bibles for guidance, and to follow the advice of their pastors regardless of the authority of
reigning monarchs or of the more ancient churches.

Some Dutch Protestants were leaving their old homes by

the dikes to seek refuge in England from the authority of the King of Spain, enforced by the armies of the Duke of Alva. Of this Ivan was aware, because Dutch trading ships as well as English ran the semiblockade of the Baltic to reach his ports of Narva and Revel (Tallinn).

Certainly Ivan desired no conflict with Protestantism as such; it had become an impalpable force opposing his will along the Baltic coast. Insensibly, the Baltic conflict had become a popular war among the small peoples opposed to him, while it became detested by his Muscovites. In vain Ivan assured his troops that the banks of the coveted Dvina were like silver, its waters gold, to be gained.

Another migration was drawing peasants from the Moscow landholdings down to the Ukraine. Under the new laws, freedom of movement was almost denied the peasantry. Serfdom had linked its first chains around them. They had not become the property of the landowners; they were simply bound now to the expanse of land which had no value to the owners unless men were chained to it, to work it. More and more of them began to escape this stress by wandering south, where the only authority—outside the few garrison posts —was that of the carefree Cossack brotherhoods.

They had heard tales of the richness of the green steppe, and they went in search of it. Like the *druijina* of Igor, they thirsted to drink of the waters of the Don. They heard the old song *"Zadonshina* [Beyond the Don River]." The Cossacks christened these refugees "the Naked."

By then the Cossack communities along the great rivers, the Dnieper and Don,[6] had managed to house themselves; the fugitives from the north appeared on rafts and along the

---

[6] How these settlements subsisted so far beyond the fringe of the growing Muscovite state remains a mystery to many modern thinkers. They were not, however, *colonies*. They were hosts, brotherhoods, of independent peoples, forming small islands of population in the steppe. So far as war is concerned, history solves the mystery by the evidence that such peoples in marginal zones usually developed a live-and-let-live understanding with neighboring populations, regardless of wars being waged by the great political states behind them.

The traditions of both the Host of the Don and the Zaporogians on the Dnieper reveal no major conflict with their powerful neighbors, the Turks and the Krim Tatars. The wars originated in Moscow, Vienna, Istanbul or Warsaw, not in the frontier zones. In this very generation the alien Moriscos subsisted peacefully enough in Spain in the mountains near Granada, although they were Moslems —until measures were taken to exterminate them by Philip's government. So the Sudeten Germans subsisted without major stress in their frontier zone until they became a part of the expansion scheme of the Hitlerian Reich.

dusty trails without shelter or goods, begging for food and the chance to work the soil. So the Cossacks called them the Naked, and the Naked began to cultivate the steppe, gradually making agriculture the mainstay of these frontier communities. The Cossacks themselves were slow to take to agriculture, preferring to hunt and fish as before, to serve in the distant wars for pay, and to raid the Muscovite trade caravans that tried to reach the Turkish Black Sea ports—which the Cossacks also raided, by ship.

On that sea the Cossack brotherhoods had built and fortified their own ports, as at Azov by the mouth of the Don. They had penetrated the steppe as far as Vladikavkas—the Lord of the Caucasus—by the muddy Terek, within sight of the cloud-veiled peaks seldom seen by the eyes of Slavs before.

Where the distant Urals—the Earth Girdle of Herberstein's legends—touched the great southern steppe, other fugitives, masterless men, hunters and miners, were streaming into the villages of the Cossack Host of the Urals.

Beyond these settlements, unmapped, lay inner Eurasia.

As yet Ivan had neglected this extension of his people into the heart of the continent. But he refused to barter or to yield either Azov or Astrakhan to the Turkish sultans.

In 1572 Ivan made one of his startling changes of policy. He abolished his own separatist government. That is, he announced the abolition of the *oprichnina* and all the mise en scène of Alexandrov, calling it merely the court henceforth. Actually, he did reduce the number of his black-robed bodyguard to the original thousand, and relaxed the pressure on the remnant of the boyar class. His *oprichniki* favorites by now had gone the way of Adashev and Sylvester.

But he could not disentangle himself from the Baltic conflict, where it still seemed as if his numbers and artillery might at least hold what he had gained. The turning point came when he failed to recapture the port of Revel after it was garrisoned by Swedes.

Ivan prepared to defend the strip of coast, won at such great cost, by digging in his armies behind his abundant cannon. It was a strange trick of fate that this man who hated campaigning, and even dreaded death at the hands of his own troops, should have made his most desperate effort to win a war such as this. He could not, or would not, summon back the Kurbskys and Vorotinskys to aid him. Nor could he depend upon the Muscovite cavalry, or the Cossack and Tatar regiments to withstand Polish lancers or Swedish infantry, when commanded by such strategists as Batory and De la Gardie.

Nor was the fortification of the Livonian coast to aid him when the Swedes struck down around Ladoga, and Batory with the new Polish army ignored the coast and moved against the strategic rivers inland, and Moscow itself. Ivan was to watch Narva fall, with Polotsk, and the network of portages pass to the enemy. In defeat, he was to try every expedient of negotiation and even to appeal to the Pope to become arbiter. In the end he had to accept his defeat.[7]

Yet during the quarter century of the Baltic conflict he had gained contact with the outer world, in extraordinary fashion, through the English. To this contact he clung with all his tenacity.

What the English Saw

The spacious days of Elizabeth had not begun and England was hardly merry England when her navigators discovered Muscovy by accident, in 1553.

At that time Ivan might have read enough in the German-printed world chronicles to understand that Albion was a small island of indeterminate shape off the western coast of Europe, populated largely by sheepherders and makers of wool and fishermen. He might have read that it exported woolen cloth, and had one large town, Londennum, on its chief river, the Thames.

It was rather more than that, however. In the very year that Ivan had put his people astride the Volga by taking Kazan, the unknown English prepared to search the northern seas for new lands. From our perspective today, we can say that these two mighty nations started to expand at the same moment in historical time—the Russians across the land mass of a continent, toward the seas, the English across the seas toward distant continents. That twofold expansion was to have great consequences.

It was not altogether a coincidence that one of the earliest English navigators should encounter Muscovites on the shore of the Frozen Ocean Sea.

England lay at the moment in dire stress, almost shut off from the continent where great empires ruled. Apparently she was doomed to isolation, in which her embryo industry

[7] One historian sums it up aptly: "Ivan needed more skill to lose as he did in the west than to win as he did in the east."

could find no markets—"vents," her chroniclers termed them.
Except for fishing craft and a few merchantmen, she had no
fleet. She had no navigators, except the Italian Cabots whose
services she had hired. Her Bristol fishermen, like the Vikings
before them, ventured out to the banks of the "New Found
Land." But her merchant cruisers had been barred from the
rich Mediterranean trade by powerful armadas, Spanish,
Venetian and Turkish. New markets had to be found at all
costs, and where was so fine a market—outside Spanish
monopoly—as in Cathay where, supposedly under the dominion of the Great Khan of Tatary, silk, tea and spices could be
had for English wool?

It was definitely ascertained by then—by 1552—that the
land across the Atlantic explored by the Genoese Columbus
and the Italian Vespuccius was a new continent, and not
islands off the coast of Cathay. Besides, Spanish shipping had
made of that obscure coast a Spanish main sea. So in natural course the first English efforts to explore toward Cathay
were directed to the northwest and northeast, to search for
a passage. What might lie upon this way to Cathay in the
northeast, the English gentlemen adventurers did not know—
beyond the North Cape of Lapland, that is. They understood
that the great motionless Ice Sea extended there, where the
sun rose with thunder.

The first adventurers to outfit three ships under the advice
of Sebastian Cabot to explore this Ice Sea formed "The
Mysterie and Company of the Merchants Adventurers of
the Citie of London, for the discovery of Cathay and other
divers regions, dominions unknown." They bore with them
letters to (in modern English wording) "all the princes and
lords, to all the judges of the earth . . . whoever possess any
high authority in all the regions under the vast sky." The
letters certainly entitled the adventurous Englishmen to treat
with any monarch they might meet.

Yet there is evidence that Sebastian Cabot, at least, anticipated his explorers would meet with Russians. One journal
mentions Cabot as "long before having this secret in his
mind." And Scandinavian interpreters who spoke Russian
were furnished the explorers.

Three ships set out, too late in the season. After rounding
Scandinavia, two were caught in the winter ice and lost,
with no survivors. The third, the *Edward Bonaventura*, had
amazing luck. Passing a great headland as the long winter's
darkness began, the *Edward* felt her way upon a warm
current into a narrow unknown sea, and thence into a river's

mouth where stood a monastery. The river was the eastern Dvina, the monastery St. Nicholas.

Instead of perishing in the ice and darkness, the master of the *Edward*, Richard Chancellor, was whisked south along the river road by sled, and found himself in Moscow. There the surprised Englishman was kept waiting only ten days before being admitted to see "the light of the majesty" of Ivan.

"He himself," Chancellor reported, "sat much higher than any of the fair company, in a gilt chair, and in a long garment of beaten gold . . . with a staff of crystal and gold in his right hand. . . . After my duty done and my letter delivered, he bade me welcome and inquired of the health of the King my master. . . . Upon the which I was required to depart, for I had charge not to speak to the Duke but when he spoke to me."

Even while he was being entertained by a legendary monarch, with all the sumptuous Muscovite hospitality, this Englishman noted nothing so much as the quality of goods, the value of treasures.

He dined in a palace "which is called the golden palace, but I have seen many fairer than it, in all points." The hall itself was "small and not great as is the King's Majesty's of England." From the images in the churches to the painted cheeks of the few women he saw, he noted down details with a merchant's eye. Yet he was struck by the sagacity and endurance of the Muscovite soldiers. "Now what might be made of these men if they were trained and broken to order, and knowledge of civil [i.e., intelligent European] wars?"

Nor did Chancellor fail to observe how, even in that early year, the Tsar commandeered the property of his nobles. "If there be a rich man, or one stricken in age and not able to do the Duke service, the Duke sends to inquire of his wealth . . . and he shall be called before the Duke and it shall be said to him, 'Friend, you have too much living' . . . whereupon his wealth shall be taken away from him at once, saving some little to find himself and his wife on. And he may not repine of that, but [must] immediately say that he has nothing—it is God's and the Duke's Grace's. He can not say as we the common people of England say, if we have anything, that it is God's and our own."

One of his officers, however, reports that while Chancellor was "nothing dismayed" and did his duty after the "manner of England" the men with him were "amazed at the majesty of the Emperor."

For Chancellor returned safely to England in his lucky little vessel. And on his testimony Cabot and the other merchant adventurers formed the Muscovy Company, to send ships regularly to the river mouth in Arctic waters.

At this stage the will to trade was all on one side, with the men of London. They were almost desperate in their need to barter their woolen cloth and stuffs for the flax, hemp, wax, silk, and the oriental goods that Chancellor's party had seen in Moscow. Here was a vent for trade outside the reach of the great Spanish-Portuguese fleets. Moreover they still hoped that this might prove to be the coveted passage to Cathay. When Chancellor returned to Moscow, three years later, he bore instructions to "use all ways and means possible to learn how men may pass either by land or by sea to Cathay."

One of his vessels, the *Searchthrift,* went on to explore east through the Ice Sea, and actually rounded the coast of the Samoyeds probed against the island of Nova Zembla. There seemed to be no way through the gathering ice fields, and the ship returned before the winter's darkness set in. On the other hand, at Moscow they learned much about the caravan routes through Asia, leading toward Cathay.

They had also learned to address Ivan as "the right High, right Mighty and right Excellent Prince, garnished with all gifts of Nature by God's grace, John the son of Vasili, Emperor of All Russia, Great Duke of Vladimir, Moscow and Novgorod, King of Kazan"—and of all the other cities and territories by name—"Commander of the north part, and Lord of many other Countries."

It sounded well. Yet Ivan does not seem to have been impressed by the matter-of-fact Chancellor or by his blunt and plainly clad companions. He regarded them as wandering traders, lacking the power and prestige of the Germans, Venetians or Turks. True, he granted them privileges to trade, east and west of the Dvina, and he consented to send back with Chancellor a Muscovite governor, to draw up a reciprocal trade agreement in London.

Only by chance did this first ambassador, Nepey, from Moscow to London survive. The English navigators had proved that they could round the fabulous North Cape without being drawn down into the watery gulf of Maelstrom; they had felt their way into the Sea of Ice; they had even recovered the two lost vessels. But almost within sight of their islands, Chancellor's ships were scattered by a storm and three of them lost; the *Edward* being driven on the rocks of the Scottish coast. Chancellor died in launching the boat that saved the life of the Muscovite envoy.

Whereupon the merchants of London and the court at Windsor joined their efforts to make impressive the arrival of this ambassador from Muscovy, saved from the sea.

"He was received twelve miles from London by fourscore merchants with chains of gold and goodly apparel who conducted him to a house and made him a riding garment. The next day he had not only the hunting of the Fox and suchlike sport shown him, but also by the Queen's Majesty's command, he was received and embraced by the right honorable Viscount Montague [and] divers lusty knights, esquires, gentlemen and yeomen who led him to the City where was presented to him a gelding, richly trapped together with a footcloth of Orient crimson velvet. The Lord Mayor accompanied with all the Aldermen in scarlet did receive him, with all sorts of Officers to attend upon him, as to such an ambassador of honor doth pertain."

Within a year, however, the records of the Muscovy Company reveal that his London hosts had some misgivings about this same Nepey.

"We do not find the Ambassador now at last so comfortable to reason as we had thought. He is very mistrustful and thinks every man will beguile him. Therefore, you have need to take heed how you have to do with him, or with any such, and to make your bargains plain, and to set them down in writing. For they be subtle people, and do not always speak the truth, and think other men to be like themselves."

In the reciprocity of privileges that they signed, the Englishmen were careful not to grant overmuch to the unpredictable Muscovites. With the death of Sebastian Cabot, who carried so many "secrets" of navigation and geography with him to the grave, and after the loss of so many ships and cargoes, the Muscovy Company might well have ceased to be. Yet a new fleet was fitted out, fresh traders enlisted, and plans made for the building of a post on the Island of Roses in the Dvina.

For the first time the English were piloting themselves out of their narrow seas, without aid of the experienced Spaniards or Italians,[8] to a gateway to Asia. And this time

[8] Fleets sent later in the Elizabethan age to the coast of America were piloted by a Portuguese, Fernandez. Even Francis Drake, in his reckless venture around the world, impressed Spanish pilots after crossing the Atlantic. The English navigators, lacking maps, were learning their geography as they explored. These first ventures into unknown seas were by no means the carefree exciting voyages of later-day imagination. Although Drake reached England eventually with a whole

the ill luck that had dogged the first ships changed to un-dreamed-of fortune.

By then (1558) the Livonian war had started; the Hanse towns and Baltic shipping had begun what amounted to a blockade of ports leading into Ivan's dominion. The Londoners noted that such towns as Dantzig, Lübeck and Hamburg "desired to stop all ships as should go out of England for Moscovia."

Very speedily Ivan realized that only by way of the White Sea and only by English shipping could he obtain the lead, iron, cloth and powder that Muscovy needed now. So the situation at Chancellor's first visit of five years before was reversed, and the Muscovites besought the English to increase their trade. Under these conditions the increased trade was to yield a profit of two or three hundred per cent.

Almost at once, after the Muscovites captured Narva on the Baltic, the Polish court wrote to Elizabeth, who had just become Queen, in protest against English trade with Muscovy. "The Muscovite, enemy to all liberty under the heavens, daily grows mightier by the increase of such things as be brought to him. Thither are brought not only merchandise but also weapons heretofore unknown to him. Even the artists, makers [of such weapons] are brought him, by whose means he maketh himself strong to vanquish all others. Your Majesty knoweth not the strength of this enemy, nor the authority he has over those who serve him."

Search for the Land Route to Cathay

The English persevered in their venture to the east, forwarding code books to their traders on the Dvina, with instructions to code all messages sent back. They added in the same letter: "We perceive that Stephen Bourroughs is returned [from Nova Zembla] with the *Searchthrift*, and wintereth at Kolmogro, and is minded to set forth in the beginning of June next to seek the river of Ob. We pray God to speed him well . . . and we will that he proceed on his voyage to discover. Also we have sent you one Anthony Jenkinson, Gentleman, a man well-traveled, whom we mind to use in further travelling, according to a Commission de-

---

ship's cargo of gold, plate and jewels and vestments, he brought back only one ship out of five, and very few survivors of the original crews. These sixteenth-century voyages set out to render a grim service to their country.

livered him. . . . He must have forty pounds a year for four years, to be paid him by the half year, or as he shall demand it of you, so let him have it from Easter last."

During each of those four years Anthony Jenkinson was to earn his forty pounds. It seems that his "Commission" was to use Ivan and the court at Moscow as a means of finding a land route to Cathay. And on the way thither to establish a chain of English markets.

Letters from the home office of the company reveal that it was close to bankruptcy, but "had hope of good trade" from Anthony Jenkinson.

What kind of a man he was, we can understand by the difficulties out of which he achieved a miracle. Before then his "travels" had been the exploration of the Mediterranean, and much of the North African coast, where he encountered the Turks. On the voyage out, although rated only as a Gentleman, he was chosen captain of his ship. On arrival, past St. Nicholas Head, he spent the summer taking soundings and keeping a record of mileage in versts, as well as learning the language and plotting the position of all towns by observation. He adapted himself quickly to post travel through the great forests, where "all the way I never came in house, but lodged in the wilderness by the river's side, and carried provisions for the way. And he that will travel these ways must carry with him a tinder box, a hatchet and a kettle, to make fire and seethe meat, when he has it; for there is small succour in these parts."

At Moscow this astute and inflexible Englishman won Ivan's interest at once—for he was placed at a small table by himself facing the Tsar during the banquets, and Ivan sent him wine and meats that he had picked out for his guest, by the hand of a boyar. More than that, Jenkinson by degrees won an extraordinary privilege for the English company. It was to trade independently throughout Muscovy and further Asia, with Ivan's authorization.

So Jenkinson did not confine the company's posts to the northern Dvina area as Ivan had expected; nor did he himself remain in Moscow, with the other foreign merchants of the German village (which had not yet been purged by Ivan's *oprichniki*). He started off to the south, on the Volga River route (then newly opened) with two young companions, a Tatar guide, a convoy of trade goods and Ivan's letters to unknown khans and princes of farther Asia.

Following the Volga waterway down through the treeless steppe, Jenkinson passed between the Cossack frontier communities—the Host of the Don and that of the Urals. Coming into the last Muscovite post, Astrakhan, on an island near the river mouths, he found himself in the stench of drying fish and the piled-up bodies of Nogai Tatars who had drifted in to the log walls of the Muscovites during a famine. "There died a great number of them for hunger, which lay all the island through in heaps, like to beasts unburied, very pitiful to behold; many of them were also sold by the Russes and the rest were banished from the island. . . . How could the Russes show compassion to other nations when they are not merciful unto their own? At my being there I could have bought many goodly Tatars' children . . . of their own fathers and mothers, to say a boy or wench for a loaf of bread worth six pence in England."

When Jenkinson left Astrakhan, he embarked on the salt waters of the unknown inland sea, the Caspian, where floated the red rust of oil. Without protection from the Muscovites he had to navigate as best he could, keeping at first to the coast, where he found himself off the mouth of the Ural River, without sign of habitation.

Here his voyage nearly came to an end. Lying sick on deck, attended by a Moslem pilgrim from Mecca, while his companions explored the shore, his bark was boarded by a wandering band searching for enemies. "Who began to enter into our bark, and our holy Tatar called Azi, perceiving that, asked them what they would have, and withal made a prayer. These rovers declared they had come to see if there were any Russes or other Christians (which they called *caphars*) in our bark. To which Azi most stoutly answered that there were none, avowing the same by great oaths of their law (which lightly they will not break). Him the rovers believed, and upon his words departed. And so through the fidelity of that Tatar, I was saved with all my company and goods."

Driven ashore on the eastern shore by a storm, Jenkinson left the sea and tried to strike directly east across the desert toward a main caravan track. Confronted by wandering Turkomans, he visited the chief of them, offering gifts—to keep from being plundered—and hiring a thousand camels for a baggage train. Guided eastward around the waste of the Black Sands Desert—"where the like of us had not before arrived"—he learned to live on mare's milk instead of bread, and to keep a semblance of authority by begging letters from each tribal group to the next.

Hearing that a great lake lay near, he investigated and found himself in the stronghold of the Khiva khans, named Urgench, below another inland sea, which he thought to be the fabulous Lake of Cathay. It proved to be the Sea of Aral which lay far indeed, as Jenkinson discovered, from the frontiers of Cathay.

But he found himself to be on the caravan route that skirted a river leading to Bokhara and Samarkand. Thither he started, with a mixed caravan, guarded by eighty riders from Urgench, who proceeded to demand a bonus as soon as they sighted a band of raiders approaching. The Englishman decided that the holdup had been prearranged, and refused to pay, whereupon their guards departed. Left to themselves, some Mecca pilgrims—who seemed to know more about the danger than the Englishmen—killed a sheep to take an omen from the markings of its shoulder blades. The oracle of the bones foretold that if they went on they should be attacked and greatly harmed but would not be captured.

"To which sorcery my companions and I gave no credit; but we found it true. For within three hours after the soldiers departed from us we escried far off divers horsemen which made toward us . . . they willed us to yield ourselves or else be slain, but we defied them, wherewith they shot at us all at once and we at them very hotly . . . divers men, horses and camels being wounded and slain on both parts. Had it not been for four hand-guns which I and my companions used, we had been overcome and destroyed, for the thieves were better armed than we. . . . Two hours within night, they asked a truce with us until the next morning, which we accepted and encamped ourselves upon a hill, walled about with packs of wares, and laid our horses and camels within, to save them. . . . The thieves encamped between us and the water, to our great discomfort, because neither we nor our camels had drunk in two days before.

"Thus keeping good watch, when half the night was spent, the Prince of the thieves sent a messenger half way to us, swearing to keep the truce so that we all heard. And then we sent a holy man of our company to talk with the messenger who cried aloud 'Our Prince demands of your caravan pasha, not wishing your blood, that you deliver up to him as many caphars—that is unbelievers—as are among you, with their goods, and by so doing you may depart in peace with your goods, but by not doing so you will be handled with the same cruelty as the caphars.'

"Our caravan pasha answered that he had no Christians in his company, nor other strangers except two Turks, and if he had, he would rather die than deliver them, and we were not afraid of threats as they should know when day appeared.

"And the thieves, contrary to their oath, carried our holy

man away to their Prince. Whereat we were much discomforted, fearing that the holy man would betray us; but he, being cruelly handled and like to die, would not confess anything touching us, nor what men they had slain and wounded of ours the day before.

"In the morning we prepared for battle, which the thieves perceiving, asked [instead] payment of us, of twenty times nine things. Having so little to lose, we gave the things and a camel to carry them, and the thieves departed into their wilderness. We came to the river and refreshed ourselves, having been then three days without water, and tarried there, making merry with our slain horses and camels to eat."

After this initiation to the trade of Eurasia, the English pioneers reached Bokhara, a religious center where their lives were forfeit. Jenkinson made good use of Ivan's letters, persuaded the reigning Sultan to recapture the lost camel load of goods. He entertained the surprised Sultan with tales of Muscovy, Turkey and England, and learned on his part what caravans came through from China with musk, rhubarb and

First coherent map of "Russia, Muscovy, and Tartary." Drawn by Anthony Jenkinson, 1562, following early English exploration of the northern polar coast and the southern Caspian Sea. This reveals Jenkinson's knowledge of the peoples of inner Asia as far as Samarkand on the way to "Cathay."

silk and satin. Before the Sultan left his city to go to war, Jenkinson promised to conduct a pair of his envoys safely to Moscow. "In spite of all this entertainment, I found him a very Tartar, for he went away to the wars owing me money." Money for which Jenkinson managed to collect goods, before he beat a hasty retreat from the city, hearing that the local war was going badly. (He left just in time, because Bokhara was sacked ten days later by raiders from Samarkand.)

Traveling back as the ostensible conductor of envoys from Bokhara to Ivan, Jenkinson collected four ambassadors at Urgench, urging upon the khans there the necessity of sending more envoys than the Bokharans to Moscow. On the road to the Caspian he freed twenty-five Muscovite captives, and improvised a guard out of them. Finding his bark stripped of sail, cordage and anchor, he recovered the anchor from the country people, and fashioned a new sail, and wove ropes out of hemp—then set a course across the sea to the Volga. There he made one theatrical gesture. He flew at his masthead the red cross of St. George for the first time on the Caspian, and perhaps for the only time.

With his recruited ambassadors, when he returned to Moscow, he presented the pleased Ivan with a Tatar yak-tail standard, and drum. He had also brought along a Tatar girl whom he called Sultana Aura, to be dispatched to Queen Elizabeth.

For himself, he had a really accurate survey of the routes and cities of his journeys, and a description of the way to Cathay from Bokhara along the "great south road" (formerly the famous Silk Road).

Not content with this, he ventured a second time far beyond the limits of Muscovy, down the Caspian, through the towering Caucasus, to the trading center of Tabriz. He reached the court of the Shah of Persia at Kasvin, near the mountains' edge.

Here, obliged to wear foot wrappings so his feet would not pollute the ground of the jealous Moslems, he found himself faced down by old antagonists, Venetian and Turkish emissaries. Yet he answered the impatient questioning of the Persian by explaining that he was from "the famous city of London, within the noble Realm of England, and that I was sent thither from the most excellent and gracious sovereign Lady Elizabeth, Queen of said Realm, for to treat of friendship and free passage of our people, for to bring in our commodities and to carry away theirs, to the honor of both princes."

Undisturbed, he left his hostile audience, while a servant

hastily scattered fresh earth to purify the ground where he had stepped. And he brought back to Ivan messages and envoys from the Armenians and Georgians of the Caucasus, as well as the "lord of Hircania."

To Ivan he rendered an accurate account and survey of the kingdoms by the Caspian. Convinced, on his own part, that the Muscovy Company could not traffic directly with faraway Cathay, he got Ivan's agreement to establish company posts in Kazan and Astrakhan, to tap such trade—"to buy barter and sell at will, without custom."

And Ivan agreed, "for our sister's sake, Elizabeth," that only the English should enter Russian ports to trade; the ships of any other kingdom would be confiscated. This was a monopoly—"heavier than tribute," Ivan complained—and by it the English gained their first trade with inner Asia.

The Obsession of Marriage and Escape

It was also a very one-sided agreement, as Ivan well knew. To Jenkinson in Muscovy he had conceded both the monopoly of foreign trade and extraterritorial rights to the English posts and personnel being set up from the White Sea to the Caspian. By then the English agents, with their secretaries and "painstaking" young men in Muscovy, might have numbered forty or more On the other hand, in London the council of the Muscovy Company and Elizabeth herself granted only the vaguest privileges to the worried ambassadors from Moscow. The profit in money went all one way, and it was becoming a great profit. Why did Ivan, a most experienced bargainer himself, grant this?

He was fascinated of course by Jenkinson's achievements in exploring new frontiers, and drawing for him the first coherent map of a greater Muscovite state. Then, too, Dutch vessels were following the English through the Baltic to Narva, where for a time a hundred foreign vessels were to be laded yearly. Regardless of his agreement, Ivan made no real attempt to bar out these Dutch and Scandinavian traders. He needed powder and guns too badly for the Livonian campaigns. In fact he seems to have been almost obsessed at that stage (1561-66) with the thought of accumulating artillery to win victories. His vast collection of guns at Moscow surprised the English observers. (England, in Elizabeth's youth, had neither a fleet built for war nor an army.)

"The Emperor's majesty," one of their letters to London relates, "useth every year in the month of December to have all his ordinance that is in the city of Moscow carried into a field which is without the suburbs of the city, and there to have it planted and bent [i.e., ranged in battery and aimed] upon two houses of wood filled with earth; against which two houses there were two fair white marks set up, at which marks they discharge all their ordinance to the end the Emperor may see what his gunners can do. They have fair ordinance of brass of all sorts—bases, falcons, minions, sakers, culverings, cannons both double and royal, and basilisks long and large. They have six great pieces whose shot is a yard of height [i.e., a cannon ball a yard in diameter] which shot a man may easily discern as they take flight. They have also a great many of mortar pieces or potguns, out of which pieces they shoot wild-fire. . . . The Emperor's majesty having on him a gown of rich tissue, and gold and silver abundantly . . . before him went 5000 harquebusiers [Streltsi] 5 and 5 in a rank in very good order, every one of them carrying his gun upon his left shoulder and his match in his right hand, and in this order they marched into the field."

After the loss of the port of Narva and the outlets from the Baltic, Ivan was more dependent than ever on the English shipping and the Arctic route (the same that the English convoys took to Murmansk in World War II). Ivan was content for the time being to take a loss in money of which he had a superabundance, to maintain this life line, not of the state of Muscovy, but of the Baltic war.

For Ivan, like his grandfather and his father, would not look to the east. Like the Romanov, Peter the Great, more than a century later, he pushed at the narrow closed door that led to the Baltic. That door was narrow, for the Baltic front extended over little more than three hundred miles. The door to the east was wide, some seventeen hundred miles, from the Dvina's mouth to the Caucasus. It stood open, except for the far brown steppe where the horsemen of Asia were still formidable. But he could not or would not realize that.

Meanwhile the English agents were thrusting further along the Siberian way, between the Urals' end and the Arctic Ocean. The closing of the Baltic ports had thrown the bulk of the great northern fur traffic toward their White Sea outlet. Here they had a true monopoly; their fleets came in convoys to the Dvina terminal after the spring thaw and departed at the summer's end. During the winter their workmen cut yew timber, and built tarring sheds and sheds for ropemaking. Within a few years they were to aid in building the hamlet on the Dvina near the monastery of Michael the Archangel, to be called by them Archangel, and by the Muscovites Archangelsk. The high prices they paid at their Dvina factory made good grades of sables and black fox scarce in Moscow. A Muscovite trapper who brought in a fine black fox skin intact might get three hundred rubles, worth at that time three hundred pounds sterling—enough wealth to last a family for a lifetime.

The young Englishmen who followed the fur routes as far as the Ob brought back also ivory of narwhals and walruses, and stories of magic practiced by the Laplanders, who put themselves together again after being pulled to pieces by a cord bound around them. But those who tried to follow Jenkinson's routes along the Caspian and to Tabriz and Aleppo for the most part died. To London went too many laconic reports like this: ". . . by reason of the hot time of year Thomas Banister with Lawrence Chapman and some other Englishmen unhappily died; which being known of M. Ducket, he immediately came from Tabriz to take possession of their goods."

A letter from a Richard Uscomb, written in August 1571, gives the news of the attack of the Krim Tatars on Moscow. ". . . very heavy news. The Mosco is burnt every stick by the Crimme, the 24th day of May last, and an innumerable number of people: and in the English house was smothered Thomas Southam, Tofild, Waverly, Greene's wife and children, two children of Rase and more to the number of 25 persons were stifled in our beer cellar; and yet in the same cellar was Rase, his wife, John Brown and John Clark preserved, which was wonderful. . . . The Emperor fled out of the field, and many of his people were carried away by the Crimme Tartar: to wit, all the young people—the old they would not meddle with, and so with exceeding much spoil and infinite prisoners, they returned home again. What with the Crimme on one side, and with his cruelty on the other, he hath but few people left. Commend me . . . to all our friends."

In spite of deaths by fire, sickness and the hostility of Turks and Persians, the stubborn Englishmen managed to tap much of the trans-Asiatic trade—especially silk and spices. Their records show that in so doing they incurred the ill will of the Muscovite traders; still, they did it. The ocean route to Persia and India was still closed by Spanish and Portuguese fleets.

Meanwhile Ivan had entrusted "a great matter" to Jenkinson. The discussion of it passed in secret papers back and forth between Moscow and London. Ivan demanded shelter for himself, his family and portable wealth, in England.

More than that, he had at first the clear conviction that the virgin Elizabeth should be his next bride. At that time he was in the throes of the *oprichnina* melodrama, the Livonian campaigns had begun to go ill, and the obsession was growing upon him that he could trust no one in Muscovy.

Without much trouble Elizabeth parried the secret marriage proposal; she had become adept at that. Apparently by word of mouth, she put Ivan off, not denying him. Ivan was in fact asking for a definite alliance between his dynasty in Muscovy and the Tudors in England. But the "great matter" itself—and she understood or was assured that this was Ivan's main point—baffled her. Openly, in beautifully illuminated parchment scrolls, Ivan besought her for a real alliance between All the Russias and England; he begged for English artisans and "an architect able to build castles, towers and palaces, a doctor, an apothecary, and artificers such as can seek for silver and gold." He pointed out how their mutual trade could enrich England; *and he required that Elizabeth sign a secret agreement to claim sanctuary in his court,* as well as he in hers.

Elizabeth knew only too well the poverty of her exchequer, the utter dependence of the English traders in Muscovy on Ivan's pleasure. How was she to answer the richest man in the world, whose private treasure, she had been told, would load four thousand wagons? Perhaps on Jenkinson's advice, she answered "her dear and loving brother" most gently, pledging him that at any time he would be welcomed and safeguarded in England, but explaining that she was not, actually, her own mistress, that she ruled by the grant of Parliament, and that it would distress her loyal subjects if she made any such plan as this to escape from them. Such a contingency she could not imagine.

Ivan was not pleased. While he did not allow his anger to appear in his negotiations with the Muscovy Company, the English traders found their privileges challenged, their claims for payment ignored, while thefts of their goods increased mysteriously. Nor did he spare Elizabeth the lash of his anger.

"We thought that you were ruler in your own land, seeking your own honor. So we proffered this weighty matter to you. But now we see you are ruled by other men, and what men—like merchants, like peasants! They do not seek the honor of our two Majesties, while you act like a stupid wench, and nothing else."

It was Elizabeth's first experience with one of Ivan's soul-searching epistles, and in all probability it amused her. But her Muscovy agents were kept oscillating between disaster and the promise of still greater privileges—of free trade with the Asiatic countries, franchise to mine for iron, to recast their own coinage, and to drive any other shipping from the White Sea. Then, after 1570, Ivan went through the conflict with the Metropolitan Philip, the purge of Novgorod, and the blow of the Krim attack on Moscow. His temper hardened.

Partly to try to gain compensation for the heavy loss in the Moscow fire, but chiefly to pacify Ivan, Anthony Jenkinson was sent back to the court where he had been a favorite, this time as an ambassador from the Crown.

He landed on Rose Island in the Dvina July 26, 1571, and found conditions very different from his earlier voyages. There was plague in the land; he was detained in the north; the watch on the roads stopped his messengers. Ivan seemed to be absent in the campaign against the Swedes. Not until March 23, 1572, did Jenkinson set foot before the throne of Ivan, for his formal reception.

"The Emperor, sitting in royal estate, stood up and said, 'How doth Queen Elizabeth, my sister, is she in health?' To whom I answered 'God doth bless her Majesty with health and peace, and doth wish the like unto thee, Lord, her loving brother.' Then his Majesty, sitting down again, commanded all his nobility and others to depart, except the chief secretary and one or two of the Council, and willing me to approach near unto him with my interpreter, said unto me these words.

" 'Anthony, the last time thou wast here, we did commit unto thee a secret and trusty Message, to be declared unto the Queen's Majesty herself, thy mistress, at thy home-coming. We did expect thee to come again to us at the time appointed, with a full answer.' "

(Ivan, Jenkinson relates, was provoked that in all the time of Jenkinson's absence he had received only evasive reports on the progress of "The princely affair whereby friendship between the Queen's Majesty and us might be sealed for ever.")

To which Jenkinson stoutly answered, "I did declare both secretly and truly unto the Queen's Majesty, herself, word for word, the message given me. Which her Highness did willingly hear and accept."

And he gave Ivan a letter from Elizabeth, adding carefully that he could explain anything that might be obscure in the letter. Instead of displaying any anger, Elizabeth had answered very frankly, and with conciliation. ". . . Our ambassador will tell you in all truth that no merchants govern this estate, but we rule ourselves with the honor befitting a virgin queen appointed by God; and no sovereign, thanks to God, hath more obedient servants."

After Ivan had time to study this letter, he summoned Jenkinson and explained pleasantly that the long delay "caused us to think our princely affairs were set aside and little regarded, wherewith we were at that time much grieved."

There began between those two habile bargainers a truly strange debate. It was a question of "princely affairs" —personal alliance and sanctuary—against "merchants' affairs" as affecting majesties. By merchants' affairs both Ivan and Jenkinson meant the profit and loss of the Muscovy Company. Princely affairs, Ivan insisted, should come before merchants' affairs. He was full of the dream of an escape, to the friendly English. (At that very time he wrote in his will that "the boyars have driven me from my possessions, and I wander through all lands.") Jenkinson knew that Elizabeth cared only for the continuance of the trade, which at the moment meant little to Ivan.

Did the aging master of the black-garbed *oprichniki*, those men "dark as night"—did he actually long for a retreat and peace in the western lands whence had come his mother and grandmother? Did he in fact believe that he would not be safe in Solovetsky on its island of birds, or beyond the Urals? It is only clear that he conceived of himself as a homeless wanderer.

Either by Jenkinson's persuasion, or by a characteristic *volte face*, he dismissed for the moment the project of the escape route to England, and paid without discussion all the company's long list of claims for damages, including the loss in the Moscow fire.

Unmistakably Ivan had put aside the idea of an English marriage, but Elizabeth was no less concerned for her trade, and her ambassadors kept bringing up the question of a personal alliance discreetly. To one of them, Ivan replied impatiently that he had forgotten it—that he was about to make an alliance with the Roman Emperor, Maximilian.

Then came the loss of Narva and the succession of defeats by Batory's new army, and Ivan dispatched an agent of the company, Jerome Horsey, overland through his enemies to ask urgently for shipments of munitions. Thirteen English ships were sent to the White Sea the next spring.

And the dream of the English marriage revived. This time Ivan requested that the bride be a kinswoman of the English Queen. Somehow the name of Mary Hastings—Maria Hatins to the Russians—crept into the bargaining. Although Ivan had just married a Maria Nogai—his sixth or seventh wife— he demanded assurance that this Mary Hastings would be betrothed to him, and her portrait sent him.

The Russians in London were shown a woman they described as "Tall, thin and pale, with blue eyes, light hair and slender hands." Possibly Elizabeth's court had staged such a demonstration of the bride-to-be. It is more certain that Ivan flew into a rage when the English ambassador of that year, Jeremy Bowes, parried his questions about Mary Hastings by saying that Elizabeth had a score of attractive kinswomen.

"A score!" Ivan screamed. "Tell me there are a thousand girls in England, and how many serving wenches! Am I to send offers to them all?"

As long as he lived, Ivan liked to discuss the phantom Mary Hastings. But after Jenkinson's departure, he does not seem to have counted on it. Instead, in such matters he was advised by the intelligent young Boris Godunov, the brother-in-law of Feodor, his feeble-minded son.

In the climax of his struggle with the Baltic peoples, Ivan hoped for aid from the Dutch and English ships of war. He hoped that by some miracle their cannon might sweep away the blockading ships of the stubborn Swedes, Danes and Livonians from the Baltic.

Nothing like that happened. The Dutch "beggars of the sea" clung to their own coast to save their ports from the invading armies of Spain; the English would deal with Muscovy only as merchants. Elizabeth was helping to build men of war, but only to tap the Spanish treasure convoys, and to prepare to do battle with the Spanish armadas for control of her own "narrow seas."

Ivan could not have known how these same Englishmen were exploring the seas of the earth. At the end of the desperate and glorious Elizabethan age, the careful chronicler of such voyages, Richard Hakluyt, was to write with naïve wonder:

"Which of the Kings of this land before her Majesty had their banners ever seen in the Caspian sea? Which of them had ever dealt with the Emperor of Persia as her Majesty hath done, and obtained for her merchants large and loving privileges? Who ever saw, before this, an English ambassador in the stately gateway of the Grand Signior of Constantinople? Who ever found English consuls at Aleppo or Babylon? What English ships did, heretofore, ever anchor in the mighty river of Plate—pass the impassible strait of Magellan . . . and all the backside of Nova Hispania, further than any Christian ever passed?"

The first English exploration and the first contact with Asia had been gained through Muscovy by the aid of Ivan the Terrible.

The Mock Tsar

The extraordinary thing about Ivan was his resilience. However bad might be the fortune that befell him, he refused to accept it as final.

Men said that he aged a generation after the burning of Moscow and the end of the *oprichnina* experiment. His ruddy beard was shot with gray and his great shoulders stooped.

He had been refused the crown of Poland, and was being denied the English alliance. The west, toward which he turned so constantly, mocked him.

What did he have to hold to? His city lay in black ashes, or sprawled haphazard in new log houses—new but old in pattern as a trader's blockhouse. When he looked from the Kremlin's wall across the gray Moskva, he saw no foreign settlement. When he rode out through the woodlands, he counted too many abandoned cabins, whose owners had marched off to the Volga lands. He was Tsar of All the Russias, yet he must have wondered in what direction lay his power, and how as the man Ivan he could face the masses who pressed around him, petitioning him for release from taxation, for more pay or simply for advice from the Emperor anointed by God.

He had become cynical about these human beings. His dream world of Moses and Tsar David had become intangible, remote from him. No longer did he invoke it in argument.

The expedient he hit upon at that time—1575–76—was startling, and still logical enough to one who thought as Ivan thought. He appointed another man to be Tsar of All the Russias.

The new potentate was given a crown and at least one out-fit of imperial robes. The man selected could not interfere with Ivan's personal authority, because he was a young Tatar, baptized Simeon by name—titular Khan of Kazan. Ostensibly Ivan retired, almost as with the *oprichnina*, to private life as the feudal lord of Moscow. When he visited Tsar Simeon he appeared plainly dressed, without his usual escort.

The young Tatar had no illusions about the situation. He continued to speak of himself as "your slave" before Ivan. Why did Ivan play this farce? Had he heard his people whispering that he had become a man "with the soul of a wild beast?" Did it please his perverted fancy to watch Simeon struggling with a host of petitioners, or attempting to lead an army in the Livonian campaign? Was Simeon serving as Ivan's whipping boy, a veritable mock king? Or did Ivan hope, by this parade, to satisfy the restless Asiatics who grieved over the loss of Kazan, and were only too quick to perceive the weakness of the Muscovite state after the raid of the Krim Tatars?

Ivan was the real lord of Kazan. He had simply changed places with the pretended lord of Kazan.

"It means nothing," he told a curious Englishman.

Tsar Simeon soon passed from the public eye, not to reappear in such state.

Stephen Batory was penetrating deeper into Muscovy. This young westerner, raised in Hungary, limping a little, abstemious of money, able to speak only in Latin to the Poles and Lithuanians who had elected him King—Batory, sworn to his mission of vengeance, was cutting off town after town, pacing the Swedes invading from the north. Batory had few men but they were disciplined—*superior*. Ivan dared not meet him in the field. This sprig of a German-Pole even dared challenge the great Tsar to a duel. Ivan made no response.

"Even a brood hen," Batory mocked in his cackling Latin, "will cover her young when the hawk attacks. The two-headed Eagle of Muscovy hides himself away."

Ivan made no answer. With all his cancerous fears, he had courage enough. But he was not a soldier, like De La Gardie or Batory. He had no leaders for his army which lay scattered, perforce, through the chain of guardian ostrogs and forts, to the south, west and north. Into the fortifications, his cannon were piled. Giles Fletcher said in 1580: "No prince of Christendom hath more munitions." In Pskov, the key to Novgorod, more than a hundred cannon had been

gathered, behind massive stone walls on the height overlooking the lake.

Batory encircled Pskov. His Lithuanian horsemen burned
the countryside that had been Muscovite for a century. His
regiments felt their way toward the spot west of Moscow
whence the headwaters of four rivers flowed, the strategic
center of the Muscovite river system.

That winter while Pskov held out and Moscow was menaced, Ivan sat with the envoy he had demanded. This was
the mediator from Rome, Antonio Possevino, a Jesuit.

Smooth-shaven, adroit, the negotiator made test of the
qualities of the strange Tsar. He found Ivan to be fanatical,
with vast understanding, brilliant in argument. The papal
envoy pressed for a union between the churches of Moscow
and Rome, before discussing a truce between Ivan and the
European states. Ivan retorted with a true flight of imagination: why not deliver Rome and Christendom entire from its
greatest enemy, the Turk; why not launch a crusade of
Swedes and Poles and Muscovites, to be rallied around Moscow? The Jesuit returned to his argument, the dignity and
power of Rome.

"Your Pope," Ivan shouted in a rage, "is a wolf."

The hardest blow of all came from his own hand. In a fit
of blind fury he struck at the head of his eldest son Ivan. He
struck with the steel-tipped *kisten* that he had as usual in his
hand and his son died.

The younger Ivan had been the Tsar's companion from the
time of the *oprichnik* raids; he was to have been his heir.
Ivan's grief tormented him.

Behind that grief lay one of the familiar haunting fears.
It had grown out of the memory of his brilliant, sickly mother
Helen, and of his shadowy half-wit of a brother. Feodor
(Theodore), the surviving son, was little better, feeble in mind,
like a monk in his devotions. In slaying Ivan, the Tsar had
put an end to his own life stream.

Down in the streets the common folk heard the rumor of
the death and made a song of it. "The Tsar Kills His Son."
Only, so strange is popular fancy and so greatly was Ivan
revered, the singers improvised how Ivan had, at the last
moment, tried to save his son.

Yet the blow had in fact brought to an end Ivan's
dynasty, and the long succession of the princes of Moscow,
the fellowship of the ancient sons of Rurik.

There was nothing to relieve Ivan's bitterness. The next

English ambassador to appear at the Red Stair testifies that he "Let loose his passion as if his will had seldom been gainsayed." (This envoy, Sir Jeremy Bowes, was a truculent and dogged soul, and nothing could have angered Ivan more than to hear Bowes argue the prosperity of England and the well-being of Elizabeth at this stage.)

"I do not think Elizabeth my equal," Ivan stormed. "Those there are who are greater than she."

Sir Jeremy would not hear Elizabeth disparaged, or yield to Ivan's anger. ("To subject myself to the angry humor of the Emperor was not the means to win aught at his hands.")

"The Queen my mistress," he retorted, "is as great a prince as any in Christendom, and wants no means to withstand any she has cause to be enemy to."

"Yes?" quoth Ivan. "How say you to the French King? And the King of Spain?"

"Marry, I hold my mistress to be great as either of them, both."

"How say you to the Roman Emperor?"

"The King, the father of my mistress, had that Emperor once in his pay."

At this Ivan's fury broke out. "If you were not ambassador, I would throw you out the doors!"

"You could. But my mistress will avenge any harm done to me."

"Get out!" Ivan screamed.

After Bowes left the chamber, Ivan lashed out at his chancellor and courtiers. "Did you hear? He would not have a word spoken against his mistress. If I could have had servants like that!"

After beating his silent chancellor with his staff, Ivan sent within an hour a message to Bowes's house, to urge him to forget their talk—that he, Ivan, would grant all the wishes of his good sister Elizabeth, and Bowes should have a gift worth a thousand rubles.

Following the death of his son and the departure of Possevino, Ivan made one of his sudden decisions. Accepting a truce from his enemies, he gave up the Baltic and the northern towns. Pskov and the river portages he kept—worse off than he had been at the beginning of the thirty years of the Baltic struggle.

The great frontier cities of Smolensk and Kiev were lost to the Muscovites. The Borderland, the Ukraine, now lay far out of their reach.

In acknowledging the defeat of his army in the west, Ivan

admitted defeat for himself.[9] Other than that army he had
no foundation for his rule—unless it was the adulation of
the populace. He was Tsar indeed, lord of all the lands and
places so carefully enumerated in his title. But what in
reality had he to bequeath to a successor, and what men
would unify the empire that had taken shape around him.

His intimates of even the last decade were dead or exiled.
One Englishman says that Ivan had at this point no more
than three hundred in his entourage. True, in his will he gave
minute instructions for the disposal of his vast property to
heirs, but no familiar name appears among them. Of himself
he said in his will, "My body is grown feeble and my soul
sick; yet for the wounds of my soul and my body there is
no physician who can make me whole. In vain I have looked
for some man to have pity on me, but I have found no one.
Yes, no comforter have I found but only such as have
rewarded me evil for good and hatred for love."

Even so, the indomitable master of the Kremlin gathered
about him a new family. Maria Nogai had borne him a son
who was christened Dmitri. In time the infant would grow
strong. Although Feodor, feeble in spirit, could never take
Ivan's place, and had no sons of his own, he could wear the
imperial crown, and be advised by the politic Boris Godunov,
the brother of Feodor's wife.

Ivan became gentle with this remnant of a family.

And at the same time he reversed the family policy of three
generations. He turned to the east.

There his fur traders had passed beyond the Urals, to find
the "great sea river," the Ob. Beyond its estuary, seeking sable
and seal and white fox, they had followed the bare shore
through the Ugrian strait, to the ice of the Kara Sea. This
was open water, extending—so the Samoyed hunters claimed
—past the land of Yal-Mal to the homeland of the great
khans of Tatary.

---

[9] Batory had only a small army, ranging from nineteen to thirty
thousand, largely outfitted at his own expense, and stiffened by Hungarian regiments. Ivan had nearly three times as many men under
arms, but he was obliged to man the southern frontier, still menaced by the Krim Tatars. Ivan's policy was to conciliate the Krim
khans—and hence the Turks, their supporters also—while holding
to Azov at the mouth of the Don and Astrakhan at the Volga
delta. In this policy he was aided by the Cossack communities of
those frontier zones.

After the truce in the west, and Ivan's death, Batory talked of
marching to Moscow, and even to Azov; but he never attempted it.
Perhaps, wiser than Charles XII of Sweden, he realized that no single
foreign army could dominate the vast lands of the Muscovite Empire. At any rate, he died two years after Ivan. Napoleon was not so
wise.

In this way the Muscovite fur traders had discovered the northeast passage, such as it was, by water to Cathay.

They had found their way to the Siberian and Mongol tribes, guardians of the snow gates of Kitai. They had heard tales of gigantic tusks of ivory, tusks of giant beasts (mammoths) frozen in the ground for uncounted ages. And they told Ivan of the snow roads leading ever "east, beneath the rising sun, along the road of the ancient Tsar Alexander [Alexander of Macedon] to the giant mountain Karkour."

That way lay the road of empire, and Ivan at last perceived it. To the ambitious frontier family of the Stroganovs, he granted lands beyond the Urals. Two years before his death, he received a surprising message from those lands of Sibir.

An army of renegade Cossacks of the Don, sent across the Urals by the Stroganovs, had wrested these new lands of Sibir from their Tatar Khan—Kuchum, the son of the Khan of Bokhara who had sent envoys to Ivan by Jenkinson. More, the Cossacks had forwarded to Ivan a wagon train of thousands of pelts, gold, and jewels, asking him to accept the conquest of Sibir.

It delighted Ivan. He forgave the erring Cossacks their long list of crimes, and accepted their grant of Sibir—taking the ermine cloak from his shoulders, to put on the messenger, and ordering two of his army commanders to move east to take possession of Sibir in his name.

Before he could hear again from Sibir, Ivan died. Although he had sat on the throne for half a century, he was only fifty-four years of age.

And the chancellor appeared in the apartments of Jeremy Bowes, the ambassador from England, to say with malice, "The English Emperor is dead."

From that moment ended the favor of the English in Muscovy.

Ivan had never been insane. Few men of his century had shown more intelligence; and few, if any, with so much to fear had evidenced such stark courage. In popular fancy, he became a favorite, linked to the legends of old time, to the names of Vladimir the Splendid, Alexander Nevsky and Dmitri Donskoi—an honor never accorded the Romanov, Peter. Yet he had in reality destroyed more than he had created.[10]

[10] Kliuchevsky sees in him a thinker rather than a doer, and says "the life of the Muscovite Empire would have developed precisely as it had done before his day, and as it did after he was gone." And "he acted rather upon the nerves and imagination of his contemporaries."

What came to be in his time, and what has endured under all stress, was the structure of a Russian nation. In his time the embryo Muscovite state lost its earlier semblance. The terms "Muscovy" and "Muscovite" ceased to have their old meaning, and were gradually forgotten. What remained was the state subject to the rule of one man, stretching from Lake Ladoga to the mouths of the Volga at Astrakhan, the Russia of Ivan the Terrible.

It is true that the life of the frontiers developed without aid from Ivan, except by the acts of his last two years. So the new empire continued to develop, almost apart from Moscow, and regardless of who or what might be ruling, for the century until Peter. By then its nature and extent were established, not to be changed.

V

MIGRATION INVADES THE EAST

Across the Urals

NO SOONER had Ivan's name become heroized in the *bylini* (ballads) of the people than another name joined his—Irmak, the son of the Don, leader of a Volga band. Irmak, so the popular fancy insisted, had found his way far indeed into darkest Siberia, had overthrown in battle the descendants of the great khans, and had thereby made a gift of all Siberia to the ailing Ivan, who blessed him with his dying breath. Thereupon Irmak, invulnerable to sword or bullet, had been slain by Tatar magic.

So ran the tale of the time. What Irmak accomplished was something quite different but quite as remarkable. And his actual achievement can be retold best by the tradition of the men of the Don themselves. If legend creeps in, it is at least the legendry of eyewitnesses.

Irmak Timofeivitch, a bastard son of a son of the Don, whose mother had been a Danish slave on the river Kama, was a blue-eyed giant with a golden beard condemned to death for stealing horses by the authorities at the age of twenty-one. Escaping to the Volga, he became leader of *ushkuiniki*—river rovers—who took toll impartially of Muscovite barges and Persian caravans, until the Volga was made too hot for him by Muscovite guard troops. Although Irmak and his *atamans*, his commanders, mocked the hired troops—"they ride two on a horse, they are good only to shell peas and feel hens for eggs"—they left the Volga's bend for the headwaters of the Kama, toward the invisible eastern frontier, in 1579.

Irmak's chief atamans were these men:

Ivan Koltzo, a Zaporogian, small and dark, could ride a horse without a whip, and boasted that he could outdrink the Devil. Burned in a blockhouse later by Tatars.

Yakub Michailov, an ex-soldier. Ambushed by Tatars.

Nikita Pan, who resembled an ape, with parchment skin, because of his Tatar blood. Cruel, a poorer swordsman than Koltzo, fond of killing dogs, and cherished a fine chain-mail shirt.

Gritzko Pounya, a Zaporogian, and Irmak's bodyguard, a Tatar hater and masterly liar, who ended his stories with "Believe me, brothers, it's true." Cherished a fine ivory and gold-inlay pipe which Pounya swore had been given him by the Sultan of the Turks in the way of ransom. Supposed to have said when he was mortally hurt in a Tatar raid, "Believe me, brothers, I'm dying."

There was also Makmoutka, the Tatar whose life had been saved by the Stroganovs, who slept outside Olga Stroganov's door, and served as a spy.

Over such men as this Irmak had made himself master. There were 540 in the band that found its way out to the stockaded log castle and village of the Stroganovs, within sight of the dark foothills of the Urals. That was a castle! So thought the wanderers from the Don, the Dnieper and Kama. Twelve feet high the wooden wall, with four cannon inside the gate. More gay with lights and music than the somber stone Kremlin of Moscow. Silk and brocade on the walls of the guest rooms. Ikons from Mount Athos on the ikon stand, and a welcome to all who came in the door of Chusavaya, as it was called. An army of servants, so the women's quarters had to be barred and guarded, to keep the girls in and the eager men out.

The lords of Chusavaya were Ivan and Sergei, sons of Anikta Stroganov, lords of cattle herds, and iron and gold mines, of forests and valleys and the fur traffic east of the Volga bend.

A sister they had, Olga, whom Makmoutka called "an angel whiter than snow." Irmak, so they say, made a bloody cross with his sword edge across the seat of Nikita Pan's breeches when Pan looked too often toward Olga.

The compact the Stroganov brothers made with these river brigands may not have been made willingly, but it was workable. Irmak was furnished weapons from the Chusavaya arsenal, and protected the Stroganov land empire, and kept his own men in hand.

On that, they feasted. Tatar neighbors, fur merchants, were invited in to meet the new guardians of Chusavaya. At this feast Irmak sat beneath the ikon stand, between the brothers, and twice Olga came in to offer him goblets of brandy, bowing and saying, "Noble lords, Cossacks, the house of my father is your house." And the Tatar guests belched, saying, "*Chok Yakshy* [That's fine]."

At this feast of sturgeon pie, and young wild boar, wild ducks and cheese-cake, and horse-meat for the Tatars, the house girls danced the *chorovod*, singing, "Here sits the eagle of the Don. . . ."

Although Irmak and his men kept their word to do no harm to Chusavaya, they burned a Tatar shaman who prophesied that Irmak would die of a two-headed eagle. Who had ever seen an eagle with two heads?

They did other things, as related in an angry letter from the Tsar, Ivan. ". . . they were to expiate their guilt, instead of which they rob and plunder as they did on the Volga . . . involving us in a quarrel with the Siberian Khan [Kuchum] . . . just as they did formerly with the Nogai Horde and the Persians. . . . WE have sent to Perm our commander with orders to take these Cossacks, Irmak and the rest. and carry them back to Perm."

When word of Ivan's wrath reached Chusavaya, Irmak consulted with the Stroganovs and it was evidently decided that they should disappear again, for that is what they did, taking with them the remaining 300 guardsmen of Chusavaya —escaped Lithuanian and Muscovite soldiers and Christian Tatars. They disappeared with their long boats up the Chusavaya River, eastward, dragging the boats over the portages of the pass through the Ural highlands.

Obviously, Irmak had convinced the Stroganovs that he could take away all the 840 experienced fighters and still protect the Stroganov settlements, because there could be no Tatar raids over the Urals while he himself was raiding the Tatars. And just as obviously, the Tsar's officers could not follow them across the mountains among the direst enemies of the Muscovites.

What the Cossacks hoped for—too obviously to mention it—was loot. Somewhere in the luxuriant "wild lands" beyond the Urals waited Sibir,[1] the town of the powerful Tatar Khan, Kuchum.

[1] Sibir, at the headwaters of the Ob and the Irtish, gave its name later under the Russian Empire to the vast domain of *Siberia* or northeast Asia. Irmak of course hardly entered Siberia; he did break the Tatar control of this midway basin, a focus of river routes. He also demonstrated that less than a regiment of Russians could stand their ground against the eastern Tatars. For two generations Muscovite power had not been able to capture Sibir, as Irmak did.

It is hardly true, as casual histories often relate, that the Tatars who faced Irmak's men were frightened by firearms. Kuchum's horde had seen Muscovite firearms; but they had never encountered a

The way toward Sibir (or Iskir) was dangerous, because over it passed the roving hordes, great and small, of central Eurasia. It was more dangerous than the well-trodden way to Kazan had been for Ivan's Muscovites, twenty-nine years before.

So Irmak's mixed frontier army felt its way, cautiously, over the Ural divide and down the little river Tura, flowing east. Camping at night around the boats and keeping sentries lying far out in the darkness, they halted when the river froze, building log huts, and hunting in sled parties for their food.

They found sable and beaver in the forest. Down the river their flotilla crept, down past the spruce growth into open larch and willows, past the boiling mouth of another river. They felt the presence of the Tatars, unseen until then, as arrows struck down their foragers and volleys of arrows raked the boats at the river bends. Cautiously the Cossacks fought back, too experienced to plunge into the shore growth after the elusive horsemen of the steppe. Carrying their sick and wounded, they entered another river flowing north, passing abandoned settlements. While Irmak's detachments raided inland for cattle and grain, the Tatars attacked in force at night, silent as the rush of the flooded river—killing and drifting out into the darkness again, but never quite breaking down the Cossack defense of matchlock, pistol and saber.

In this vast fertile basin, cut by the rivers, Irmak felt for Sibir. At the great juncture of the upper Ob and the Irtish, he fortified a bluff, guarding his precious boats beneath, unable to go on. It would have been madness to venture afoot out into the tranquil-seeming green prairies. So Irmak sat on his bluff and waited patiently.

Koltzo took a detachment across the river and surprised a Tatar settlement on the far bank that the lieutenant had located by observation. Tatar captives, interrogated by red-hot spits thrust into them, revealed the direction of Sibir—within a few miles across the river. Thither Irmak led his whole force in a sudden thrust, and found the wooden stronghold deserted by Kuchum's Tatars.

Here, in the enemy's citadel, the Cossacks were secure. Yet they were hemmed in by Tatar forces that could not be tracked down. Irmak investigated the plains around Sibir, and took liberal tribute as conqueror from the peaceful hunting tribes, the Voguls.

---

small army of westerners who occupied the ground they advanced over.

Kuchum's Tatars had withdrawn toward the southern steppe.

Before the rivers froze that autumn (1583) Irmak decided to winter in Sibir, instead of trying to fight his way back up the river road to the Ural pine forests. Perhaps the Cossacks did not dare venture back among the Muscovite officials; perhaps, as often happened with their breed, they wished stubbornly to hold the new land they had taken. But their decision helped shape a new Russian frontier.

Irmak knew that they could not survive long, cut off in Sibir. Aware that the Stroganovs had no real force to send to his aid, he gambled on a greater chance, and sent a detachment with captured furs and treasure by way of Chusavaya and Kazan to the Tsar in Moscow, seven hundred miles away.

According to the Cossacks, Koltzo headed the treasure party, with "a gift for the Tsar, the Terrible, of 1592 sable skins, 6182 ermine" (hardly that many!) "192 white fox, 610 bearskins, and emeralds, rubies, diamonds and hundreds of *bersacks* of gold and silver."

To the Tsar, Koltzo delivered this message: "Mighty Tsar, Irmak the son of the Don, needs only gunpowder from you. To you Sibir and its riches are a gift."

To Koltzo, the Tsar gave the splendid ermine cloak from his own shoulders. And that very day, the Cossacks say, Koltzo was found stretched out in the cloak, deliriously drunk, in one of the Moscow streets.

The Muscovite chronicles do not say that much; yet Ivan evidently dispatched by Koltzo the famous double breastplate (or hauberk) with the gold two-headed eagle upon it, as a token for Irmak, at the same time granting title to the new lands beyond the Urals to the Stroganovs, and ordering a relief force of regulars to journey to Sibir.

No further mention was made of the punishment of "those Cossacks, Irmak and the rest," for their former crimes.

Irmak had survived the winter. On snowshoes, his foraging parties worked northward, taking tribute and food from villages and coming back safely by boat in the spring thaw— only one detachment being massacred. The Cossacks surprised a Tatar encampment and took Kuchum's nephew captive.

Evidently Koltzo got back that spring with the good news from Moscow, because Irmak left him and Michailov in command at Sibir and started back along the river route with half his surviving force to meet the hoped-for relief division under Prince Bolkhovsky.

But the Streltsi could not travel the frontier as the Cossacks did. Upriver, Irmak waited out the summer, and most of the fall, without sight or word of his relief. He waited too long, and was caught by the river ice before reaching the Irtish. On foot, his party cut across the snowbound land, keeping to the timber and moving only at night. For the plains around Sibir were alive with Tatar horsemen.

At Sibir, Irmak found only a remnant of the garrison. In the last months Koltzo had been ambushed and killed with forty men outside the stockade; Michailov, searching for the missing detachment, had been trapped and killed with all his party.

Instead of trying to get out with the survivors, Irmak prepared to defend Sibir for another winter. Before the worst storms, the missing Muscovites appeared along the river, guided in by frontiersmen.

But they were in a sorry state, half starved, with sick and wounded loading their sledges, and their heavy stores of powder and food abandoned on the way. Instead of aiding Irmak to occupy the country, their condition obliged him to defend and feed them in Sibir. Prince Bolkovsky died, and Irmak sent a second message to Moscow, explaining the desperate situation, with the captive Tatar Khan as a new gift to Ivan (who had died in the meanwhile).

Throughout that winter (1584–85) Irmak kept his weakening force inside Sibir, and the Tatars out. When open water came in the spring, he was told by his lieutenant Pan—and, the Cossacks say, by the treachery of Pan—of a Moslem trade caravan arriving from the southern steppe and seeking for Kuchum. Irmak took some fifty men in boats up the Irtish to wait for the caravan at a ford used by the Tatars. When it did not appear and he saw no sign of Tatars for days, he seems to have realized that he had been tricked because he started back down the river, going ashore the first night to sleep during a rainstorm.

A sudden rush of horsemen caught the Cossacks asleep. They did not reach their boats. Irmak got to the bank and jumped for a boat but fell heavily into the water, and could not swim because he had, strapped on him, the new breastplates, the gift of the Tsar. With him, all his men were killed.

"So it happened," the Cossacks say, "that Irmak, the son of the Don, died as the shaman prophesied by a two-headed eagle."

To the Tatars who had killed him, Irmak appeared to be

more than human; he had become a *force* against which
struggle was unavailing. The Cossacks say that while the
Tatars sent the ornamented breastplate to Sibir as evidence
that Irmak, the unconquerable, had been slain, they buried the
body by the river and hid the spot—which became marked
by night lights visible only to Tatar eyes—so that they might
come back to it and take earth from it, to act as a charm
against their enemies. So, as the Tatars prayed to the spirit of
a bear they had killed, they prayed to the spirit of Irmak to
aid them, instead of harming them.

The Cossacks say that when the lovely Olga Stroganov
heard the news of Irmak's death, she leaped her horse from a
cliff into the swift waters of the Chusavaya.

Certain it is that to the mass of land seekers pressing
through the barrier of the Urals in the next century, Irmak's
name became a talisman of fortune in the new land, to be
prayed to along with the good saints Andrew and Nicholas,
the protectors of wanderers.

Opening of the Lone Siberian Way

Moscow, at last, became intent on the development of the
eastern continent. Boris Godunov (whether as adviser to Ivan,
or regent for Feodor, or Tsar himself) followed out Ivan's
last measures for opening up the east. In fact, he may have
suggested them to Ivan.

The relief forces sent into the new province of Sibir
stayed there. Without scruple, they assassinated a Tatar khan
invited as a guest to a banquet, and eventually drove the
blind Kuchum farther east, after capturing most of his
family—who were paraded in triumph through the streets
of Moscow, as visual evidence of the subjection of the east.

After the troops came Muscovite engineering. A road was
built up the Kama and Chusavaya to the Ural pass. The Stroganov plantations moved across the mountains. Blockhouse
settlements—ostrogs—Tiumen on the Tura River, and Tobolsk
near the site of Sibir, fortified the new frontier. Fur traders
worked their boats up the Kama and Chusavaya across the
portage, down to the Tobol River, hence to the Irtish and the
Ob headwaters. After five years of consolidation, new lines
of ostrogs pushed south as far as the open steppe, and
rapidly north along the wide Ob—jumping across to Mangazeia on the northward-flowing Taz River, from which a
short haul by portage and tributary gave access to another
giant of the east, the Yenisei.

This took place swiftly because Moscow, under the guidance of Boris Godunov, was feeding men and stores into the

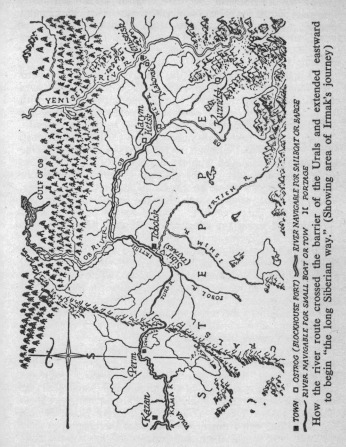

■ TOWN □ OSTROG (BLOCKHOUSE FORT) 〜 RIVER NAVIGABLE FOR SAILBOAT OR BARGE
▬ RIVER NAVIGABLE FOR SMALL BOAT OR TOW)(PORTAGE

How the river route crossed the barrier of the Urals and extended eastward to begin "the long Siberian way." (Showing area of Irmak's journey)

new territory, and because no such warlike horde as Kuchum's Tatars barred the way. Village people like the Ostiaks and Voguls—hunters—merely paid tribute to the Muscovites as they had done before to the Tatar khans.

Mangazeia opened up a new world to Muscovite enterprisers. That world was the real Siberia.

Toward that same Siberia European ships were questing,

still seeking the hidden Northwest Passage to Cathay. The Europeans knew more about Cathay—actually northern China—but they still hungered to find the sea route thither. Explorers along the coasts and islands of "The New Found Lands" now being called American returned, if they returned at all, with tantalizing reports of inlets, bays and frozen seas; yet no clear passage by water had been found, to the northwest.

In London the directors of the Muscovy Company realized after Jenkinson's reports that the land route to Cathay was closed. After Bourroughs's daring venture eastward with the little *Searchthrift*, the company directors hoped that this Arctic coast of Muscovy might fall away to the southward.

They ordered two small vessels to try to follow the coast, where the light of the moon and stars was brighter than the sun, and the Samoyed hunters quested over the ice packs for seals. The exploring ships got through (in the summer of 1580) the narrow strait at the Urals' end into open water, where *the coast tended south.* But the ice closed in around them and they barely got out.

Again and again the directors urged their shipmasters to follow that dangerous coast to the east.

On the first of August 1588, two days after the surviving ships of the Spanish Armada had been driven out of sight of England by a storm, these same directors wrote carefully to their agents in Muscovy, urging that a new try be made for the elusive passage, "for searching of the sea." While they advised caution to the three voyagers, Bassendine, Woodcock and Brown, it is clear that the company was desperately anxious to discover the passage.

"When your bark is ready"—so ran the instructions—"at the beginning of the year, go over to the eastern part of the Pechora [river], thence you shall pass eastward along the coast of Iugur; you shall pass within seven leagues of the island of Waigats which is in the strait almost half way from the coast to Nova Zembla. Which island and Nova Zembla you shall find noted down on your plan; therefore you shall not need to discover them, but proceed on toward the river Ob.

"There is a bay between the said Waigats and the river Ob that bites to the southward, as will appear on the notes which are given to you herewith. In the which bay you shall not spend any time in the searching of it, but direct your course to the river Ob (unless you are constrained to keep along the shore) and when you come to the river Ob you shall not enter into it but pass over to the eastern part of its mouth.

"Thence you shall pass to the eastward along the border of the said coast, describing the same as you can best do it. You shall not leave the sight of the said coast until you have sailed so far eastward and the time of year be so far spent that you do think it time to return with your bark for Winter—which travel may be 300 or 400 leagues to the eastward of the Ob, as our hope is. You shall leave no part of the coast unsearched or unseen, unless it be some bay or river that you do certainly know by report of the people. For our hope is that the said coast doth shortly after you pass the Ob incline east and so to the southward. Therefore leave no land on your starboard side left undiscovered.

"But and if the land trends northward, to join with Nova Zembla making the sea from Waigats eastward but a bay, yet we will that you bring us certain report of the form of that same bay . . . which discovery, if it be made by you, shall not only prove profitable to you, but will also purchase perpetual fame to you and to your country. And thus not doubting of your willing desires, we pray God happily to end the same. Amen."

The bark did find open water northerly from the great mouth of the Ob, but the rocky coast bestrewn with islands led full into the great ice pack that barred the way beyond the Kara Sea.

Englishmen like Davis and Frobisher tried the northwest instead, and lacking any coherent maps, struck upon straits and lands that they could not identify—calling the coasts Mistaken Land, and Baffin Land, among other things.

Meanwhile the hardy Dutch had been following close on the course of the English, both to the White Sea and in probing the polar waters. Cut off like the English by Spanish sea power from the growing markets of India and the Indies—as well as the half-mythical Cathay—the Netherlanders tried for the passage farther north, striking upon Spitsbergen. Barents explored the open stretch named for him.

No passage seemed to lead east of the Kara Sea.

Rivalry grew tense in the search for the missing passage. An English factor, Anthony Marsh, sent his Russian servant, Bogdan, east of the Ob through the country of the Samoyeds, only to learn that his man had been caught on his return by Muscovite river guards, and sent to Moscow, where he was lashed. "It seems they are jealous," Anthony Marsh wrote, "that any foreigner should grow acquainted with the northeast border, for there is some great secret that way which they would keep to themselves only. "

From the Russian who had served them as interpreter, to Ivan—who seemed to be dependent on them now—the English learned: "Beyond the river Ob is a warm sea where sea fowl gather in winter; it may pierce far south into Asia."

The venture of Bassendine, Woodcock and Brown may have been the last attempt of the Muscovy Company to find the Northeast Passage. Soon after the catastrophe of the Armada, Spanish control of the southern seas was broken, and English and Dutch ships began to make the long voyage direct to India, and the East India Company was chartered.

This shift in the direction of exploration did not, however, diminish the trade that was carried on between the Dutch and English ports and the White Sea inlet to Muscovy. St. Nicholas monastery, Rose Island—so named for the wild roses that grew there in the brief summer—the Dvina River, with its old town of Kholmogory and its new trading post of Archangel, became familiar indeed to the ship masters and crews that made the summer voyage thither, along the open water of the Gulf Stream's end.

There was even a French master, a certain Jehan Savvage of Dieppe, who left a journal of his first visit to the Arctic and to the Muscovites, in 1586. "*Item*—we reached St. Michael the Archangel on the twenty-sixth of June, and there our merchants went ashore to make report to the governor . . . and when he knew that we were French he became very happy, saying that he felt good would come of it. He then took a great goblet of silver and filled it and emptied it himself; and straightway another he filled and emptied; then a third went the way of the others. Having disposed of the third [our merchants] thought to be done with it; but the worst was a glass of *eau de vie* which is so strong it sets throat and belly on fire. When you have drunk such a cup, it is still not enough, for it is required again to drink, to the health of your king, which you dare not refuse, and besides it is the custom of the country to drink so well."

In spite of the ordeal of toasts drunk down so rapidly in vudka, Jehan Savvage and his fellow traffickers prospered on their voyage. All the traders around the White Sea and down the Dvina prospered. Archangel and Kholmogory became ocean terminals of the increasing fur output of Siberia.

The fisherfolk prospered from the salmon runs—which had

been one of Ivan's monopolies, but which the villagers now kept for themselves. Miners prospered by working outcroppings of shining copper along the headlands, and splitting off sheets of mica to be made into windowpanes.

Young English factors whiling away the long winter nights in this northland marveled at the Muscovite's birch cups and wooden dishes and bearskin coverlets. As for games, the foreigners found that "almost the simplest" men of Rus would beat them at chess. "The poorest rogues of all" were dice addicts, breathing on the cubes before they cast. "They cast suspiciously." And the peasants cared for their cattle during the winter's cold as tenderly as for their children. "Sheep, colts and cows come in then, to lodge by the *moujik's* bedside, where he feeds them with fodder, holding them dear as life; thus they live out the winter with the *moujik* and his wife."

Something unexpected was taking place in the north. The towns, far removed from Moscow, developed their own trade, and thrived as far south as Vologda and Ustiug on the Sukhona River which led from the Dvina toward Moscow.

This economic well-being matched that of the Stroganov estates farther south, of the boom towns like Tobolsk, and in fact of all the country "beyond the Volga." It was to have an important effect on the city of Moscow after the turn of the century.

The Fur Route to the Northeast

As the agents and factors of Novgorod had probed toward this far northeast, the Muscovite fur traders and trappers had been pushing eastward as the supply of sable and fox and beaver thinned out. In armed bands they traveled after the spring thaw, outfitted by backers in the Muscovite cities. Reaching their hunting grounds, they built log houses for the winter, setting their lines of traps—each man taking a route of his own—catching the animals when the fur was heaviest in the cold, hunting them into nets with dogs, and shooting them out of trees with blunt shafts from crossbows (not to injure the valuable skins).

Some of Irmak's surviving veterans had drifted north along the new Ob route, looking for more "wild lands" to conquer, and they had fine pelts to show the northerners. Tales of the treasure gleaned by the Cossacks grew in the telling. But there were riches enough to be had, when even beavers brought the price of a pair of cows back home, and a single fine black fox would yield a whole farm in the Moscow area. The fever of wealth gripped these traders and trappers who quested eastward, like the *coureurs de bois* of Canada in the west two centuries later.

No dour fighting Tatars opposed them. The Finnish folk, the shy Samoyeds and fearful Ostiaks retreated or submitted, when the Muscovites claimed *yasak*, tribute, and took their women, the young ones, into the log forts. It was a simple matter to strip native hunters such as these of all their furs. Through the northern forest belt, across the Ob and on to the Yenisei, the trappers raced the looters, and traders built fortified posts at the main river crossings, to sell vudka and brandy, powder and barley, and to take payment in furs. Under the northern lights, the Muscovites searched for new routes to the east, by native sled and dogs, by river boat and skis over the snow roads.

But something different was taking place now. Government bureau agents followed the traders, with troops and authority to tax the fur intake, to claim the "wild lands" thus occupied, and especially to take yearly tribute from the tribes. In a way, it became a race between the individual enterprisers and the state monopoly on fur and fish. But whoever reached a territory first stayed there.

A few colonists were appearing at Siberian terminals like Mangazeia, drawn by the lure of free land, timber and virgin earth to be worked. Even the bureaus in now remote Moscow became aware of clear profit to be had in the unmapped *Siberia*. Their agents could tax the traders and claim the territory almost without expense. In return the Moscow bureaus made some attempts to aid the settlements, sending out batches of women—"not the choicest meats," the settlers complained.

At the same time a new grim trek began, eastward to Siberia. Condemned prisoners, troublesome foreigners and prisoners of war could be dispatched out to such new towns as Obdursk and Mangazeia, there to work out their keep in communities from which the only escape would be into the wastelands.

Some of the men who appeared in these new convict shipments were of good caliber, educated Swedish officers, Polish priests. They helped to organize the communities. Also members of antagonistic boyar families like the Romanovs began to turn up in the frontier settlements, to be kept there under observation, in some comfort, but far from contact with the court at Moscow.

Isaac Massa, a merchant of Holland visiting Muscovy, relates, "numbers of people were sent thither daily, so that in course of time in some places whole communities arose of Poles, Tartars, Russians and other nationalities, mixed together. For all exiles, and murderers, thieves and traitors, being the scum of humanity who had merited death, were banished thither, some to be held prisoners for certain periods, while others were commanded to dwell their lives there— according to the measure of their misdeeds."

This sudden thrust of human beings eastward lasted for some twenty years, from 1585 to 1605. Mangazeia was fortified in 1601, and Tomsk far to the southeast of ruined Sibir, and the new town of Tobolsk, in 1604. Between them and the Kara Ice Sea lay an enormous territory now subject to Moscow's authority.

In his brief years of power Godunov, who had urged Ivan to explore the eastern frontier, made some attempt to have maps drawn of that limbo of land. At least once, he set free some atamans of the Don and Ural Cossacks, penned up for their misdeeds in Moscow, on condition that they would lead an expedition south of the Urals into the salt desert of the Aral Sea, to probe toward Khiva (visited two generations before by Jenkinson).

The Cossacks succeeded only too well. Learning from a captured caravan that the Khiva Khan had left the city with his small army during the summer heat, they surprised Khiva itself by a night march, entering on the desert side, and plundering the half-empty streets at will. They loaded a wagon train with loot, including their pick of the women, and celebrated their capture before starting back across the plain.

They were cut off at a defile in the hills by the armed force of the Khan. For a while they defended their wagon train. Being without water—the khivans say the Cossacks drank the blood of the dying men—they had to abandon their loot and the wagon train and scatter by night toward distant rivers, where most of them were hunted down before they could reach the safety of the Urals and the blockhouse forts.

On their own initiative, on the Black Sea, the Cossacks made an extraordinary gain a little later and had to give it up when Moscow would not support them.

A small army of Zaporogians crossed over from the Dnieper to the Don and joined with several thousand Donskoi. These allied Cossacks somehow worked their way down through the

Krim Tatars to the mouths of the Don, where they occupied the main channel with their boats and settled down happily between the sea and the land to besiege the strong fortress of Azov.

It was one of those reckless ventures that can succeed only by surprise or unexpected chance. The Cossacks reasoned that by occupying Azov—after looting the town—they could hold the mouth of the Don, levy tribute on the river traffic and raid out into the Black Sea. But they had no siege artillery, and the fortifications of Azov, held by a Turkish garrison, had too many cannon to be stormed.

Clinging to the river in this fashion, the Cossack atamans sent to Moscow for help, only to be told that the Kremlin could not afford to anger the Turks by assisting them. However, instead of dispatching visible artillery, the Muscovites sent a boatload of gunpowder down the river accompanied by a German mining engineer, who supervised the building of a tunnel under the Azov redoubt. The powder was used in a mine, and exploded—the Cossacks rushed the crater and drove out the garrison in bitter fighting.

This in turn brought a full-scale field army with Janizaries and Krim cavalry from the Turkish commands to win back Azov. (And in Moscow, the Turkish ambassador was given two thousand sables, to pacify him.) Against this combat army, the Cossacks held the river and forts for years until the Turks, disheartened and weakened by sickness, withdrew. But Moscow would not support the Cossacks openly, and in time they had to relinquish their conquest.

After the year 1605, the year of the death of Boris, the rush across the Urals dwindled, and changed in character. For a dozen years authority in Moscow almost ceased to be, and one of the Russian periodic times of trouble began.

The Ringing of the Warning Bells

The common folk of Muscovy[2] murmured under Boris Godunov. No matter how many silver coins he scattered from the Gate of the Saviour, no matter how many cart caravans of wheat rumbled through the Moscow streets, the folk murmured.

---

[2] The strange Muscovite state at this time bore many names, ranging from All the Russias to the Muscovite Tsardom. An English ambassador, Giles Fletcher, called it in 1590 the "Russe Commonwealth." John Milton, in 1630–40, wrote of "the empire of Moscovia, or as others call it, Russia." The false Dmitri on assuming the throne christened himself Emperor, not Tsar.

Clear-sighted, well taught, quick to adopt western ways, Boris found, like Ivan, that he had no means of ruling except by an army and the inclination of the unpredictable people. A parliamentarian by nature, Boris had no parliament. After the passing of the weak figure of Feodor without children, evil omens were perceived throughout the land. Rumor had it that Dmitri, the boy born to Ivan by Maria Nogai, lay buried beneath the stone floor of a monastery. Who had slain the boy Dmitri, unless Boris the Tsar? Who had appointed a Patriarch over Holy Mother Moscow, whose churches now numbered forty times forty, if not Boris? True, Ivan had named a certain Simeon to be Tsar in his time. Yet Boris had not the blood of Rurik and Dmitri Donskoi in his veins. He was descended from the Tatars.

The Tatars had never bowed to him. Boris had sent the great family of the Romanovs into exile to the frontier, or into monasteries and convents. Boris had called upon foreign artists to cast the greatest of all bells, the *Tsar-Kolokol*, and when this huge bell had been made with the face of Boris upon it, it had refused to be elevated into place over Moscow, beside the new Tower of Ivan. No, *Tsar-Kolokol* had broken every scaffolding built to raise him, and he lay broken in the court of the Kremlin.

Boris, said the people of Moscow, did not know the ancient ways like Ivan. Under him, the landowners, who provided horsemen for the army, forbade the peasantry to leave their lands, even on the Feast of St. George, when after the harvest was in men had been free to go to other land. Now, like serfs, they were bound, they and their families, to their fields to give value to land by their blood and sweat.

Pilgrims, going along the roads, said that the ghost of the murdered Dmitri had been seen above earth. Some said Dmitri's coffin was being carried in a scarlet cloth to Moscow from Uglitch; others declared that the last son of Ivan had

---

Except for the popular tales and songs and the religious ritual, no national literature existed; barely twenty books had been published by 1600; the architecture alone strained away from the Italo-Byzantine toward some national expression but succeeded only in imitating the wooden Scandinavian churches, with oriental adjuncts, such as the Persian bulbed dome; the art of illuminated painting had declined since the devastation of Novgorod and the north.

This poverty of national life in Muscovy contrasts with the Elizabethan theater and music and the Tudor architecture in England, with the reign of Henri Quatre in France, and the afterglow of the Renaissance in the Italian cities.

As before, the true literature of Muscovy lay in the *bylini* of its folk—the music in their songs.

never been slain, and that he was riding in from the south. Boris gave out charity, when the crowds gathered, and people murmured, "It is the blood of the innocent, in a gold vase."

Drought came, and seed grain was eaten up. Famine came, for four years. Starving bands trapped, killed and ate humans, like beasts. Through Holy Mother Moscow of the White Walls the bells rang in darkness, when no hand touched the bell ropes. Throughout the land the bells echoed the warning. Astrologers had said Boris Godunov would reign for seven years, and at the end of seven years he died. Perhaps he was poisoned. But his son and wife were slain out of hand. And Dmitri lived, again.

Tsar-Kolokol could not be hung in a belfry because Boris Godunov had ordered an enormous bell to be made weighing 140 tons—too great a mass of metal to be elevated to a tower. Like the monarch of all cannon, made for Ivan III, it stood in the Kremlin useless, an object of superstitious awe. The Kremlin's coinage had sunk low in value; its human integers, the peasantry, had grown weary of cultivating the exhausted soil of the Moscow area. The boyar class, decimated and impoverished, could not influence the populace.

Toward the vacuum left by the extreme weakness of Moscow, the vital forces of the outer regions flowed in—the Cossack brotherhoods from the south, the Swedes moving unchecked into the north, the Poles possessing themselves of the long-disputed western frontier.

With the Cossacks came the former monk who called himself Dmitri, the young son of Ivan the Terrible, and Muscovite regiments refused to stand in his way, saying, "It's a sin to go against the son of Ivan."

The common folk wanted to believe that this false Dmitri was the true Dmitri. Had not his mother, Maria Nogai, at her convent recognized him as her son? Had not the Polish nobles fetched him a princess of their own for a bride?

The fate of the pretended Dmitri, after a short month of marriage and rule, remains one of the paradoxes of Muscovy. Brilliant, able to read as a monk, and to ride as a Cossack, he threw himself with abandon into the task of bringing reality to his throne—working cannon with his own hands, exercising the stolid Muscovite soldiery against foreigners, begging money from the monasteries, planning to send boyars' sons to school in the west, hoping to strike up friendship with Henri Quatre. Who was this man, shuffled into a throne by the forces about that throne? No one can answer.

He was awkward and he had red hair. His name was Gregory Otrepiev and perhaps the priests, boyars and Poles around him had convinced him that he was actually the son of Ivan the Terrible.

Almost at once popular opinion turned against this Dmitri. The Kremlin servants complained that he passed by the shrines of saints without saluting them; he ate at a table unblessed by holy water. The boyars noted that he pardoned the stubborn Vasily Shuisky who swore that the boy Dmitri had been killed. Would a true son of Ivan have spared a Shuisky in such a case? Crowds of people saw this *Emperor* ride at a gallop, like a postillion, through the Gate of the Saviour. Men said that this stranger sacrificed to Satan with unholy rites, wearing an obscene mask the while. Officers pointed out that he kept foreigners like the French captain Margeret around him in command of his guard.

"In the beginning," relates Isaac Massa, the Hollander, who was in Moscow at the downfall of the false Dmitri, "he was very friendly, and made himself accessible to even the little folk; but after understanding the evil mind the Russians had toward him, he took care to provide himself with a guard of Livonians, and after that of Germans and other foreigners commanded by three captains, one French, one English, and one Scotch.

"The French captain, who called himself Jacques Margeret had a hundred archers under him; Matthew Knowtson, as the English captain was named, commanded a hundred halberdiers; and the Scotch captain, Albert Fancie [actually a Captain Gilbert], had a third hundred, ornamented with fine velvet for holy-days."

Even more than the other masters of Moscow, the pretender Dmitri put his trust in foreign mercenaries. Giles Fletcher, the English ambassador of the time, testifies that "of mercenary soldiers, that are foreigners whom they call *Nemschi* [dumb—i.e., not speaking Russian; usually the Germans] they have at this time 4300 Poles, about 4000 Cherkess—of which 3500 are distant in the garrisons—about 150 Dutch and Scots, and 100 of Greeks, Turks, Danes and Swedes. But these they use only upon the Tartar side, as they do the Tartar soldiers whom they hire sometimes but only for an interval, on the side against the Poles and Swedes." [3]

---

[3] Fletcher says that in his day the Streltsi "gunners" numbered 12,000, of which 2000 "stirrup gunners" were kept always on duty at Moscow. Some 1500 "court officers" were also kept in Moscow mounted. Outside these special troops, the bulk of the army num-

Besides the strong Tatar contingents, the tsars had invoked the host of the Don Cossacks. They had even devised rank, for these foreigners, of "sons of boyars," and the frontier contingents called into service for pay came to be called "cossacks" after the Don and Dnieper brotherhoods.

Never had the military force of Moscow been greater than at the beginning of this time of troubles. But the best of it was the mercenaries and the contingents drawn from the frontiers. It had no accepted leader; it lacked a common impulse; and in this crisis, it collapsed into its fragments.

No failure on the part of the false Dmitri caused the collapse. Quite simply, the divergent forces that had been held together by the two Ivans and Vasily, after a fashion, and had been held in check for a few years by Boris Godunov, now separated and struggled against each other—the peasantry, fast becoming serfs, the warring cliques of boyars, the voiceless middle class of artisans, small officials, merchants and settlers, the strong Cossack brotherhoods, the remnants of Tatar families, the incoming Swedes and Poles. All these pressed in different ways against the central point of Moscow, which had claimed so much authority over them. The man who called himself Dmitri was caught in the vortex of these forces and destroyed in a few days.

That Dmitri was doomed seemed to be evident to both Isaac Massa and Jacques Margeret, the one a merchant who had lent money to this prince of a fortnight, the other the chief officer of Dmitri's bodyguard. "From the first," Massa declares, "we heard rumors of nothing but treachery and conspiracy."

Outwardly, Moscow staged a pageant of splendor. The gilded carriage of Dmitri's bride, Marina of Sandomir, was drawn by matched white Tatar-bred horses; the boyars, friends or antagonists, appeared in long brocade court robes. At the coronation of the young pair, performed by the Patriarch himself, "the cathedral was hung with cloth-of-gold

---

bered 80,000. So, according to Fletcher, the armed forces totaled some 105,000, a very large number for that time.

Jacques Margeret estimates that the foreign contingents and friendly Tatars in the service numbered 28,000. With 80,000 Russian levies, this would give a total of 108,000.

One field army mustered in 1576 numbered 56,000. With the garrison and fortress troops that year the Muscovites would have had some 110,000 men under arms. Such forces dwarfed the smaller commands of western Europe. Henry of Navarre had 9000 men at Ivry; the Duke of Alva led some 15,000 at Jemmingen. Only the Turks could raise armies comparable in numbers to the Muscovites.

and silver embroidery . . . they carried before the Tsar the
crown and gauntlet and orb, and on a cushion of cramoisy,
the crown for the Tsarina."

Marina herself seemed happy, speaking affably with the
wives of the bourgeois as well as the great boyarinas; she
hungered for music at the banquets, and *dancing* in the
evenings. She even begged Dmitri to hold a masked ball, in
this city that knew neither mixed dancing nor masks for
entertainment. Perhaps she trusted in the presence of her
kinsmen, the lord of Sandomir, and Vishnevetsky, and the
exalted ambassador of Poland.

"The Tsar," Isaac Massa states, "had his eye and ear open,
and he advised the Poles to be on their guard, and ordered
his own bodyguard to report to the castle with harquebuses
loaded, and with bullets and matches in their cartouches."
To Massa at least the situation was very clear on that last
day of quiet. "The time of festivity was over, the silence of
death had come. On Friday no one would sell powder or
other weapons."

Marina, unaware, planned a festivity for Sunday.

"Saturday, by six o'clock in the morning," Margeret relates,
"there was no longer any doubt that this was the day appointed." At dawn of that day the French captain of the
guard was sick in his lodging, either poisoned, or suffering
from too keen an anticipation of what was coming.

"That day of terrible memory," Massa continues, "we saw
boyars riding at the head of their fighting men, covered with
mail, while the common folk ran hither and yon armed with
iron bars, stones and scimitars. All this multitude rushed
swiftly to the castle [the Kremlin enclosure] crying in the
streets as they passed 'To death! To the fire!' assuring each
other that the Poles were slaying the boyars in the castle;
yet in fact there were few boyars staying in the castle at the
time.

"So great was the confusion that they killed several Russians dressed like Poles; the residences of the Poles were
surrounded, so that no one could escape therefrom or enter
with aid. The Russian archers of the guard made common
cause with the rebels. So it befell that the poor prince who
ordinarily had a hundred guardsmen about him, had no
more than thirty, and they without a captain.

"Seeing only such a small band of guardsmen, the Muscovites called to them to put down their arms and join the
people, promising no harm would come if they did that. Once
the guards had been disarmed, the crowd ran up to the
great hall. There Peter Basmanov, the intimate friend of the

Tsar, appeared in front of them. A servant of Basmanov's ran at him and killed him.

"Then the crowd spread through the chambers, hurrying toward that of the Tsar.

"At the noise of the revolt, prince Dmitri jumped from his bed and pulled on a smock, demanding of the attendant at the bed the meaning of the uproar.

" 'I don't know,' replied the Russian. 'Perhaps, a fire.'

" 'No,' cried Dmitri, 'perhaps no fire—or all the bells would be sounding. Idiot—do you think you have another Boris here?'

"Rolling back his sleeves, he demanded the two swords that were usually kept by him, well sharpened. But the man in charge of them looked for the swords in vain. Then the crowd came nearer; Dmitri called to the halberdiers at the door not to give him up to the boyars. He locked the door himself, and dashed through the inner rooms to the bath room. Here, seeing that he was closely pursued, he jumped from the window.

"The window was high, under the roof. One of the halberdiers, a man named Farstenberg, ran down the stairs quickly and found Dmitri still alive but hurt in the chest from which blood ran freely; his head was also bruised and bleeding.

"This halberdier, helped by others, carried him back to his bed chamber where he was revived with cold water and drugs. When Dmitri became fully conscious the boyars talked with him a long time—no one knows about what. For they silenced the halberdier by killing him, and soon afterward they killed the prince himself by many blows. They threw down his body, after roping it to the bodies of his followers. Mutilated in this way, it was dragged to the public square and left naked and torn lying on the carcass of Basmanov, exposed on a wooden stand.

"Someone put a flower in the dead Dmitri's mouth, a bagpipe under his arm, and between his legs a hideous mask found among the spoils taken from the Tsarina. Men and women came in great numbers to see this spectacle."

Even so, the rumor ran through Moscow that Dmitri the Tsar had not been killed, but had sacrificed one of his men, to make this test of his people's loyalty and—shades of Ivan! —to avenge himself on all rebels. Stablemen were found who had been ordered to hold three fine Turkish horses saddled that night—horses which, it seemed, had vanished mysteriously.

Captain Gilbert, who had got out safely with his Scots to

a suburb, where a Polish general joined him, received a few days later a letter which seemed to be in Dmitri's writing. The letter asked where Gilbert had been during the attack on the palace, and quoted a conversation which the Scot had had with the pretender, when the two of them had thought themselves alone. The Pole was all for searching out the writer of the letter.

"If he is the wrong Dmitri, he may be the right man for us."

But Gilbert would have no more of Moscow's intrigue.

Witnesses repeated that the real Dmitri had had a mole under one eye, while the body in the public square showed only a cut where the mole should have been. Captain Margeret himself insists that the face on the body had traces of a downy beard, whereas the real Dmitri had been shaven clean the day before the attack on him.

Vasily Shuisky, the leader of the revolt—the same who had been pardoned by the Tsar of two weeks—had the body of a boy fetched in state from Uglitch, which was declared to be the true son of Ivan. The mutilated corpse of the pretender was dug up and fired from the mouth of a great cannon, to make it impossible for the mob to believe that he had come to life again through black sorcery. And a long list of the crimes of the false Dmitri was proclaimed throughout the lands of Rus.

"First," Isaac Massa summarizes, "that as a monk, he had broken his vows . . . second, by sorcery he had gained victories, and had himself crowned over the Russians . . . third, as a heretic he had shown no reverence for the sacred images . . . fourth, as a papist, he had conspired with Rome against the Orthodox Faith . . . fifth, by his letters he had promised Smolensk to the lord of Sandomir, and Novgorod to the Swedes (*but I do not believe that*) . . . sixth, as Tsar, he had kept the boyars away from him by his halberdiers and had consorted with the Poles instead . . . seventh, he had profaned a convent by entering it when his bride-to-be was quartered there . . . eighth, he had caused disaster along the Volga by summoning the Cossacks there to his aid, thereby ruining the rich Persian trade."

These charges were intended to appeal to popular superstition, to religious zeal, and the good will of the merchants. But the dramatization of the pretender's death did not help Moscow, which fell into chaos after the hasty crowning of Vasily Shuisky.

"The Council, the people and the country divided, one against the other," Margeret relates. "The provinces revolted, without being able to know for a long time what was happening. Many towns along the Tartar frontier rebelled, seizing their Generals and garrisons."

At this point Margeret decided that France under the League was preferable to Moscow in anarchy, and he fled still convinced that Dmitri had been a true prince of the blood royal, and regretting that he could not take Dmitri with him to the safety of the English ships at Archangel.

An Army of the People, and the Russian Nation

The first rising in Moscow during this time of troubles, resulting in the death of the unfortunate Dmitri, had been a popular movement, directed against the foreigners by a few boyars, especially by Shuisky. But the mob had not been in accord with the boyars. The Polish prince, Vishnevetsky, besieged by the mob in his quarters near the Kremlin, blasted his way out by first scattering gold coins from the doorway and then discharging a cannon into the swarm of Russians that struggled for the coins. After Vishnevetsky and his group of Poles got clear of the mob, they surrendered to the boyars, and were spared.

But neither in the Moscow mob nor in the boyars was there any enduring leadership. Control of the Kremlin shifted with kaleidoscopic rapidity. After Shuisky there appeared still another Dmitri, after him a Cossack ataman who had taken Marina for his mistress, then a Prince Trubetskoy, and a fragment of an army led by an escaped slave. And then disciplined Polish cavalry that took over the city, in spite of an attempt by the Muscovites to hire five thousand Swedish infantry and De la Gardie to drive off the Poles. The Swedes, in fact, took over Novgorod, while Polish forces occupied the bitterly contested Smolensk, and pushed deep into the Ukraine, beyond ancient Kiev, toward the Crimea.

At the same time the Don Cossacks advanced into the territory above their river, to the south of Moscow.

So by the end of its time of troubles, Moscow had lost the ancient river routes of the west, the lakes around Novgorod and all contact with the Baltic. Moscow, with a Polish garrison in the Kremlin, seemed to have at that time no power within itself to endure.

The city was helped to survive by aid from the east, and the northeast.

Moscow was Holy Mother Moscow, of the Russians, the heart of that entity which had become stronger during these last generations. And the Patriarch of Moscow led the new national movement, from his cell. To the folk along the Dvina, the Sukhona and the mighty Volga it was intolerable to watch Holy Mother Moscow held by armed foreigners, especially after the Patriarch, imprisoned by the foreigners, had died of starvation. Militia formed in the far cities of Vologda, Ustiug, Kazan and Nizhni Novgorod. The militia chose its own leaders, a merchant of Nizhni, K. Minin, among them.

A prince, Pozharsky, won the wayward allegiance of the Don Cossack brotherhood, which had always been hostile to the Catholic Poles. Marching out of the trading towns of the north, and up the Volga to the Oka, this army of the middle class had no candidate for the throne and no plan of government. It was moved by religious impulse, and held together by a sense of nationality. It sought to end misrule in Moscow and restore the channels of Russian life.

And it set Moscow free. It relied on the much abused Zemsky Sobor—which actually at this time (1611–12) began to act as a rudimentary parliament—to maintain law. For a ruler the new council decided upon a sixteen-year-old boy, Michael Romanov, a grandnephew of the beloved Anastasia, the first wife of Ivan. Michael, then in a monastery, had no special qualification to govern a state, nor did the new Zemsky Sobor place any restrictions on his authority. It was enough that he assumed the crown of Ivan, as Tsar. When he did so, it was over the Russians, as a nation.

Although Moscow had been unable to aid the new frontiers in the east and north during the first years of the troubles, from 1605–13, migration thither had set in again. New exiles and escaped prisoners sought safety beyond the Volga; impoverished merchants turned to the Siberian fur routes or the new mines in the Urals.

With them appeared two new persecuted classes, the *kabalni,* oppressed by debts, and the *opalni,* under official sentence. In the "wild lands" of the Ob, within the brotherhoods of the Cossacks, and even out in the Irtish steppe they could live far from debt or sentence.

They brought new blood to the thin-bodied eastern frontier because they appeared as colonists, to work the soil and trade with the native peoples.

The new nation had a strange contour shaped around

Moscow. In the west its frontier lay some 175 miles distant. To the east, it stretched over forest, plain and tundra 1700 miles or more.

Under the new government, in which all classes blended for a time, *Russia* lay passive in the west. Moscow, licking its wounds, recovered its strength, gaining force without direction. It held fast to the strategic portage system, west of Mozhaisk, but made only feeble efforts to recover the Novgorod and Smolensk regions, and it hardly stirred toward the Ukraine, where a blended people lived almost free from domination.

Toward the east, however, after 1610 a giant's stride was taken at once. Where the Englishmen still quested along the shore beyond the Ob, fur traders advanced over the tundras, seeking untouched hunting grounds for the Arctic animals, the sable, marten and the now coveted ermine. By breaking into new ground, they escaped the state taxation, which in turn pressed close after them. In the older territories the fur industry was fast becoming a state monopoly.

Discovery of the Continent beyond the River Ob

The Englishmen who had failed to get through the ice beyond the Ob told of at least one discovery. They had found, they thought, the Golden Old Woman of Asia's legendry.

"The Samoyeds, who are subject at this time to the *Emperor of Russia,* tell this of the Slata Baba, or Golden Hag, that it is not an idol shaped like an old woman, or an oracle. At the mouth of the mighty river Ob on the side of the sea there is a great rock which by its nature (being somewhat aided by imagination) does resemble a woman holding a child in her arms (as does the North Cape cliff resemble a friar). Thither resort the Samoyeds for their fishing, and there also they practice their sorcery (as their manner is) and conjecture about good or evil to come."

But the greatest outward thrust was made far to the south of this landmark of the Golden Old Woman. In fact, it took place more than a thousand miles south, among the headwaters of the gigantic Ob. Before the time of troubles had fairly ended in Moscow, hunters and cossacks, former soldiers released or escaping from the wars, former prisoners or exiles, and plain wanderers known as Waders—a human mixture, without class or rank—drifted out along the waterways through swamps and forests.

Its members kept beyond reach of the Moscow taxgatherers —who had moved into the Stroganov conquests, which were being taken over by the state. Their movement deviated sharply east, avoiding the open steppe still dominated by hordes of horsemen between the Irtish (where Irmak had drowned) and the Ishim. An ostrog to house the pioneers (Ketsk) was built in 1610 at the juncture of the Ket River. Following the Ket eastward, up into its highlands, they fortified Makovsk in 1618, and in the same year flanked it with the ostrog of Kuznetsk (now Stalinsk) far south where the main tributary of the Ob branched into three streams. Kuznetsk was thirteen hundred miles south of the Golden Old Woman, and some two thousand miles by road from Moscow.

In the highlands around Makovsk, hunters heard of a river greater than the Ob, to the eastward. Such rumors now drew throngs of traders to the frontier terminals.

As the first migration had been *away* from the frontier of the steppes of Asia, from the Polovtsi and the Tatars, *toward* the security of the Moscow area, this last migration was away from Moscow. In these years of trouble Moscow stood almost upon the new frontier of the west, subject to endemic war. From that war the populace escaped toward the Urals, toward fresh soil and peace.

To these headwaters of the Ob ventured young Isaac Massa, who had served his apprenticeship in more ways than one as merchant in Moscow during the time of troubles. By sled and boat he traveled to the outstations where "a great trade is now carried on in furs with the Muscovites by the Tartars and Samoyeds; but many go seeking farther, yea, far beyond the river Ob to the east and the south as well. And Tartars journey hither from the south, which is very profitable to the Muscovites. Churches are found everywhere. Would to God the cruel Spaniards had taken possession of America as peacefully."

Massa believed that these soldiers and traders, who towed him upstream in their barges, had orders "to spy out the land farther and farther, toward a warmer climate; but it was commanded to show friendliness to any people who might be found on the land, in order to have more settlers [come out]. When they ventured inland [from the rivers] they went in troops, and for a space of four hundred miles they found fertile country, without cultivation or inhabitants . . . until the huts of the people called Tungusi who gobbled like turkey-cocks, saying that they dwelt along the great river which they called *Yeniseia*, which spring from the southeast, but they knew not its source. . . . This river Yeniseia, much larger than the Ob, has high mountains on the east, among which volcanoes cast out fiery brimstone."

These pioneers had sighted the mountainous spine of the mid-continent. Beyond those heights, unknown to them as yet, lay the sandy basin of Sin-kiang (West River), the grasslands of the Mongols and the wind-swept wastes of the Gobi, bordering upon China itself.

Swiftly the pioneer groups pushed on. "The Muscovites, having heard of this from the Samoyeds who came from the land of the Tungusi, were anxious to search further, begging men of the Governor [at Tobolsk, near ruined Sibir] who granted their request, even sending soldiers with them to examine into everything. About seven hundred men set out," Massa relates, "across the river Ob through the country of the Tungusi, beyond the large river Yeniseia, going farther with the Tungusi to guide them. These Tungusi caught food for them skilfully on the way—birds, reindeer, and other strange animals. . . . It was early spring when they reached a farther river, but did not venture to cross, hearing what they understood to be the sound of bells. When the wind came from across the river it often brought a noise of people and horses. Ships with square sails passed upon the river, with a din of great guns. The river rose very high, and they rejoiced in their hearts at sight of the beautiful country . . . and rare trees and strange birds. But as to those the Muscovites were not inquisitive, caring only for profit everywhere for they are a rude people. . . . Being persuaded against crossing the river by the Tungusi, they saw flames rising from the mountains there, from which they brought out sulphur and gold-rock—so it appears as if valuable mines might be found there."

Isaac Massa himself collected diligently any accounts of the new lands to the eastward. He could get for himself only one sketch map, which proved to be of the coast on the Arctic side, at the mouth of the Ob where the English navigators had failed to get through. "It is a pity that the Dutch have not managed to get through Waygats [strait]," Massa comments, "nor do they know how to attempt it; for ships will not get through once in a hundred times. They could send people in boats as the Russians do, and so the way would be discovered."

The industrious Massa copied this map of the Ob belonging to a Russian who lent the map "at risk of his life."

The Dutch were trying, also, for the Northeast Passage. And even Massa, along the Ob about 1611, is aware of descriptions of the ocean lying beyond China. "It is to be doubted if America is not connected with China and these parts of the world by an isthmus like the one which joins Africa to Asia at the Red Sea. This, indeed, is very possible, for the only assertion that it is open sea is found in some pagan writings."

Already the Russians were musing on the nature of this farthest sea, spoken of as the "Eastern Ocean Sea."

And in Westminster a certain Master Richard Hakluyt, who collected maps and narratives of voyages, pondered letters from traders on the Pechora in the north. "Samoieds come hither in winter with commodities such as we dreamed not on yet. For by chance one came to us with a piece of an elephant's tooth which he said he had bought of a Samoied. And here are men called Tungussies, whose country is beyond the river Ob and borders upon the great river Yenisse . . . And it should seem it is not far from China."

These elephants' "teeth" weighed close to two hundred pounds. To the Englishmen they were the first tangible token of the mystery lying upon that farthest coast where spirit fires climbed the sky and ice broke with a thunderclap, where rose basalt rocks carved in grim shapes as if by spirit hands, and prehistoric people crawled and hunted through the darkness.

These were mammoths' tusks, preserved for millenniums in ground frozen four hundred feet deep, where only the topmost foot thawed under the faint midsummer sun. The Chinese had bought them for long from the folk who found them on the "Island of Bones" off the mouth of a river still beyond the ken of the Muscovites, or in the fantastic graveyard of the mammoths where the beasts still lay intact with flesh and hair covering their bones, preserved by the extreme cold. The natives said these beasts had dwelt in the darkness of the caverns of Erlik Khan, under the earth, and had died when they made their way up to the light.

In 1619 Russian settlers from Makovsk took possession of the bank of the Yenisei, which the hunters and cossacks had explored, and built the log walls of their stockade there on a bluff, the nucleus of the town of Yeniseisk—more than twenty-one hundred miles from Moscow.

In December of that year a ukase—imperial order—was sent by the new ruler, "the Lord Tsar and Grand Prince Michael, son of Feodor, of all Russia," to the governor at Tobolsk and the officers along the Ob. "We learned from Tobolsk from cossacks and fur hunters who had been on the

Yenisei that the land as you go up is Tungus land . . . and in these countries there are good quality sables, and that it is [from there] two weeks going and two days portage to a great river. But on that river sail large ships with great bells on them, and the sound of people and the firing of cannon is often heard. But what people, of what faith, and with what merchandise, or whether they are people of war, no one knew. The water in that great river was salt, and whatever you threw into it was cast up again on the shore. And there are many great islands and all sorts of good lands along that great river.

"Now when you have this order and the *yasak*-[tribute] paying people come in to the new Tungus ostrog, give them to eat, make gifts to them and persuade them in the way of service to His Majesty [i.e., the Tsar Michael] to go with the Russian cossacks to discover that great river . . . and to build of timber whatever kind of vessel can navigate that great river, so that they can go on that river and learn for certain if it be really a river, or a sea or arm of the sea. They are to explore its banks on both sides, and see if there be special peculiarities, timber for shipbuilding, and if mountains, what sort of mountains. Rocky? And how high? And are the banks tree-lined or steppes, and whence that river flows and whither—into what sea? Is it rife with fish, the water fresh or salt, and does it cast up on the shore any kind of beast? If so, what beast?"

Grotesque as these instructions from Moscow to the explorers on the Ob frontier may seem, they give clear indications of the reports coming in about the vast hinterland to the east of Eurasia.

There was of course no such "great river" lying sixteen days beyond the Yenisei. But there were mountains enough, some volcanic; there was the great Lake Baikal near the homeland of the Golden Khan, a descendant of the Mongol kha khans, near the birthplace of Genghis Khan; there were rivers in Cathay on which junks passed with square sails, exploding gunpowder; there were islands enough and arms of the sea along the far northeast coast, where mammoths lay buried and whales might be cast up; there was water salt enough in the Eastern Ocean Sea.

It lay thousands of miles beyond the Ob—farther than Moscow dreamed; but in one short generation, by one of the most amazing feats in history, "cossacks and hunters" like these were to reach the last great river where sailed Chinese ships, and taste the salt water of that ocean, the Pacific.

This rush across the breadth of a continent was on so vast

a scale that it is more easily conceived in degrees of longitude than in miles. Four hundred years before, the Mongol *ordas* directed by Genghis Khan and his staff had swept over ninety degrees of longitude, from the China Sea to the river Khalka in the Ukraine. The Mongols had traversed from east to west.

The Russians were advancing from Moscow toward the

Procession of Muscovite ambassador, with letter of credentials and gifts of furs, at German court. (From contemporary wood engraving)

China Sea, over a hundred degrees of longitude, more than one fourth the circuit of the earth. From the point of Irmak's crossing in the Urals, in 1582, they were penetrating eighty degrees to the east, at the rate—as it proved to be—of nearly two degrees a year. The breadth of the North American continent, soon to be traversed by the colonists in America, was somewhat less than sixty degrees, and it took the pioneers of America more than a century and a half to arrive in any numbers on the western coast, bordering the Pacific.

The Race from the Ob to the Lena

While the Russian nation was barred from the west, weakened by its own time of troubles and by its failures to advance in culture as the western nations had been doing after the Renaissance, much had been happening in that west, beyond the invisible Riga-Constantinople line.

After the turn of the century, middle Europe became involved in the long internecine struggle known as the Thirty Years' War, while—unperceived as yet—Turkish military power degenerated as that of Spain had done. Like the Mon-

gols before them, the Othman Turks who had come a long way from the steppes of mid-Asia were losing their vitality after contact with the softer civilization of the west. While the splendid mosque of Suleiman had been built, with the dream city of Brusa, and the pleasure palaces along the Bosporus, the Turkish grip on the eastern Mediterranean had been shaken after the defeat at Malta, and the fleet action of Lepanto. At the same time Turkish control of the Caucasus barrier and the Azerbaijan corridor, with its key of Tabriz, had yielded to the power of the cultured Persians, then ruled by Shah Abbas, when "Isfahan was half the world."

While the Turkish hold on the Balkan peoples remained firm, the Hungarians were emerging again as a nation, and Poland—now extending into the Ukraine—was enjoying, like Persia, one of its periods of advancement.

Statesmen in the west—and there were many as thoughtful as Gustavus Adolphus and Richelieu—understanding that the tide of Turkish invasion was receding, pondered the nature of that other colossus of Asia, Russia. For the new Russia was even more of an enigma than the Muscovy of Ivan IV. Would this renascent Moscow turn more to the knowledge and the customs of the west? Would its growing manpower be mustered again to break through the frontier in the west? Or would it remain quiescent within its steppes, barred from the Baltic and the Black Sea?

Addressing the Swedish Parliament in 1617, the young Gustavus Adolphus said: "The Russian . . . could justly boast that he was lord and master over a large part of Europe and Asia, the most prominent regions in the world. His power is not to be belittled, for these countries are filled with a numerous nobility, many peasants and many populous cities, and this might he has often demonstrated by the inordinately large armies he has led into the field. . . . It is not necessary to describe the appallingly large armies he has led in the field against us, as there are many living today who have seen them with their own eyes.

"This great power of his swells the strength of the naturally well-situated lakes and rivers which cover his country, for in a short while he could easily transport his forces on the Caspian Sea up the Volga and down the Volkhov River to the Baltic; and along the Dvina and the Niemen he could easily transport his forces from all the corners of his empire . . . and has been able to sail back and forth along the aforementioned rivers with lighters, and sweep over the entire Finnish archipelago. . . . He has thousands of lighters at his disposal. . . . But by the mercy of God he is now prevented from doing it since he can no longer show himself in the Baltic with a single boat. . . . The Russians have been cut off from the shores of the Baltic, through which the trade of Russia has to go. . . .

"It is not their custom to remain at peace." [4]

These same Europeans had been finding their way in two directions over the long sea routes. One was to the far east, where missionaries other than St. Francis Xavier, Matteo Ricci and Benedict Goës had discovered that Cathay and China were one, and that Japan existed, as Marco Polo had maintained when few believed him. With the breakup of Spanish control of the ocean lanes, English, French and Dutch merchantmen probed toward the Spice Islands, while the

---

[4] From *The Urge to the Sea: the Course of Russian History— the Role of Rivers, Portages, Ostrogs, Monasteries and Furs*, by Robert J. Kerner, University of California Press, Berkeley, 1946.

East India Company prepared to monopolize the trade with India, now under the rule of a Mongol dynasty (the "Moghuls") from central Asia.

European shipping, men-of-war and merchantmen bearing traders and colonists quested along the shores of South and North America, seeking trading ports and sites for settlement. Here to the north, English and Dutch still searched spasmodically for the Northwest Passage to Cathay, while Champlain opened up the fur trade along the St. Lawrence River, and the Plymouth Company prepared to land its shiploads of colonists south of the St. Lawrence.

Other ships, Portuguese, Dutch and Spanish, explored up the west coast of South America, finding what they called the peninsula of California instead of the islands of Japan which were thought to be so near.

Neither the navigators from the western ports nor the Russian pioneers in central Eurasia could have been aware of the significance of their movements. Nor that in another century the advanced detachments of the English settlers in the New World and the Russian colonists of the Old World would meet at a place which was neither California nor Japan but Alaska, whither both had been led by the search for furs.

That small forces of men, in bands no larger than a few hundreds, should have mastered the northeastern quarter of Eurasia in a generation appears incredible. They had no guiding leadership; the names of the leaders remain obscure. The forerunners had almost no aid from the state—in fact many of them were attempting to escape from the state.

Along the eastern frontier at that time raged something like a discovery fever. Even the heads of the bureaus in Moscow shared this fever. (Michael, the Tsar, of Anastasia's Romanov blood, was lame, a man of no force—intent on collecting clocks—managed by the stronger minds around him.) Instructions were sent—almost broadcast—to the frontier to search for the most incredible things. For sulphur and volcanoes, for silver and "gold-rock"—(probably nuggets washed out of rock by the heavy spring freshets)—for the Golden Khan, and rare jewels, river routes and wild horses. To the minds in Moscow, Siberia appeared to be a land of marvels, from which a quick profit could be made.

As early as 1618, "the Lord Tsar and Grand Prince Michael ordered the Siberian cossack Ivan Petlin of Tomsk to seek tidings of the Chinese Empire and . . . other kingdoms."

But the particular reason for dispatching Ivan Petlin

seems to have been a rumor of rare precious stones to be
found near Lake Baikal. Stones, in fact, "suitable for His
Tsarish Majesty's treasure"—by which was meant the Moscow exchequer.

The Cossack Petlin and his comrade Andriushko did reach
the "large lake" Baikal, and wandered at risk of their lives
among the Mongol encampments without finding the rare
precious stones [5]—only "silver which comes by trade from
China."

From the lake the Cossacks found their way to the Great
Wall, "where is a wall made of stone fifteen fathoms high,
along the side of which they went ten days, where they saw
small towns and villages belonging to the Manchu Queen;
but in those ten days they saw no people upon the wall at
all . . . they came to a gate where lie great cannon and in
said gate three thousand men stand watch. The Altyn king's
[Golden Khan's] also journey to this gate with horses to
sell to the men of Cathay, but are not permitted to come
within the wall except very few at a time."

Asked why they had appeared within the frontier of China,
Petlin answered, "to find the empire of China, and other
kingdoms."

Through some cities of China he journeyed, keeping his
route so carefully memorized that he was able to repeat it
afterward, with the aid of his sketch map. In so doing, he
discovered much about Mongol and Chinese women, which
were clean and which were not; he found parrots and pea-
cocks and dwarfs, and giant painted statues in Buddhist temples which frightened him. He entered the White City where

---

[5] John Milton, writing his *Brief History of Moscovia, And of
Other Less-Known Countries Lying Eastward of Russia as far as
Cathay,* had seen a published account of Petlin's journey, with
others, a generation afterward. He mentions "a Lake, where Rubies
and Saphirs grow." He knows the Mongol country "where reigned a
Queen called Manchika" and that the explorers came to "a stone
Wall, 15 fathom high; along the side of which, having on the other
hand many pretty towns belonging to Queen Manchika, they
travail'd ten daies without seeing any on the Wall till they came to
the Gate. Where they saw very great Ordnance lying, and 3000 men
in watch." That is Petlin's wall and gate.

Milton's interest, in this little work, lay with the wonders of the
farther east rather than with Moscovia itself. He had read in
Hakluyt and in Purchas the voyages of the English into Russia, and
the fruits of his reading appear in descriptions of *Paradise Lost,*
as where Satan returns to Hell and finds his host gathering about
Pandemonium

> *As when the Tartar, from his Russian foe,*
> *By Astracan, over the snowy plains*
> *Retires . . .*

"the Chinese Tsar dwells among beautiful and wonderful things."

The most wonderful thing, the cossack Ivan Petlin relates, was a rare precious stone (iridescent) that gave out light, day and night. He says he could have seen the face of the Chinese Tsar if he had had a gift to offer. Without a gift, there was no audience possible.

So the first Russian was received at the Chinese court. Like most of his fellows Ivan Petlin got back safely.

Such pioneers got through because they were wilderness-bred, able to hunt for their meat, and to house themselves during winter storms and spring freshets. Accustomed to the forest, they kept pretty closely to the forests. Amphibious, they followed the rivers where possible, going like the *coureurs de bois* by canoe, longboat and raft, or by sled and skis. Soon after 1620 they worked out a portage from a tributary of the Yenisei to a stream that led into the Lena, which took its course out of the fir-coated mountains, far to the northeast. These swift rushing streams falling in cascades through clean birch and fir forests delighted the voyagers from the monotonous plains and sedge-lined water channels of Russia. They learned the native way of fishing at night with spears, with a brazier burning over the bow of the boat.

Having better firearms than the natives, they could impose on the forest villages. Always they took guides from folk they had subdued and forced to pay *yasak* (tribute) when they ventured on to the unknown peoples to the eastward. Samoyeds escorted them into the territory of the Tungusi (Reindeer Folk) who shaved their heads and obeyed the orders of shamans; the Tungusi cared for them and guided them among the Yakuts, who were bolder, being of Turkish stock. The Yakut villages stretched along the Lena; beyond them were the snow-dwelling folk, the Chukchi and (toward Baikal) the Buriats and nomad Mongols, who were still dangerous, although they had fallen under Buddhist influence.

Neither the Buriats nor the Mongols—even the remnants gathered in yurt villages about the Altyn Khan—were disposed to pay tribute or to serve the Russian pioneer bands.

But the first pioneers in following the forest routes had also followed an invisible ethnological line, extending through the native forest dwellers, all the way from the Finns, Samoyeds, through the Tungusi and Chukchi.

They were the older stock of northeastern Asia, keepers of animals—especially reindeer and dogs—unwarlike. Moreover from the memory of their ancestors, they had paid *hechen,* the "law-gift," to the great Turkish or Mongol kha khans.

When the first Russians came in, with superior weapons, ordering them to submit to the White Tsar in Moscow and pay up to the speakers, it was an old story to the aboriginal Siberian tribes. In fact, these Russians used familiar Tatar words in making their demands. Like the Tatars before them, they promised protection to the natives, once payment had been made; unlike the Tatars, they did not keep their promises in that respect, because other Russians came after them, making the same demands. Then came the officers of the White Tsar, making the demands anew and taking hostages, to force the tribes to obey.

Black-bearded priests, like shamans, appeared with the uniformed officers, who took the pick of the furs, paying little, and took the younger women. These women were passed among the Russians, bought and sold, and out of them came native Russian offspring. But to resist was unthinkable to the Siberian forest folk, who had been servants of the Mongol khans.

When angered, the Tungusi would steal and raid the voyagers' post for stores, or murder men caught alone. More than that, they could not conceive of doing.

As they shaped their course, the Russians were retreading the routes of Mongol dominion, scantily populated. Under their plundering the native Siberians lived more leanly, and decreased in numbers.

Close on the heels of the exploring parties—the small bands of cossack pioneers outdistanced the others—came the officials. Krasnoyarsk was fortified at a source of the Yenisei in 1628. Three years later the Bratsk stockade protected the passage to the Lena, and in 1632 the strong Yakutsk ostrog was built at the great fork of the Lena, above the homeland of the Mongols—thirty-one hundred miles, as the birds fly, from Moscow.

Hunters and traders moved on, in almost desperate haste, to have the first kill of animals in new grounds, and to be first to take toll of the natives. Ahead, somewhere, fortunes waited.

On the other hand, some of these voyagers were murderers, condemned and then pardoned on condition that they "discovered new lands"; many were exiles who had nothing to hope for from Moscow; many more were driven by need to smuggle out their gains.

The arrival of officials on the scene meant bribes to be

paid, fur catches to be confiscated, or at the least taxes to be imposed. And state agents had a way of paying low prices in the Siberian posts, while entering the purchases at the higher fixed rates on their books. The very *voevodes* (governors) and inspectors were timeservers, condemned to duty in Siberia for two years, and so naturally inclined to compensate themselves for their sufferings.

Naïvely enough the Moscow bureaus issued statements to the native peoples, who had become the "Tsar's people," arguing that the taking of many tributes, and of women and children as slaves, were the sins of the erring officials and distasteful to the benevolent Tsar, who disavowed the actions of his "governor, inspector, bureau agents, sons of boyars, military commanders, soldiers (Streltsi) and cossacks."

This was quite a complete roster of the official agents who followed the pioneers to an eastern outpost.

Moscow had written to the commanders at a danger spot on the frontier, warning them they might be attacked by "hostiles." "And at Tomsk, sirs, you have, according to the service rosters, boyars' sons and cossacks, Lithuanians and captains both mounted and afoot no more than 280, with those in the Kuznetsky ostrog. And these are no-account fellows, burdened with debts, and besides scattered in government duties, so that Tomsk and Kuznetsky cannot possibly be defended by them."

By Lithuanians, the communiqué meant Swedish or Polish or other prisoners of war, who were sent to serve in Siberia at that time.

These prisoners of one kind or another, these hunters, miners, "Waders" and ordinary looters were the firstcomers. Russian officials called them the *starozili* or "old dwellers," while the peasants who followed them were called *novosyoli*, "new settlers."

In fact, during this rush into an unknown world, the peasant cultivator, the true colonist, lagged far behind. Driven eastward by the urge toward fertile soil, and the desire to escape the hardships of the west, the peasants drifted only slowly along the river basins, building cabins where the soil seemed good for wheat or barley, then moving on with their families when they heard of better settlements elsewhere. As always, the peasants proved to be hard to contain in a district. They tended to drift south, and they stuck for a long time along the old Volga-Ob frontiers, in the good feathergrass steppe where wheat could be grown easily. They were still there when the advance pioneers, the old dwellers, were exploring up and down the Lena, two thousand miles to the eastward.

Like the colonists, the monasteries lagged—but not so far behind. Priests and monks joined the Siberian rush as individuals. (Even in Irmak's band there had been a priest, Upanas, a hardy soul who wore chains under his habit and wandered the forest alone, so that the natives brought *hechen* to Upanas, believing him to be a new kind of shaman, whom it was good to propitiate.) The state officials discouraged the priesthood in Siberia at first because Christian converts were not supposed to be taxed. Still, Isaac Massa had seen many churches in the new Ob settlements.

After a few years small churches, quickly followed by monasteries, appeared in terminals like Yeniseisk and Yakutsk.

As Massa believed, the priests accommodated themselves to native life rather than imposed Christianity upon it. Often the bearded priests took native women for temporary wives.

The Russians at this point and for long afterward were hardly *foreigners* to the natives. The first pioneers at the Ob had lived a generation or more in the melting pot of the Ukraine and among the Volga "Tatars"—that is, among the blond, horse-riding Bashkirs and Mordvas who still retained the old nomad pride that holds its folk to be superior to those who grubbed in the earth for a living. The Don Cossacks had been a blend of such peoples. Many of the explorers of the 3200-mile-long Lena were the tough mixed stock spawned along the earlier frontiers. They followed native ways and even superstitions closely.

The cossack Elisha Buza who traced the Lena to its end in the Arctic waters during 1632 must have been a Christian, of Tatar stock.

But there in the waste of snow tundra, Buza had gone among strange folk, the old people of the mountains, he called them—people who sucked blood from dogs and slept for days at a time, chanting monotonously in their sleep. They told him of the icy waste that was *kanun kotan*, the land of the gods beneath the spirit gate in the sky. Buza himself saw the spirit flames soaring up the sky in darkness, lighting the white frozen world beneath, where shadows danced under the sky fires.

From the Lena's mouth the old people of the mountains— the people of the far mountains at the continent's end —brought to the cossacks a gigantic tusk, too heavy for two men to lift, a veritable fortune in ivory. The old people said this had been one of two tusks protruding from the frozen earth by the river. The tusks belonged to a beast that was the reindeer of the evil spirits. Reindeer brought good to the owners; the great beasts of the earth brought evil. So the old people were glad to give the tusk to the cossacks.

The Way from the Lena to the Great Lake

To the simple minds of these far Siberians such as the Chukchi, and in a measure the Tungusi, there was nothing strange in the coming of the cossacks from the west. The dwellers on the frozen tundras and the bare hills had known of small parties of such masters, arriving to give orders and take away fish and ivory. The Siberians merely said, "Some are slaves and some are masters." The Yakka Mongols and the dour Manchus had been masters; so, obviously, were the cossacks.

Yet if a stranger, even a Russian—an *Urusse*—killed a reindeer, the natives avoided that man as if he had the plague. For the spirit lord of the reindeer, the *vairgin*, was akin to the spirit lord of the Chukchi and Tungusi. By the reindeer these men lived, without harming them. One who slew a reindeer, even by accident, was doomed, and might be put to death by his own brother without blame or blood revenge.

It was held against these Russian masters that they slew reindeer, bears and other animals with their firearms for food, and for the skins without waiting until the animals died a lawful, natural death.

So also believed other reindeer-keepers, the Urianghi in the lands south of Baikal.

From the middle Lena toward the Arctic—directly under the invisible Arctic Circle—the Russian pioneers built their ostrogs unhindered. Up and down the river, and out to other rivers, they fortified seven posts in the seven years between 1632 and 1639, in a wide sweep of five hundred miles around Yakutsk, which had grown in that time to a stockaded town with four watchtowers at the corners, and a church inside.

Swiftly as they had made progress in the forest belt and frozen tundras, the Russian patrols faltered and penetrated only slowly to the south, from the headwaters of the Yenisei to the storm-lashed shores of Baikal. Here the forest gave way to more open *taiga*, sprinkled with willow and larch, where snow packs on the heights watered open grazing lands.

Here the Urianghi and Mongols kept their reindeer and their cattle, hunting with falcons and listening to the chants of minstrels. They were people with memories, still active and restless.

The Urianghi minstrels remembered that a man of that people had been one of the Four Torrents of Genghis Khan. When the Russians rode down from the crests, armed, they found mute stone figures standing in the open plains, facing toward the east, marking the site of old burials. The Urianghi and the Mongols would not allow the graves under these stone guardians to be dug up, to yield the gold death mask placed on the heads of the dead.

Even though the Russians sat with them in council, asking for *yasak* with words familiar to the Mongols; even though they had the same name for the long overland way, the *darogha,* to reach the ancestral graves of these eastern folk, the Mongols did not believe they had come with authority of the Great Khan.

The living Altyn Khan, titular head of the surviving western Mongols acknowledged first of all the supreme authority of the Dalai Lama in Tibet; as to the power and authority of the White Tsar, he was uncertain, having heard little news of the outer world in his fastness except what came by way of the tea caravans from China.

The Altyn Khan was willing to take the gifts sent from the White Tsar, and to place his horde under the protection of the White Tsar, but not to take oath of subservience.

"It has never been our custom," he informed the Russians, "for the Khan himself to take oath. So my envoys in Tomsk could not do that, for myself and my horde [*orda*]. They were forced to do that by your *voevodes,* who gave them bread only at the point of a knife and held swords above their necks. That kind of oath was never known to us."

Behind the Altyn Khan, across the waters of Baikal (Great Lake) and south of the Mountain of Power lay the open grasslands watered by five small rivers, the ancestral homeland of the Yakka Mongols. Somewhere there, carefully hidden, lay the grave of Genghis Khan where, the Mongol minstrels said, a white horse from the spirit world appeared on the first day of spring.

Farther on, at the caravan track, stood the ruins of the clay walls of Karakorum (Black Sands), battered by the winds, and ground by the blown sand, the site from which the Mongol kha khans had ruled their empire of the steppes, extending over Cathay and beyond Moscow.

The Russian envoys and soldiers quartered within sight of Baikal had traced their way thither from Moscow.

But they had come the northern way, along the river and portage route, through the forests, not over the great caravan routes used by the Mongols formerly, far to the south.

Failing to win the subjection of the Altyn Khan, they talked of trade agreements by which they might get furs and silver. They explained that the peoples behind them acknowledged the White Tsar and paid tribute.

The Altyn Khan of that day was a man of peace, attentive to trade but more attentive to his own honor. "I, the Altyn Khan, with all my children and blood-kin and clan and horde will be under the high hand of the Tsar's Majesty," he agreed. "But as a subject, not as a servant."

At least so the Russians said. They complained that the Altyn Khan had had the word "servant" stricken out of the agreement, and the word "subject" written instead. And the Russians in Moscow soon discovered that the Mongol Khan considered himself to be a lesser ruler than the Tsar only because the number of his people was less. Instead of paying tribute he sent gifts to Moscow with a Buddhist lama as ambassador, expecting greater gifts to be sent him by the Tsar's Majesty. The lama brought two hundred sable skins as present from his Khan, and one hundred from himself. In return, the lama presented a list of gifts that would be acceptable to the Mongols.

"For the Khan there should be things of gold and silver, and shining beadwork, strings of coral and precious stones of different colors, a good coat of iron chain-mail with a sword and a firearm with six barrels; the gift of cloth should have gold brocade; the gift of a horse should be Turkish breed—also a bell, a drum and horns for service in the temple, a telescope and a clock that strikes, along with a monk from Jerusalem to teach Christian prayers, an interpreter knowing Russian and Mongolian speech and writing, a doctor with the medicines he uses, a silversmith, a gunsmith, and a skilled leather tanner."

The lama specified for himself red coral and damask cloth, with silverwork, large and small tents, among other things. The Russians did their best to fill out the list of wanted articles; but when their envoys reached the pastures near Baikal, they discovered that the Altyn Khan now considered himself to be the faithful *ally* of the Tsar instead of a subject; when the envoys were slow to deliver the presents, the Khan parted company with them by striking his tents in the night. Whereupon the bewildered Russians found themselves beset by unruly Mongol riders, who wrested the presents from them, and carried them off—to the Altyn Khan, as it developed later. By degrees the Russians were learning the diplomacy of the far east. But they were slow to discover that the Altyn Khan, whose name had seemed so noble to them, was only a small figure among the Kirghiz, the Kalmuks and the Kazaks and the Mongols themselves.

From these the Russians received no offer to become either subjects or allies.

Curiously enough, in repeating to the Mongol the list of Michael Romanov's titles, the envoys had said that he was: "grand prince of Novgorod and Smolensk, Lifland [Livonia] . . . ruler and lord of the Karthian kings, of the Circassian and Mountain princes"—among other things. Now Moscow at that time had lost the Livonian coast, and Smolensk. And no Russian was then within close sight of the Caucasus heights where dwelt the other princes spoken of. Perhaps at one time Moscow had been able to claim sovereignty over such regions, but not now.

Yet while Moscow exaggerated its holdings in the west, it understated its territories in the east, mentioning only the Volga lands, the Urals, the Yugorian coast and the northern region of Ob.

Either the Bureau of Ceremony in Moscow had not caught up with the enormous gains in the east, or it did not care to claim sovereignty beyond the Urals. The truth seems to be that officials in Moscow were too intent on other matters to grasp the significance of Siberia, except for the wealth taken out of it. Not for another century was any semblance of government set up over the new provinces. For the time being—and for long after—the political exiles who had to stay in the country did the best work in bringing some kind of order to the Siberian settlements.

The great advance was being carried out not by war but by subjection and fusion. The native peoples were treated as the "Tsar's servants" at the time when the peasantry in the western half of the dominion was being chained to the land in serfdom.

For a generation the pioneers had made their way through subservient peoples; they had endured the bitter cold of the northernmost tundras—they had reached the Oimyakon, the "Cold Pole"; they had charted the river routes of a new continent. Nowhere had they encountered a people that could not be reduced to submission to the Tsar in Moscow, by the methodical thrusting forth of log blockhouses, armed with small cannon.

The Tungusi had been intractable as the Mordvas and Bashkirs back in the Volga territory, yet they had proved to be even more incapable of organized resistance. Never had the harvest of furs been as great in the east as during these last two generations. (In 1586 the Muscovite state had reaped more than two hundred thousand sable and black fox pelts, and a half million squirrel skins, besides the ordinary beaver and marten and the now rare ermine from "Siberia" alone. This did not include the catches of smugglers and private traders. One fourth to one third the yearly revenue of the Moscow government now came from this expanding fur trade.)

From Yakutsk to Moscow, furs had become as good a currency as silver coins. In the east they were traded for vudka, cloth, gunpowder and grain. In the cellars of Moscow they lay stored by the tens of thousands; merchants dealt in them by the "frame" of forty skins, and passed them on to foreigners by the hundreds in exchange for luxuries from abroad. Again as in the century before, in Ivan's time, Moscow was accumulating huge stocks of raw stuff which could not easily be converted into wealth by exchange with the west.

In the account books of the Kremlin, "Siberia" had become a gold mine without gold; its *expenses* for nondescript soldiery and staffs of inspectors and taxgatherers at the few terminals and ostrogs were measured in hundreds of rubles, against an intake of thousands. And the bureaus at Moscow still pressed the eastern frontier posts for more silver, and the always illusive precious stones and gold. Outcroppings and mines opened up through the Urals and around Baikal only whetted the appetite of the bureaus for more of the precious metals. "Siberia" had been added to the list of dominions of the Muscovite Tsar; in official orders the native peoples of the far east had become "servants" to be administered by "those who served" the Tsar's government.

As Batu Khan, with his census takers and taxgatherers, had dominated the Muscovites four centuries before, the Muscovites of 1640 dominated the mild peoples of Siberia, drawing wealth from them but making no attempt to colonize their territories.

In taking this toll of the east the men of Moscow seemed not to realize that they were in turn accepting the influence of the east. While the fortified stockades of Yakutsk and Yeniseisk remained closed to the native folk (who were not allowed to remain inside the walls) the settlers themselves interbred with the natives and adapted themselves to the native way of life.

There was not then—nor for long centuries—any cultural influence emanating from Moscow strong enough to infuse energy into the easterners. Before such influence appeared (in the middle of the nineteenth century) the passive way of life in the east had made its impress on the Russian character.

The Eastern Ocean Sea

The long Siberian way had taken a most curious course. It had not been a thrust directly to the east; from the very start it tended sharply north, away from the warmest and most fertile land.

Down at the barrier of the Caucasus, the Cossack outposts stood at latitude 43; midway across Eurasia, at Kuznetsk, they were as far up as 52 degrees; Yakutsk lay about 63. It was as if, in journeying east, the pioneers had climbed invisible steps toward the region of Arctic cold.

There were two reasons for this slant to the north. The voyagers had been following the rivers which all flowed to the Arctic, seeking above all things the best fur regions, which also lay within the forest belt, and toward extreme cold. But the compelling reason was that the hunters, the adventurers and settlers *could not* enter the southlands.

Below the forest belt lay the open steppe and desert where the warlike peoples of mid-Eurasia dominated. These were still nomadic at heart, and their strong hosts of horsemen were still too powerful for the Russians to meet in the open plains. Jenkinson, among the Turkomans and Uzbeks of the Bokhara deserts, had tasted their fierce temper; the Don Cossacks had been decimated in their raid on Khiva.

Farther on, in the open plains between the Sea of Aral and Baikal, the wild Kazaks, the three hordes of the Kirghiz, and the Black Kalmuks held fast to the former Mongol khanates.

The pagan Kalmuks in fact were never to submit to outside rule. "The Kalmuks," their chieftains were to inform the Russian authorities long after, "have always been free; they have not been slaves to anyone, nor will they ever be."

In their own steppes the Mongols were too dangerous to warrant an intrusion. These Turkic-Mongol peoples, formidable as the Krim khans, extended in a long oblique line up to the very shore of the Eastern Ocean Sea, where the Manchus had been descending from their homeland and possessing themselves of China, as the Moghuls had done in India, from the northern mountains.

Where the Russian advance had tended south at all or had left the protection of the forest belt, it had come into collision with the steppe peoples. At the headwaters of the Ob, where timber and hills projected into the plains, the Kirghiz attacked the ostrogs at Kuznetsk and Krasnoyarsk on the Yenisei, burning crops and storming at the log forts persistently.

These posts were abandoned later, temporarily.

The power of the middle Eurasian peoples centered about the through caravan routes, the great trade cities of Khiva, Bokhara, Samarkand and Kashgar. Not for generations would the Russians make any real impression upon their dominion.

Nor did Moscow try to set up any defense for Siberia at first. The defense cordons, the carefully prepared lines and outposts of the west manned by "those who served," ended at the Volga. Only about Moscow itself, to the south and west, in that corner of the dominion, was the frontier fortified. Beyond the Volga, Moscow would only send some powder and men, with advice on how the settlers were to protect themselves—and to keep the outer hostile peoples embroiled against each other. Moscow referred to the Kirghiz and Kalmuks as "His Majesty's traitors" and "rebels."

The way to Cathay lay far to the south. At the least, it should have taken the Russians along the Altai (Golden) Mountains, and the Blue Lake, past the ruins of Karakorum, down the caravan track to the Great Wall and the gates of Pe-king (The North Court).

Perhaps the counselors in Moscow knew this. They had heard from an explorer other than the cossack Petlin that China must be a small country, because it was all enclosed in a high brick·wall! They had tried to drink the strange effusion called *chai*, tea, made out of dark leaves soaked in hot water, flavored with milk—that the Altyn Khan had sent as his latest tribute, and they had not liked it.

But out in the far frontier, at Yakutsk, and Krasnoyarsk, the settlers had discovered that they could not advance in that direction. The Mongols and Kara Kirghiz held fast to the region around Lake Baikal; there was no getting past such mobile horsemen. The "cossacks and hunters" could maintain themselves behind log fortifications, with cannon and guns; they could not advance with their hundreds into the open, in the face of thousands of intractable horsemen.

Yet they heard accounts from the Tungusi and Mongols of rich forest land to the east, or a river that wound south to a warmer climate, and of the open sea that lay

Dutch navigators killing a bear, during their search for the northeast passage through the Ice Sea, beginning of seventeenth century. The phenomenon of manifold polar suns seemed to them to be "a wonder in the sky." (Hakluyt Society)

beyond. They knew the name of that river, the Amur (the River of Peace).

Checked in their advance eastward from Baikal, the pioneer forces did what they had done often before—they swung north, and around the obstacles.

Search parties quested northeast from Yakutsk, building winter quarters, and feeling their way from river to river, over the mountain ridges. Some went as far as the Lena's mouth, into the true Arctic, and followed that barren coast to descend the next river. In so doing they were advancing toward the exteme northeastern tip of the continent, where the natives were mild Chukchi and Tungusi.

After three years of this, in 1639, a band of no more than twenty men, circling far north, came out at the mouth of a small river to the ice-coated shore and the horizon of the sea to the east. This was the coastal bend known as the Okhotsk Sea. They brought back sables taken from the natives but no gold or silver.

They brought back word from the native fishing tribes that this mist- and ice-filled stretch of the Eastern Sea was really no more than a great arm of that sea between an island (Sakhalin) and a jutting peninsula (Kamchatka). Probably they had no idea that a little to the south of the island lay a chain of other islands populated by unknown natives, Japan.

Still, they had set foot on the shore of the Eastern Ocean Sea. And that shore was marked down vaguely on their sketch maps, which they turned in to the military commanders at Yakutsk.

The searchers went out as volunteers, asking permission and begging money for supplies. They were the hunters and cossacks who had spearheaded the long march into the northeast that had paid such rich returns in furs, tribute and glory to the court at Moscow. Still unaware that they had reached the end of a continent, they probed again and again through the ridges of the barrier mountains and along the ice of the rivers, learning to build the skin canoes, the *kayaks,* of the natives. But for once they had no tidings of people existing somewhere beyond—only of a region of unknown gods. Nor, this time, did they have the rumored report of some voyager to give them an inkling of what they might find.

At times the natives, the Chuchi, resisted with their spears, saying that the strangers "dipped their hands in blood."

As before, the explorers were plotting the courses of the small rivers patiently. Yet here in the Arctic, no convenient portages led from watercourse to watercourse. They had to find the river mouths by pushing further along the coast. In 1644 they built a winter post in the ice of the Kolima's mouth.

At times they found small troves of walrus tusks in the dunes, and they still found good sables and white fox. Only, what lay *beyond* they could not ascertain. On the eastern arm of the ocean (Okhotsk) they erected an ostrog for the use of the hunters.

In 1647 an expedition set out for this unknown terrain, between the farthest river of the Arctic shore, the Kolima, and that great bay of the Eastern Ocean Sea, the Okhotsk. Like the others, it left Yakutsk in the brief breath of warm autumn air when water flowed freely down the rivers into the Arctic ice, making a channel for large boats. It was headed by a merchant, Aleksiev, and a Cossack of Yakutsk, Semen Dezhnev; it sought walrus tusks and tribute from the Arctic tribes, and it disappeared into the gathering winter's night.

For seven years only fragments of the expedition turned up. Aleksiev had died. Some tusks had been found along

the coast: some scanty furs were sent in. The Cossack Dezhnev continued to search the bare mountains, and to feel his
way mile by mile along the coast, changing from sleds to
boats made by his men.

While Dezhnev was lost to sight in the northern mountains, the pioneer forces of Yakutsk sought for the mysterious Amur River. They heard of gold to be found on its
banks. And as always, they searched for tributaries that
would lead to the great river, dragging their boats from
stream to stream, working to the south.

South they went, out of the frozen lands, finding themselves in good forests swarming with dark fur-bearing animals. They found grain growing in the wide Amur valley.

Under the leader Poyarkov a small force traded and fought
its way down the widening Amur, to emerge at the edge of
the familiar Sea of Okhotsk. Hunters found a shorter portage route cutting across from the Lena to the great Amur.

Beyond the Amur, however, they entered cultivated fields
that had been abandoned, where the standing grain was
burned. Instead of isolated villages that could be plundered
piecemeal, they met here a sullen countryside and learned
that these people were subject to the Manchus who had
captured Pe-king a few years before.

At Baikal, the Mongols warned the Russians of the power
of the Manchu Emperor: "The Bogdi Tsar of the North
Court holds silver mines and iron mines; he has brass cannon and firearms just as your Tsar has."

A flotilla manned by three hundred pioneers sent to explore the Amur met constant combat from elusive bands of
horsemen who refused to be driven off. The three hundred,
eager to occupy the fertile banks, fought off a massed attack
by the horsemen yet could not maintain their hold on the
river and were forced back to the ostrog in the highlands.

Here the ostrogs could not be pushed along the river basin,
where crops had been destroyed and herds driven off. The
pioneers could raid down the river, subsisting on meat
and fish. Lacking colonists to follow them and occupy the
land, they were forced to turn back again after a raid. They
could not wrest the soil from a hostile peasantry.

Here on the Amur, they were thousands of miles from
Moscow, and no army came from Moscow to aid them.
By 1648 the Russian advance was stopped at the Amur.
Irkutsk was built on the west shore of Lake Baikal.

There was no way around. Below Baikal the Mongol horsemen barred the road across the steppe.

And soon the Cossack Dezhnev appeared again. He had been missing for seven years and he brought back few survivors, and little gain. But he had worked his way from the rivers on the Arctic coast to the Anadyr on the eastern coast.

He had rounded the tip of the continent, passing through the strait that would be named after another navigator, Bering, a century later. Certainly he had seen no other land seaward, only ice.

There seemed to be nothing more beyond.

At this time, in the middle of the century, a chronicler writing in Moscow, by the river, paused in his narration to wonder, "What man ever thought or divined that Moscow would become a kingdom, or what man ever knew that Moscow would be accounted an Empire?"

By then the town of Moscow had become the Russian Empire.

VI

THE FORCE OF THE EMPIRE, AND THE RESISTANCE OF THE FRONTIERS

Moscow, 1648

IN THE events of these few years the forces that created the empire are perceptible. When it took shape, it assumed the strangest of shapes, with Moscow, its central power, almost at its far western edge. There, too, was concentrated its population, for there were little more than fifty thousand *Russians* in the three million square miles of its dominion to the east. It had formed around the river routes, keeping to the forest zone. It had been shaped in this fashion by the pioneers, the traders, and by the government agents who followed trade, except where its course had been opposed.

Colonists following the pioneers were occupying the land very slowly. But what they occupied, they would keep. Patiently, almost imperceptibly, they were pushing down into the better grain-producing lands of the south.

In Moscow, at the middle of this century, there reigned a hereditary Tsar, a Romanov, beside a Patriarch of the Orthodox Church. It would not matter henceforth, except in rare cases like that of Peter the great Romanov, what man headed the state in Moscow. The growth would go on, as a glacier adheres together in small particles and moves by the force of inward stress.

In the Kremlin, on the height now almost treeless, were grouped the cathedrals, the palaces and the council halls of an empire, within the battlements designed by Fioraventi's architects.

To these had been added an arsenal.

By the Neglina brook a factory had risen where foreigners and Russians cast cannon and ammunition. (Other factories made glass, potash and clocks.)

At Tula, near by, munition works turned out cannon and

matchlocks. For the Russian army was being remodeled on the new European plan, drilled by foreign officers, veterans of the Thirty Years' War which had just ended. A chronicler of Moscow wrote that never before had so many Russian infantry been seen armed with the new firearms. In 1647 a pamphlet was printed by the Razriadni Prikaz, entitled *The Teaching and Skill of Our Warlike Body of Foot Soldiers*.

To the west of Moscow and toward the Baltic these armed forces had resumed action against the Polish plain and the Lake Ladoga region.

By 1648 the new southern frontier defense line—breast-works in the forest, ditches and ramparts in the open, and wooden *gulai gorodi* by the "black roads"—had been moved south of Voronezh (some three hundred miles from Moscow) to Bielgorod and the ostrog at Kharkov in the steppe, and had been finished at great expense.

Against such heavy taxation and the demand for labor there had been mute rebellion in Moscow. This happened also in towns like Tver and Viatka, which remained agricultural, keeping to the old ways and not sharing in the industrial development of Moscow.

Such disturbances in the cities brought about an assembly of the land, which passed rigid laws confining peasants to their fields and shops. In 1649 serfdom became a fact, in the west.

With serfdom in the Moscow region, men were joined to the land as property. After that, the state dealt with its human occupants of the land in terms of the land itself. At long last the earth of Rus had absorbed its cultivators.

Inarticulate, popular resentment against the new laws and foreign ways brought about a drift of peasantry and workers away from Moscow. In churches and monasteries a cleavage grew between "Old Believers" and the followers of new ritual. Religious persecution led to flight from churches in the west, into the east. Priests joined the peasantry seeking to escape from serfdom into the "wild lands."

A greater cleavage separated the new Russia from Europe beyond the Constantinople-Riga axis—as utterly as under the Tatar dominion. Western Europe, turning to the new sciences, had forged far ahead of this still medieval Russia.

There was growing in Moscow a great hunger for the knowledge of books. Savants, "men of wisdom," were sought from the west, to develop mines, build ships, dye cloth.

At the same time the merchants of Moscow rebelled against the long-standing control of trade by foreigners—forcing the Kremlin to end the special privileges of the English and the

Dutch in 1649. (Few English vessels put in at Archangel then; the loss fell heaviest upon the Dutch shipping, which virtually served as Moscow's merchant marine.)

Silently the people resisted service in the enlarged army, trained by foreign officers.

By 1650 so far was Moscow from control of the vast new land and its peoples that it was a question whether the city could in the end master the continent, or whether it would pass from power like Kiev, or Karakorum or Constantinople.

In this empire, like no other within the old world, the heart of the people lay not in Moscow but out in the new lands beyond the Urals, in the settlements where the folk formed the old pattern of communal *mirs,* aiding each other with food and labor, reading for the first time the Scriptures printed in Slavonic—even if by candlelight—slowly, like very young children.

Down in the fertile Ukraine unrest had burst into revolt against the authority of the north, in this case that of Poland. Here, too, it was partly a rising of the ill-armed peasantry, partly religious reaction, against the Catholic priesthood. Cossacks from the Dnieper encampment—the Zaporogians— spearheaded it. A Cossack, Bogdan Khmielnitsky, led this uprising. The Krim Tatars were enlisted as allies, their *orda* moving in force from the Black Sea shore.

The resistance movement grew in strength, sweeping up the Dnieper, blotting out garrisons, looting the towns, drawing contingents of masterless men from the swamps by the river and the "wild lands" and hermits from roadside shrines. For a while its untamed force broke through opposition. Khmielnitsky was called "chief of the Zaporogian host, and of all the Cossack-Russian Ukraine."

This struggle aimed at self-rule for the Ukraine, and— vaguely in the hopes of its followers—for release from land and war service. But in spite of Khmielnitsky's daring and cunning it broke down in discord. The Tatars drew off with their loot, leaving the Dnieper Cossacks alone to act as masters in a disordered land. The Cossacks themselves knew no authority except that of their military commanders, nor could they forge an effective army out of the vagrant peasantry. Khmielnitsky discovered that an independent Ukraine could not stand between the frontiers of Turkey, Poland and Russia.

In the end his Ukrainians retreated back to their river, and drifted across it to the left bank. Here the tie of religion bound them to Moscow. In 1654 Khmielnitsky, Hetman of the Ukraine, and his Cossacks acknowledged the suzerainty of Moscow.

By doing so they added to Russia all the lower Dnieper, the ancient road of the Variags, the city of Kiev—now thriving again and making an advance of its own in culture—and a strip of the Black Sea coast. This lost land of the Ukraine came to be called Little Russia. It lay 130 degrees of longitude distant from the Kolima River, and the shore of the Eastern Ocean Sea.

Farther north, up the ancient river route, the mixed Slavs of the "western lands"—called White Russia—turned toward the authority of Moscow.

There followed an explosion of conflict between Russian and Polish forces in the Ukraine, in the years that became "the time of ruin" of the Ukraine.

Revolt of Stenka Razin

As the western Ukraine had risen against authority, so the Volga lands resisted Moscow, from the year 1667. As the Zaporogian Cossacks had headed the first movement, the Don brotherhood and the Cossacks of the Urals joined in the second. As the Krim Tatars had aided the first, the pagan Kalmuks from mid-Asia linked their forces to the second for a time. With them at least two other native peoples rose against authority—the restless Mordvas and the wild Bashkir breeders of cattle.

So, in a true sense, the former Volga frontier marched against the central authority of Moscow, as the Tatars had done before the loss of Kazan.

Not that these Cossacks and the subjected people did not acknowledge the sovereignty of a tsar. As the Cossacks took their own atamans for granted, and the native peoples their khans, mirzas and princes, so they accepted the person of a ruler. "To war we will go," the Don Cossack spokesmen said, "for the sovereign tsar and grand prince of Great and Little and White Russia, the Autocrat, and Lord of many Hordes." They even had with them a boy who was declared to be the rightful son (a memory of the many Dmitris) of the Tsar. They rebelled against the rapacious officials, the taxation and the conscripted soldiery of Moscow.

"*Saryn na Kitchkou!*" they cried along the river. "Kindle up, and slay. Kill the guardsmen, and go to Moscow to burn the oppressors." This revolt against Moscow soon reacted upon officials and great property owners in the scattered towns, and particularly upon the Streltsi garrisons. Against these garrisons surged masses of Tatar tribesmen, "Naked" wanderers, peasants, small traders and Volga boatmen.

Mixed as these elements appear to be, in reality they formed an entity, the population of the Volga River lands. And they clung to one idea, liberation. The man at the head of the revolt they called the Liberator. He was Stenka (Stephen) Razin.

"They called him Father," relates John Struys, a young Dutch merchant-adventurer who found himself on the Volga at the time. "He had the ability to make himself feared, and the gift of being loved."

Stenka Razin was from the Don Cossacks, like Irmak a physical giant, with an instinct for action, able to hold the devotion of his followers. The Cossacks say his front teeth had been broken off in fighting, his nostrils torn out in prison, and that his left shoulder had been branded with the name of Cain. They insist that when Stenka Razin was going to sentence men to death, he had a way of baring that shoulder and saying, "That is the mark of Cain you see on me, and I bear it for good reason."

Struys believed he vowed enmity against all Muscovites for a wrong done his brother. At first he plundered merchants' ships along the Volga, his men drifting up to anchored vessels at night in longboats camouflaged with sheaves of rushes to look like islets floating down the tide. There a large force of Don Cossacks joined him, and together they ranged the waterways, down into the blue Caspian, and back through the salt marshes up the Ural River.

The Cossacks—who seemed to have confused Razin a little in their memories with Irmak—tell that he feared nothing, and was impervious to sword cuts or bullets. His first lieutenant was Filka the Devil; he enjoyed the mock religious ceremonies practiced by a renegade priest, Chvedar, and the other mockeries of a Tatar jester—that he was *zakoldovan*, by which they mean that he had gone into a church on Easter night, and spat out the Communion wine and bread. Chvedar officiated at many marriages of women to Razin—a hundred and fifty, the Cossacks say.

At the masthead of his ship hung a red rag and a dog's skull as a pledge that he would bite the Muscovite boyars. His men had a song:

> From the white island
> On Mother Volga
> Stenka Razin's brethren
> Sail with a merry song——

Stenka Razin our Father,
The Devil our admiral—
Sing a song, princess,
For we are merry today.

The Cossack fleet cruised the Caspian, putting in at ports
where they were not known. "He had a trick," Struys says,
"of sending in word that he planned no injury to the people
of the town but only wished to buy goods of which his
army had need. After reassuring them in this manner, so
that they did not flee, he went among them himself, speaking
in friendly fashion, and buying some stuff or other from
them, for which he paid. Then he turned his cap around
on his head as a signal. His troops fell upon the townspeople,
killing them quickly and seizing and carrying off their goods."

Apparently at this time Razin was content to range the
Caspian, making an island near the Persian coast his base.
On their part, the Persians have a tradition that he landed
there, calling himself simply "lord of the sea," and occupied
a castle, which he shared with a girl of noble blood and her
brother.

The Persian girl seems to have accompanied Razin on his
voyages because the Cossacks of his ship remonstrated—
distrusting his obsession with the woman—that she would
bring them all ill luck, and that he must get rid of her.

Struys, who was in Astrakhan near the Volga mouths at
the time, claims to have seen the Persian. According to him,
Razin appeared from the islands off the river's mouth with
twenty vessels and six hundred men, "even the meanest of
them wearing silk or cloth of gold, so that Razin himself
could only be distinguished by the respect they paid him."
But the Volga pirates were then in want of food, having eaten
up the thoroughbred horses sent by the Shah of Persia as a
gift to the Tsar, and they were glad to accept a truce from
the governor-commander of Astrakhan, to sell stuff in the
markets for food. Razin himself was offered amnesty by the
officials if he would swear to serve the government.

"We found him," John Struys relates, "on the river, in a
bark all painted and gilded, with his confidant, called Devil's
Mustache, drinking and making merry with some officers.
He had with him a Persian princess whom he had brought
off on one of his last raids, with her brother. The brother he
presented to the Governor of Astrakhan, and kept the princess
whom he loved . . . he had a way of being drunk at the
end of the day, and that habit cost the miserable Persian dear.

"Heavy with drink, he leaned against the rail of the bark,
and looked down in a muse for a while at the water of the

Volga. 'There's no river like you,' he said then. 'All that I am I owe to you, and what have I ever done to satisfy you? Nothing! I will give you the best thing I have.'

"Then hurrying to the princess he threw her into the river, all dressed up as she was in cloth-of-gold, pearls and precious stones. This poor princess did not deserve such a fate, and there was no one who did not grieve for her. Disgusted as she was at being penned up on the vessel with him, she still had a liking for him, and let him do what he wished with her. . . . Brutal as Razin was, he would hardly have done that if he had not been drunk."

The Cossacks believed that he sacrificed the girl to prove his loyalty to them, and to "Mother Volga." Behind this belief of theirs and the imaginative report of the young Hollander there is the shadowy outline of a Stenka Razin intent on more then revelry and plundering.

This Razin never became articulate. In 1669 he sat in talk with the Kalmuk khans and then crossed over to the Don, to observe the situation among the brotherhood there. The unrest of the countryside invoked a leader, and he accepted the leadership of the revolt rather than the amnesty from Moscow. With the Volga rivermen, the Cossack *kurens* and Tatar tribes, with fisherfolk and the aroused peasantry trooping into his bark on the great river, he raised the strangest of all war cries, "For God and Allah, for our Sovereign and the Cossack Host."

The river became the thoroughfare of the revolt against the governors, the hired soldiery, the secretaries and the tax collectors of Moscow. Stenka Razin's fleet moved on the towns, while Cossack and Tatar horsemen cut the communications of the garrisons by land.

The first town approached was Astrakhan, formidable on its island, defended by a strong city wall mounted with cannon, and the citadel of the governor's palace. One of the foreign officers, a certain David Butler, perhaps a Scot, kept a dispassionate diary of the days during which the countryside rose against the garrison in Astrakhan, and this diary is quoted by John Struys.

"The first day of March in the year sixteen hundred and seventy an order came from the Court for all men of the river service to return to Moscow. Very gladly, everyone in our crew set about obeying, and for my part I was charged to see that the ship was provided with new gear and supplies, in readiness to serve at need against the Cossacks. My bark was equipped, and fresh water taken in by April.

"On the tenth of that month a detachment was formed of eight hundred men, half Muscovites, half Tatars, and sent up to Saritzin under the lord Bogdanov. Saritzin is the town on the Volga nearest the river Don to which the Cossacks drag their barks—which are built of heavy timber crudely shaped—by a long road over land.

"On the twenty-eighth we discovered from a hostile prisoner that the Cossacks had taken Saritzin where the garrison of a thousand or twelve hundred was cut to pieces. At the same time news came in that the Tatars were divided and fighting among themselves. Bogdanov had withdrawn to Charnojar, a town fifty leagues above Astrakhan. As soon as we learned that, the Governor fitted out all vessels at hand and sent them to aid him, under command of John Rusinsky, a Polish colonel. Monday, the twenty-fifth May, forty barks were sent with fifteen hundred men, all Poles or Muscovites except for a reserve of some Germans of the English captain Robert Hein and Nicholas Schak my lieutenant who had been made a captain.

"This same day they hung the Cossack prisoner of whom I spoke in sight of all the [remaining] troops after making him endure extraordinary tortures. From that day we heard nothing in the city but mutinous grumbling. I bought some silks and furs from the Surgeon of the Ambassador who had just returned from the court of Persia.

"The fourth June we heard from a Nobleman that the very day our Muscovite troops appeared before Charnojar they had mutinied under the excuse that the enemy forces were stronger than they had been told, and that the officers who remonstrated with them had all been killed. This news alarmed everyone, and the Governor ordered me to take charge of the cannon, and to make very sure that nothing lacked for them. The trouble worsening, on the fifth we fetched ashore the gear and ammunition from our ship, loaded the cannon [on the Astrakhan fortifications] and made ready to drive off the dog-pack that only waited to unmask itself and mock the Governor. The Surgeon I have mentioned knew the humors of the Muscovites and he assured me that if the popular murmuring lasted from day to day, it would break out [in action] before the eighth day. In such case, the foreigners would be the first attacked. He added that since our wages had not been paid, we were no longer employed, and we had better contrive how to get away while there was still time.

"I put it up to my officers, what they thought best to do. All wanted to get away quietly, even agreeing to take nothing

THE FORCE OF THE EMPIRE

with them but the clothes they were in. My store of precious stuffs—which I did not want to lose—they decided to pack into two small chests. I ordered them to carry out some supplies to the ship secretly, without being observed. But the crewmen took also two of their women who had borne children, and these were seen. . . .

"I decided to wait out the troubles, and the Surgeon agreed with me. I sent the ship's master to warn our other people who were on the bark of our change of plan. But, finding the gate closed before the usual hour, he could not speak with them. I spent the night uneasily. In the morning as soon as the gate was opened I sent a sailor out to the vessel; then I went after him, and found as I had suspected that everyone was gone, with the vessel.

"The same day the Governor ordered the Nobleman who had brought the news of the mutiny up the river, to leave for Moscow with word of the situation. He told me before starting out that he had never seen anger like that of the Cossacks against the Muscovites—that they were unquestionably in touch with the townspeople.

"The ninth June I made the round of the city fortifications with an English Reformist [i.e., Cromwell veteran] colonel up from the Caspian. When we came in the Governor asked our opinion how the city could be defended. For my part I advised that, instead of going through so many useless antics, we announce an amnesty for all who had joined the rebellion, if they returned to their duty—and offer largesse to their leaders. My advice was not taken.

"However, our garrison troops were carrying out orders scrupulously, the Persians, Circassians and Kalmuks even making the rounds in step to their trumpets and cymbals, with unseasonable enjoyment.

"On the fifteenth, I dined at the Governor's table, and afterwards he gave me a fine satin robe, with boots and shirts, thanking me courteously for the good discipline I kept among my hundred men. The nineteenth, we had word that the Cossacks were approaching by fast marches, and the news was confirmed by fishermen and peasants who thronged into the city.

"In the alarm that followed the commanding officers got the idea somehow that our cannon, instead of being properly loaded, had been charged with the wadding driven in before the powder and shot. I discharged one cannon to show the Governor that the loading had been as it should be. That day my shipmaster gave some ridiculous advice about the defense of the city, and was put in charge of the Wosnosinsky gate. Two days later I was posted where the city wall is weakest, after the Governor promoted me to be Lieutenant.

"That same day the Cossacks came in sight. They sent a man and a priest with a summons to the city to surrender. Besides, they brought a letter in German to me, advising me to keep my men out of action, and to do nothing myself if I wished to live. The Governor tore his letter in two before reading to its end, and immediately ordered the two envoys to be beheaded.

"Next day some three hundred barks of the enemy sailed in to the shore, at a vineyard half a league from the city. As they landed, we set fire to the Tatar suburb. Observing from the roof of the Governor's house that some fishing craft came and went up the river, I told him we should not allow that—poor stuff as the fisherman might be, they could carry intelligence out to the enemy and back. Taking my advice, he had the fishing craft destroyed. He had two fishermen hung, and two drowned.

"On the twenty-third we gave out a hogshead of strong beer to the soldiers, and some tobacco also, which one of the Emperor's agents had given us. That night, after making the round of the ramparts with two of my fellows, I threw myself down on a mattress to sleep for an hour or two. But some one woke me, saying that the rebels had begun to attack and were at the Wosnosinsky gate.

"Being able to make out a company of them advancing, I began to fire our cannon. At the same time Thomas Bailly, an English colonel armed with a breastplate, came to find me with several German officers. He let me know that they were betrayed, and that his soldiers had injured him in the face and arms when he had tried to make them resist the attack.

"Although treason was clearly to be seen, and I did not doubt him, I pretended to believe that things were not as bad as he made out, and advised him to go back to his post. He went back with the others, and at first their soldiers seemed ready to follow out orders. But an hour later I was told they had all been massacred by their men. At the same time a German captain standing very near me was seized by his servants, and tied and killed.

"This sight frightened the Surgeon who was with me then, who wanted, in spite of me, to jump from the parapet of the wall to the ground, to escape the traitors. I stopped him by saying I knew a better way than that.

"I had noticed a sally door at the base of a tower, very near. To this I led him, with his valet and two men of my crew. When we descended to the door, the sentries there recognized me and let us pass—the Surgeon first, then me. But we saw nothing more of the valet and the sailors.

"As soon as we were out, we plunged into the water up to our necks, to try to reach the Tatar suburb, which would be our best chance of safety—guilding ourselves by the musket shots overhead. We went on for a quarter of an hour and found a small boat in which a man was sleeping. Him we made take us to the other shore of the river. Then he led us to a village, where there were only fishermen.

"Seeing that we were still too near the city to be safe, I worked to persuade our guide to lead us on. I had some thirty-five Holland francs on me with which I bought a tent, ten pounds of bread and an ax. After two or three hours we met fishermen who took us to their huts, where we found a colonel and two captains, all Muscovites, with forty-six soldiers. This company was on the way to Astrakhan, not knowing that it had fallen into the hands of the Cossacks.

"The colonel made up his mind to go back, down river with his two captains, leaving the men at the huts. All five of us got into a small boat, launching it down stream but keeping close to the bank for fear of being seen.

"Toward the end of the day we noticed a bark following us. As it made sail to come up with us, we strained to make speed with our oars. But it was a useless effort—we fell into the hands of the pursuers. They were the forty-six soldiers we had left behind. Angered, they had determined to get back at us. We were so few and badly armed we could make no fight of it, nor keep them from stripping us naked. After that they tied our feet and rowed us back to the fishermen we had left that morning.

"There they shut the colonel up in a church, telling him to pray all he liked, and tied up the rest of us cruelly while they drew cards for our gear . . . the Surgeon offered them five hundred florins for my ransom and two hundred and fifty for his, but the men said they would have to take us over to Astrakhan, but they would do what they could to keep us alive.

"About six or seven in the evening we entered Astrakhan and were taken at once before Razin, Chief of the Cossacks. This Chief demanded of the Surgeon who he was, and, finding out, sent him to treat the wounded, assuring him his life.

"Razin asked me the same question, and the Surgeon answered that I was his comrade, before they took him away.

" 'But you,' Stenka Razin persisted, 'what do you know how to do?' I said nothing, because the Surgeon who had spoken up for me well had claimed me. So I stood there alone, thinking death inevitable.

"Razin was sitting in the street in front of the Bishop's house, drinking with his officers who were as drunk as he or almost so. They questioned the colonel, and sentenced him to be thrown from top to bottom of the tower known as the Ruscat, whence the Governor and his Chancellor had been thrown after being made to suffer all that the cruelty of these barbarians could imagine. The rest of the officers were either hewn into separate pieces or drowned.

"While I waited my time, Stenka turned to look at me steadily, and ordered spirits given me. I was on the point of falling down from weakness. Two great mugs of this drink stiffened me comfortably. I was able to walk over to his armed men, where he ordered me to go.

"They took me to a boat near that of the general. There I was recognised by a soldier who said to the widow of an officer I was luckier than her husband because I was still breathing. This he kept repeating to others, among them a young German who, after seeing the carnage wrought among the foreigners, had joined the Cossacks, pretending friendship for them. When he discovered where I was, he sought me out and promised that he would look out for me, but I did not think my life would last much longer. . . .

"For four or five days I stayed there, and hardly an hour passed that I did not see some one die, either cut to pieces or hung up by the heels. They fixed a hook in the side of the Secretary, Alexis and hung him up by it. . . .

"On the twenty-first, the general left Astrakhan, taking twelve hundred men in a swarm of small boats with him. He left twenty men out of every hundred in the city, under two Governors, both Cossacks like himself."

Stenka Razin found, as others were to discover after him, that he could not hold such an army together for long. The populace that joined his Cossacks at each town melted away during the campaign in the field. He hoped to march on Moscow, yet had no allies within that important city. When he moved west from the Volga region he was defeated by government troops, and the rebellion broke down. Razin himself sought safety on the Don, the sanctuary of escaping men. There he was betrayed to a government detachment by some wealthy Cossacks.

"In a house near the river," the Cossack tradition has it, "he was with his woman Alena, who was really his woman. The Voevode Prince Gagarin and a company of musketeers surrounded the house, and after Razin had killed some of them, he came out and gave himself up, saying, 'Take me, dogs. I am ready.'

"In the great square by the Kremlin, many thousands of people watched Stenka Razin drawn to his execution in a cart by six black oxen. He held a candle burning in his hand, and he listened to the music that was playing. As a last favor, he asked to smoke two pipes. His body was burned for three days, and the ashes were sprinkled with holy water to exorcise evil spirits."

By the curious selectivity of Russian popular memory, Stenka Razin's name became linked to that of the fabulous Ilya of Murom, and Irmak, the son of the Don, and Ivan the Terrible, who captured Kazan and killed his son. Razin's song was sung as often as the chant of the nameless Volga boatmen.

To his following, Razin had personified freedom (if not license) to follow their own way of life. His memory was bound up in that hope, the more because after his death Cossack autonomy from the Dnieper to the Don, Volga and Urals began to yield to Muscovite overlordship.

Paradoxically, these revolts did not arise against the authority of a tsar, as such, nor against Moscow as the seat of government. The popular concept never questioned the Tsar as *guardian* of his many peoples, even as guardian ordained by God. Nor did it question the physical Moscow as the city that was at the same time the abode of Tsar and Patriarch, of shrines and miracle-working images.

These outlying lands, in the Ukraine, the Volga plain and the Urals had developed their own resources, their growth had been almost entirely spontaneous; their varied peoples had coalesced after a rude fashion of their own; they remained agricultural and pastoral, engaged for the most part only in local trade which still relied on barter. They rebelled against Moscow as the base of serfdom and conscription, the metropolis of foreign ways and trade. Moscow was revered as "Holy Mother Moscow" and hated as the breeding ground of officials avid for gain as the Mongol "Squeezers" of the past.

Retreat of the Old Believers

While the lands of the Volga revolted under Stenka Razin, another struggle convulsed the Russians inwardly. The Old Believers, the *Raskolniki*—Dissenters—withdrew themselves forcibly from the authority of Church and State in Moscow, as the Puritans had done the generation before in England. Moved by mysticism, aroused to defend an intangible belief, the Raskolniks drew apart by thousands, turning their backs on the ritual of the Metropolitan in Moscow, on the imported science of the west, on "German-lovers" and newly published prayer books, these uncounted thousands sought escape in the "wild lands" as flocks followed their priests into the steppe, or along the river roads of the pioneers into the eastern forests.

Their resistance of the spirit never came to a single head; they merged into no one group but scattered, seeking sanctuary, beyond the Urals, finding their way to the far Altai and even across the Dnieper to the border towns of the Turks.

With them wandered elderly souls who looked for vampires in dark ravines, vagrants questing for new beginnings, throngs that fled with the dread of Antichrist at their heels, as well as hardheaded farmers and men of wealth who made good colonists beyond the Volga.

While controversy raged within the churches and monasteries of the Moscow area as to whether a blessing must be given with two fingers or three outstretched, or whether the Alleluia should be repeated twice, a deep emotional cleavage grew between the Old Believers and the New. It came from the tenacity of the Russian spirit, holding to what was peculiarly its own—to the ikon painting of old Novgorod, the choral music of the Slavs, the legends of the Russian saints.

Groups sought to purify themselves by flagellation; willingly they endured exile, or burned themselves, locked in their churches, rather than be made to endure what seemed to them to be the ritual of Antichrist.

They tended to vanish into obscurity, and they left almost no records even when they swelled the increasing drift of population to the eastward (beyond the Urals that population might have been seventy thousand in 1662; it would be close to a million in 1783). One of their voices has come down to us in written words, that of the Archpriest Avvakum. And Avvakum had a tongue to defend himself, when he did not use his fists.

Somehow his words echo the spirit of an inarticulate people, and in them is renewed the refrain of the Song of Igor's Arming, the fiery letters of Ivan the Terrible, the music of a Rimsky-Korsakov.

"In the morning came the Archimandrite with the brothers," Avvakum relates,[1] "and they led me away; they spoke

[1] Quoted from the remarkable translation by Jane Harrison and Hope Mirrlees of the seventeenth-century text, *The Life of the Archpriest Avvakum by Himself*, published by Leonard and Virginia Woolf at the Hogarth Press, London.

to me coaxingly, that I should yield to the Patriarch, but I thundered against them from the Scriptures, and snarled at them. . . . they drove me to the minster-church that they might shear me, and during Mass they kept me for a long time on the threshold. The Emperor rose from his place and going up to the Patriarch entreated him that he should not shear me, and they took me away to the Siberia Office and handed me over to the scribe."

Stubborn, bearded Avvakum was sent with his family to the far east to minister to a Cossack garrison, that he might mend his ways, and that he would not do. The journey became for him a test of his faith, and so upon rafts in the rivers and carts in the muddy trails, he felt himself strong against the abominations of Antichrist. "Dame Avvakum bore a sickly child in the cart and we brought it as far as Tobolsk . . . on our journey from Enisiesk—it would be on the great Tunguska river—a storm sank my raft . . . in other rapids—called the long rapids—he, Pashov, set about driving me from the raft. 'You bring bad luck,' says he, 'to the raft. You're a heretic,' says he, 'off with you to the mountains! It's not fit for such as you to keep company with Cossacks.'

"Alackaday! The mountains were high, there was a stone crag that stood there like a wall—you'd crick your neck before you saw its top. In these mountains great serpents were to be found, and in them dwelt ducks with red feathers . . . and wild goats, and deer and bison, and elk, and boars and wolves and wild sheep—clearly to be seen but not to be caught."

Yet this animal life became supremely important to the exiles because it provided them with food. "The folk would wander over the steppes, digging up grasses and roots, and we with them. And in winter we would live on fir cones, and sometimes God would send mare's flesh, and some would eat frozen wolves and foxes. Who will pour water on my head and unseal for me the fountain of tears, even that I may weep for the poor soul that is mine, which I have been destroying with my daily appetites? . . . This poor hapless wretch of an arch-priest set to fashion a dog-sleigh for himself, and started hauling. . . . I was made to pull a towing rope on the Khilok river, and up-stream it was mighty hard going . . . it was the fourth summer of my journey from Tobolsk; they were floating logs for the building of houses. . . . There remained to Dame Avvakum one Moscow gown that had not been rotted with damp. It would have fetched twenty-five rubles and more in Moscow; but in these parts they gave us four sacks of rye for it, and we dragged on for another year. . . .

"And we had a pet, a black hen, and she laid two eggs a day to feed the children, by God's will, helping us in our need. But when they were carrying out the baggage to the dog-sled, she was crushed to death, for our sins, and to this day whenever I think of that hen my heart aches for her. I know not an it were hen or miracle: all the year round she laid two eggs a day, and we would not have taken a hundred rubles for her—nay, we would have spat on them! Mere dross!

"And that hen, God's living creature, fed us, and she would take her meals with us, pecking at the porridge of fir-cones in the caldron, and pecking at the fish, and in exchange she gave us two eggs a day. Glory to God, who fashions all things well! . . . But enough of this matter; it was not the first miracle that Christ had brought to pass. . . .

"When I was at Dauria [beyond Lake Baikal] and I labored as a fisherman, I went in the winter to my children, and I went along the lake on snow-shoes; there was no snow but great frosts, and the ice froze well-nigh the thickness of a man. I began to want to drink, and I suffered much from thirst. I couldn't go on, I was midway upon the lake; I couldn't get to the water; the lake was eight versts. I began to look up to heaven and to say, 'O Lord, thou didst cause water to flow in the desert for the thirsty people of Israel. Give me to drink by whatever means seem good to thee. O Lord my God! I know not how to pray—forgive me, for the Lord's sake. Who am I, a dead dog?' The ice gave a crack beneath me and split up to either side across the whole lake and came together again, and a great mountain of ice rose up.

"While this was going on I stood in my place, and looking toward the east I bowed twice or thrice, pronouncing the name of the Lord in a loud voice from the depths of my heart. God had left me a small hole in the ice, and I, falling down, slaked my thirst. After that the hole in the ice sealed up, and I bowed down to the Lord, and then ran again along the ice whither I must needs go to my children. . . .

"So I left Dauria. The food then began to grow scarce so I prayed together with my company, and Christ gave us a roebuck, a huge beast, and on him we lived until we reached Baikal. There by the lake we came on Russian folk—a settlement of sable hunters and fishermen; they were right glad to see us, dear souls, and they dragged us and our boat to shore. They snowed meat and drink on us; they brought me forty fresh water sturgeons, saying 'There, Father, take them all!' And from dire need I accepted some from them. . . .

"So we reached Russian settlements, and I was informed concerning the Church, and like Pilate, I saw that I *'could prevail nothing, but that rather a tumult was made.'* My mind was troubled and, sitting down, I began to ponder what I should do—should I continue preaching God's word, or should I hide myself? For I was tied by my wife and children. And, seeing that I was troubled, my wife came up to me timidly, delicately, and said, 'How comes it, my lord, that you are troubled?' And I acquainted her with all my thoughts. 'Wife, what must I do? The winter of Heresy is at the door. Am I to speak or to hold my peace? I am tied by you.'

"And she said to me, 'Lord have mercy! What are you saying, Petrovitch? I and the children we give you our blessing, continue preaching the Word of God and take no thought for us. Get thee gone, get thee gone to church, Petrovitch!'

"From town to town I taught the people of God and denounced those others, the spotted beasts . . . they sent us a letter, saying thus and thus: 'Wilt thou so long vex us? Be reconciled to us, dear old Avvakum!' But I refused as though they were devils. And they flew in my face . . . they took me again to Moscow, and in the room of the Crosses, the bishops held disputation with me. They led me to the Cathedral church and after the Elevation of the Host they sheared me and the deacon Theodor, and then they cursed us, and I cursed them back. And I was heavy at heart for the Mass. And after I had stayed for a time at the patriarchal court, they took us by night to Ugresha, to the monastery of St. Nicholas—and the enemies of God shaved off my beard. What would you? It is like unto wolves not to pity the sheep; they tore at my hair like dogs, and left only one forelock—such as the Poles wear on their foreheads. They did it carrying me not along the road to the monastery, but by the marshes and the quagmires that people might not see me. . . . Look, thou that readest! Our misery was of necessity, we might not escape it. . . . Satan has asked and obtained from God our bright shining Russia that he might purple it with martyrs' blood."

The Archpriest Avvakum was burned at the stake at Pustozersk in the year 1681.

The monks of Solovetsky on their island in the White Sea refused to accept the new authority, and the new ritual, holding with Avvakum, the spokesman of the Old Believers, that "truth hath come to the land of Rus from the early fathers, and we may not set bounds to that which is eternal."

When the monks persisted in their revolt, troops were sent from Moscow to the northern sea, where they besieged the island with its monastic citadel for years before they occupied it. In time Solovetsky became an internment prison.

Journey of Isbrant Ides

Moscow was eager to establish transcontinental trade with the Chinese cities. On their part the Chinese knew little of the Russians except for the scattered raiders and traders who had appeared unexpectedly along the western woodlands. At Peking the Jesuits like Fathers Gerbillon and Verbiest had explained a little more about the peculiar Muscovite dominion. On the whole the Manchu emperors, preoccupied with other matters, desired little contact with the unintelligible newcomers.

The first embassies from Moscow had miscarried badly.

"In the year 1656," the Jesuit De Mailla records, "the king of the Urus, which is to say the Russians or Muscovites, sent some of his grandees to Pe King, to establish a free commerce between the two states. The emperor ordered them treated with honor . . . and a guard corps posted before their residence.

"The Court required in the first place that the Russian monarch acknowledge himself to be a vassal of China, and that the gifts he sent be offered as tribute. . . . These conditions made the stay of the Russians very short, because they refused to subscribe to them."

During the years of fighting around the Amur, no diplomats came through. But by 1676 an envoy, Nicholas Spatar, managed to reach Peking and to stay for three months in talk with Manchu ministers and Father Berbiest, with the result that he advised withdrawal from the Chinese frontier when he returned to Yakutsk.

Then, in 1692, a German-born Hollander, Isbrant Ides, was sent by Moscow to try his luck with the Chinese court. (This was after the retreat of the Russian hunters and colonists from the Amur basin, the founding of Irkutsk west of Baikal, and the frontier agreement drawn up between Manchu and Muscovite envoys at Nerchinsk—an agreement in which the Jesuits, who officiated as peacemakers in this first meeting of Russian and Chinese envoys, related that "the Russians insisted for long on the regions where the black fox and finest sables were hunted.")

The narrative of Everard Isbrant Ides, of his journey across the new empire to the court of the Manchus, gives a clear picture of the restless people along that almost roadless thoroughfare. First of the German observers to reach the far east, Ides ventured into what was a new world to him. And it took him five years to reach Moscow again.

Ides headed a largish embassy, with a secretary and servants and interpreters. Delaying to stock up with food and presents, he started late in the season from Moscow, on March 14, moving his train by sled over hard ice and snow up to Vologda before turning easterly along the frozen Sukhona.

Although he carried the Tsar's letters to the Chinese court, and traveled with authority from Moscow, he seemed to be prepared to make his own way, at his own risk, from town to ostrog. That way led along the rivers.

When he reached a terminal town like Great Ustiug, he was feasted by the *voevode*—staying over a night to do so. Beyond, at Solovy city, he found salt pits and workers in copper and silver. Here at the juncture with the north-flowing Dvina (the route to Archangel) his mission turned due south to reach the Kama. Ides's curiosity was stirred by villages of German-speaking folk, who could not explain how they had got there, although he suspected they were descendants of évacuées of some old war. Early in April he was halted by the beginning of the great spring thaw.

"In a forest we were assailed again by violent rain. In the space of one night the waters rose so . . . our sleds floated continually and from each side streams and freshets poured in on us, so we were like within a sea and could proceed neither forward nor backward for four days. Nor would the ice in the larger rivers bear any longer. By the help of bridges at last we reached Kaigorod."

Here he had to wait several weeks for open water on the rivers, discovering the while that Kaigorod had just been raided by bandits.

"About noon on a Sunday, several well-manned barks sailed in upon the river with flags flying and drums and trumpets sounding. The townspeople, taking them for friendly visitors from neighboring villages, gathered along the shore to divert themselves, suspecting no harm. The men [from the barks] leaped on shore and set the southern end of

the town on fire. Then they fell upon the inhabitants of the
north end, cutting all to pieces who came in their way. At
last they reached the voevode's building, which they plundered. After outraging his servants and carrying off what
they pleased, they returned to their boats and, undisturbed,
sailed down the Kama."

The raiders proved to be runaway serfs and slaves, most
of whom were run down and tortured; but after that Ides
was careful to post a watch by day and night, and to demand
firewood to keep large fires burning.

Not until April 27 did he arrive by ship at the point
where the Urals could be crossed. Owing to the spring thaw,
travel by land was impossible, and he was furnished with
"small barks" to ascend to the portage because he was an
envoy of the Tsar. Going up, he passed great salt barges
that made the trip down the Kama to the Volga. When his
flotilla sailed into the swift Chusavaya (where Irmak's war
band had ventured a century before) he "went on shore and
ate dinner on a high and beautiful green hill—my last
dinner in *Europe*. I drank a glass of wine as a farewell to
dear *Europe*."

The methodical German had reason to regret the corn-
fields, fruit gardens and salt works of the Kama basin; entering a wilder country where his vessels had to be towed
by animals on shore, he met the first eastern folk, the Vogul
Tatars, who "live on what their bows provide." The land
itself was fragrant with flowers and rife with game, which
the Tatars trapped by pits and bow snares.

"Daily we see numbers of wretched Russians," they assured Ides, "who can hardly get the pieces of dry bread by
which they live . . . we pay tribute to the Russians and live
our own way in peace."

By June the expedition had shifted from boats to wagons
and was traversing the marshy woodlands explored by Irmak's men. This stretch went easily, past still lakes and
villages of Russian settlers. At Tiumen, near the Ob, Ides
found that the only furs to be had were red fox, wolf and
bear, although a very fine breed of gray squirrel was protected by law against hunters.

Here the expedition was following Irmak's track, down the
Tura, to the Tobol River, into the wide Ob. But at Tiumen,
"its inhabitants and all the neighborhood were in great fear
of the Kalmuk and Kazak Tatars who had joined together to
make a raid and lay several villages waste, cutting the people to pieces, and threatening this city, from which they
were not more than 15 [45 English miles] distant. For

this reason I was not willing to stay longer here but as soon as I obtained fresh rowers and soldiers for convoy, I left on the twenty-sixth and went farther down the river Tobol ... the shores of which were under water, and not inhabited."

At the mouth of the Irtish, Ides found safety within the high palisades of Tobolsk, where troops were quartered, and the governor of "Siberia" resided, and a great stone monastery provided a citadel of refuge. Outside the palisade on the bluff Moslems from Bokhara were encamped, who carried on caravan trade between the Kalmuks and China. Yet Ides did not dare follow their route, up the Irtish toward the dry steppe. That way, he discovered, lay the danger of attack from Kalmuks, the Kirghiz Kazaks, the raiders from Bokhara and even the Bashkirs. Instead, he had masts fitted into his boats and sailed north along the Ob, seeking the safer forest route.

The countryside he found well settled by Russian peasants, who got along with the Tatar hunters—elk, stag, swans and wild geese filled the woods beside the flooded rivers, and a hundred German pounds of rye flour could be bought for sixteen kopecks, the flesh of a whole ox for two *rixdollars* (about eleven shillings).

Here also, along the Ob, was some evidence of a post service, because the villagers were paid to transport government officials, by water in summer, by sled in winter. "These people keep a great number of dogs ... sharp nosed, carrying their tails crooked up, like wolves ... which they use to travel with in winter. The dogs are yoked two to a sled which is made very light and thin. If, on the way, the master is minded to hunt he takes his gun on his shoulder, puts on his long sliding shoes, takes the dogs with him and steps a little way into the wood. There he turns up all manner of game, even a black fox. The master keeps the skins, and gives the meat to the dogs. . . . The best of the fox skins are reserved for his Tsarish Majesty, and are valued at from two to three hundred rubles."

From the Surgut junction, Ides's flotilla veered up the Ob, where the boats had to be towed through the midsummer months, to the fortified post at Narym, garrisoned by Cossacks. This was fairly into the great Siberian plain, with good furs to be hunted—beaver, ermine and sable. They saw no tilled land here, and when they worked up the Ket River portage they had only a gang of Ostiaks to aid them, meeting no other human beings.

The Ostiaks Ides found to be reddish-haired and weak, unable to labor hard at the towing, and fearful of war. They wore loose garments of fishskins, even in the winter cold. "If, as sometimes happens, they are caught by a severe frost —so incredibly hard does it freeze on these rivers—and if it seems impossible to escape with their lives, they throw off their fishskin coat with the greatest haste and fling themselves into the deepest snow and willingly freeze to death. The reason why they pull off their coat is that they may die the sooner, with less pain.

"When they have killed a bear with their short spears, they cut off his head and stick it upon a tree with the deepest respect; then they run to the dead body with cries, asking as follows: *'Who killed you?'* They answer themselves, 'The Russians.' *'What cut off your head?'* 'A Russian ax.' *'What cut up your belly?'* 'A knife made by a Russian.' By this folly, they make it appear that the Russians are to blame and they are innocent of the murder of the bear."

On the haul up the Ket they were caught by the autumn snow and wind, and one of Ides's retinue died in this seemingly limitless forest. The Ostiak couriers became so weak with towing up the winding river that Ides's men had to keep an armed watch on them, to prevent their deserting in a body. "No day passed in which some of them did not run away. And at last the cold and their unceasing labor made them entirely unserviceable." The expedition was out of food, except for fish and game, and was almost halted by the freezing of the river, when a relief party brought them in to the Makovsk post, and on to Yeniseisk.

Here, as at Tobolsk, Ides found himself in a rambling government town, with cloisters and a garrison. "About seven years past, the citizens of Yeniseisk fitted out a ship and sent her [down the river to the Arctic coast] on a Whale fishery. They never yet heard where their ship was lost."

While he waited for the rivers to freeze hard in mid-January, Ides heard the tales of mammoth hunting. "Among the hills to the northeast . . . particularly on the banks of the Lena to the Frozen Sea, the Mammuths tongues and legs are found. In the spring when the ice of this river breaks up, it is driven by the swollen waters with such great force that . . . it frequently breaks off the sides of hills. These falling down, reveal these Animals whole, or their teeth only, frozen to the earth, which thaw by degrees.

"I had a person with me . . . who told me as a truth that he had found a head of one of these Animals, disclosed by a fall of earth. Opening it, he found the flesh rotten, and only with great trouble did they break out the teeth, which thrust out of the mouth like those of an Elephant. After-wards, he and his companions cut off its fore-foot which was as large around as the waist of an ordinary man.

"About these animals there are different reports. The heathen Yakuts, Tungusi and Ostiaks say that by reason of the very hard frosts they live continually or at least mostly underground. To confirm which they tell us they have often seen the earth heaved up when one of these animals was on the march, and the place sink in after he passed. They further believe that if these beasts which are never seen come so near to the surface that they feel the air, they immediately die. That is the reason why several were found dead on the banks of the river where they came out of the ground unaware.

"But old Siberian Russians affirm that the Mammuth were in this country before the Deluge, when the climate was warmer. Their drowned bodies, floating on the waters of that Noah's Deluge were at last washed into subterranean cavi-ties. After the Deluge, the warmth here changed to cold, and so these carcasses have lain frozen in the earth ever since—which is no very unreasonable conjecture."

Starting from the protection of Yeniseisk in mid-January, the Ides expedition took to sleds and for almost the first time in its long journey was able to travel due east, up the ice of the Tunguska River. Slowly, in the devastating cold, the sleds climbed the high plateau northwest of Lake Baikal. Here they found only scattered Russian hunting posts and occasional Tungusi villages of bark huts.

And they passed by one of the worst portages of the long Siberian way—a mile and a half of rapids called the Sha-man's Fall. Natives and Russians alike believed there was something supernatural about the torrential fall which burst through ice in midwinter. The sound of it could be heard for nine miles on a still day. It could be ascended by boats only when the river was low in midsummer.

Then the vessels were worked up the rapids by towrope, and anchor and windlass, taking six or seven days to make the ascent, although they came down in twelve minutes, as Ides relates—and he watched some of them do it.

"The ships are always unloaded, and their lading carried by land until they get past, when it is again loaded on board. I myself have seen ships which sail down this torrent do it in twelve minutes, so prodigiously rapid is their descent. Very few Russians or Tungusis know how to bring down the ships, which must be provided with a rudder fore and aft, and

rowers on both sides. The pilots give orders to the rowers by
waving a handkerchief, for no voice can be heard over the
hideous noise of the water. The ships are also closely covered
in, so that the raging water which frequently flies over
them, may not enter and sink them.

"Several ships are cast away here every year, especially
when inexperienced pilots try to bring them down. Often they
are shattered to pieces against hidden rocks. The men are inevitably lost, either drowned in the rapid torrent or shattered on the rocks. Wherefore their bodies are rarely found,
and the banks are filled with crosses erected in memory
of those buried in the water."

Ides was moved by curiosity to visit the shaman for
whom the rapids were named, and found him to be "a tall
old man with twelve wives and not at all ashamed of the
magic he professed to do." This necromancer of the waters,
who would prophesy or insure safe passage of the falls for a
fee, had accumulated great herds of cattle around his dwelling, the gift of his clients.

While the ice and snow still held, they worked their way
to the south, up the small Ilim River, moving from one
fortified post to another—for this was near the Mongol
frontier.

The tents here were hung with horses' manes; the boats
were birchbark canoes in which men knelt with double-ended
paddles; hunting ranged over the prairies—throngs of horsemen circling around game and driving the antelope and deer
against a barrier.

From the monastery of St. Nicholas, Ides descended the
steep shore of Baikal, crossing it hurriedly while the ice
was still firm—"full two Holland ells thick. It is dangerous
when those crossing it are overtaken by a high wind or
heavy snow. There are broken places and wind holes. If
the horses are not sharp-shod they are driven by the wind so
violently that they can not tread sure, but slide and fall on
the ice until they and the sled with them are swallowed up in
a hole. Besides, the ice is sometimes torn open for several
fathoms by storms, making a noise like a thunder clap."

Feeling its way along the rivers, the expedition entered
the rolling, treeless hills of the Mongols, where Cossacks
garrisoned the posts. "In summer the Mongolians often come
and drive off the horses of the inhabitants, even when they
are grazing within sight of the town."

Here there was no cultivation, and only a little hunting
down around the frontier posts. The expedition shifted its

stores to horses and camels, and joined company with a traders' caravan.

At times, as the prairie grass dried, it was fired by Mongols who hoped to deprive the animals of the caravan of forage. The expedition followed the course of the small rivers and got through to Nerchinsk, where Siberian Cossacks and brass cannon guarded an enclosure large enough for their herds to graze, and a *Taidchi* of the Horse Tungusi gave fealty to the Tsar and served as protector in chief of the post—"this prince can in one day raise three thousand riders all equipped and with good bows."

When the Russians climbed the last dividing mountain ridge, marveling at the girls who rode horses like men, and the women who dressed in pantaloons like men, and the lamas who had worn down their thumbs numbering the beads of their rosaries, "as we climbed, we observed a remarkable alteration of the country on the south side of the hills . . . these valleys are covered with fine grass, and herds of deer and wild-sheep appear numbering hundreds of heads. Flocks of wild duck and water fowl pass overhead. Turning my eyes to the south, I can not help but own that the river's side here is like paradise."

Here in what seemed to be paradise after the long Siberian way, to the envoys as to the explorers who had gone before them, they sighted their first Chinese guard post.

Ides's mission to Peking failed, and his letters were not ever read, because in them the name of the Tsar (Peter) had been written before that of the Manchu Emperor, K'ang-hsi.

When the Hollander published the book of his journey he dedicated it to Peter, and in so doing gave to the young Tsar some new titles.

"To . . . Peter, son of Alexis, by the grace of God, *Emperor* of the whole Great, Little and White Russia; *Monarch* of Moscow, Kiev, . . . *Tsar* of Kazan, Tsar of Astrakhan, Tsar of Sibiria (etc.), . . . *Lord and Great Prince* of Novgorod . . . and of the whole North [Baltic] Sea . . ."

The Tsar, then, was to be addressed as lord of the ancient sea of the Variags. Some of the Siberian regions such as "Obdoria" appear in the newest style. Peter is *"Commander and Lord"* of several Caucasus princes and peoples, and of ". . . many other countries and territories to the East, West and North, the inheritance of his ancestors." The "and other countries" of the earlier styles have become part of the imperial inheritance.

While the politic German who had hopes of a high diplomatic career under Peter invoked all the flattery of his time, he stressed what he knew would interest Peter. He lists natural resources—"treasures and minerals, such as gold, silver, copper, iron, saltpetre, sulphur, salt." He alludes to the "men of war" which have broken into the barred-off Caspian, and freed the mouth of the Don, "by which means the Black Sea is become accessible, and affords a communication South and Westward, with the Mediterranean."

Nor does Ides omit the Dvina and the White Sea, "which hands on commerce to the ocean." In Siberia itself he names the rivers that will lead to the Amur, and thence to the Eastern Sea.

Peter, however, like Ivan, devoted his own energies and the resources of his people to the west.

The tsars between Ivan IV, last of the sons of Rurik, and Peter I had served as little more than the heads of the state, however they might have been torn at times between old tradition and the new ideas of the west. But the dynamic Peter left the impress of his personality (1689-1725) upon the new empire.

Self-taught like Ivan, impatient of the old-fashioned thought around him, he experimented continually—particularly with the new model army, with an inland and seagoing shipping, and the inevitable artillery. After his journey into Holland, to Vienna and England, where Ivan had thought to take sanctuary, Peter Romanov became convinced that his empire must be extended physically into the west, and must develop along the lines of western science (hence the activation of the Finland-Baltic waterways foreseen by Gustavus Adolphus, the building at terrible cost of Peter's-town, where the Neva enters the gulf, the training of the "new regular army" on Prussian lines, and the long wars that began at Narva and ended at Riga).

The force of Peter's very active personality, then, was thrown toward compelling his own people to shift toward the west, and to think as westerners. Like Ivan, Peter felt himself to be not so much the tsar of a Eurasian state as the servant of a Russia that must recover a lost heritage in the west. He thought of himself realistically enough as an emperor who owed nothing to Byzantine tradition, to Slavic customs, or to Asia.

Yet Peter was inwardly as Russian as any other soul of his time. For all he made his entourage shave their beards and wear European dress, he accepted the responsibilities of the *land* that had now become a huge dominion. Behind his own efforts lay the anonymous pressure of his people, impelling him to navigate the river routes outward, to control the junctures of the rivers with the seas, to compete with the Dutch and English in western trade, and to create a military force that could reach these objectives (in spite of the Russian aversion to militarism).

While Peter's policy toward Europe was clear enough, his policy toward Eurasia—toward the regions east of Moscow—followed a hit-and-miss course. In this quarter, like Ivan in his final years, Peter planned much and accomplished little. Almost his first outward thrust recaptured Azov, at the mouth of the Don, from the Turks—yet his government yielded Azov later to secure an advantageous peace. The early occupation of the Ukraine, with the aid of the Kalmuk horsemen, was not followed up; the movement into the Caucasus gained much that was abandoned later; two Cossack-Russian expeditions across the southern deserts to capture Khiva in the Aral littoral and to drive into the Kirghiz steppe, along the Irtish, met disastrous defeat, even while Peter talked of using Persia as a steppingstone to gain access to India. The shipping that dominated the Caspian for a while was allowed to deteriorate. (On the other hand, Peter's effort helped launch the Bering-Chirikov exploration of the Siberian coast, which penetrated to America seven years after his death.)

It was almost as if the Kremlin, under Peter, exploited the resources of inner Eurasia to batter at the west.

In any case, this policy brought continued reaction from the populace east and south of Moscow.

Even while Peter carried out his rapid self-educational tour of the European cities, the Streltsi, stirred up by Old Believers, rebelled within Moscow (1698).

After the early defeat in the Baltic and the conscription of labor to build Petersburg, revolts in Astrakhan and among the Volga people like the Bashkirs flared up (1705-08).

Down the Volga, Razin's old stronghold, the populace turned against the officials. Their priests of the countryside echoed the cry of the Old Believers against "Latin prating and German teaching" and the new ideas imported from the west. The rebellion spread to the shipyards along the Volga and the mines in the Urals, which had been laboring to meet Moscow's demands for ships and metal. It spread to the cloth and leather factories in the Oka-Volga valley.

But it did not reach the proportion of a national revolt, and it remained Russian in sympathy. When the Swedish army under Charles XII invaded western Russia it was joined by no more than a division of Cossacks led by Mazepa. (Whose name, thereafter, unlike Razin's, was shunned by the Cossacks, as a whole.)

A century after Razin, a third resistance movement swept this line of the old frontiers. This time the Mordvas and Chuvashes linked up with the pastoral Bashkirs and the Cossacks, under Pugachev, and the revolt was serious—although it did not spread to the Ukraine or other frontiers.

The Open Frontier

Like a tide the great advance had swept across the north of the continent, ebbing back a little from the Amur to Baikal, but only a little.

By the second half of the seventeenth century, it was taking on a New World semblance. The river systems were linked together by portages. Some sort of roads joined the stockaded towns growing up around the ostrogs, as Moscow had grown around the Kremlin. The resistance of native peoples like the Tungusi and Yakuts had ceased.

The long southern flank of the advance had little to safeguard it. There it dug in, at the edge of the forest areas, as colonists trickled into the settlements.

This northern domain of the forest fronted the southern belt of the plains, mountains and inland lakes—the age-old nomad highway from Baikal and the Altai to the Volga. Above this invisible line of demarcation stood the churches of Orthodox Christianity, facing Islam, Buddhism and shamanism. The stockaded towns faced the moving peoples of the steppes. Over this line horse and sheep trading went on, with barter for rugs, weapons and grain.

Along this open frontier the Manchu government extended its control westward among the Mongols, by influencing their priesthood and confining them to fixed areas. On the far side the only advance was by the Russian colonists, who pushed tilled fields and cabins forward almost imperceptibly into the grazing lands of the tribes.

One powerful tribe of Mongol descent, the Oirat—called Kalmuks by the Russians—migrated along this open frontier as late as 1771 and still passed south of the Russian settlements. With their barbaric horse-tail standards and their Buddhist shrines mounted in carts, the Kalmuks to the number of some sixty-five thousand tents had occupied the brown steppe extending from the Don past the Volga to the Urals—where the Turkomans of the Aral region and the scattered Nogais took care not to interfere with them.

Apparently they had thrived on the rich grazing lands, thick with antelope and wild horse herds. But as herdsmen themselves and a formidable army of horsemen, they had blocked the way to penetration of this western steppe by the Russians, who were advancing slowly toward the Caucasus. At times divisions of Kalmuks had joined the Russian armies, or the Cossack revolts.

But when part of them were moved by the Russian government into a dry area where drought killed off their herds, they felt themselves finally challenged by the Russian advance.

To the protest of their Khan, Ubasha, the Russian governor retorted by demanding hostages from the Asiatics. "You think you can remove yourselves elsewhere," he added, "but you are like a bear chained to a stake. You cannot go where you will; you must go where you are led."

Whether aroused beyond endurance by the misconduct of Russian officials, or realizing that they could no longer hold their steppe, the Kalmuks gathered along the banks of the Volga and started eastward in January 1771, when the rivers were frozen. Only a remnant of them chose to remain under Russian authority.

Some sixty thousand tents joined the migration from the Volga back to their ancestral homeland. They followed the age-old "road of peoples" over which William of Rubruk and Carpini had been rushed by Mongol couriers—below the Ural Mountains and above the salt deserts.

Ural Cossacks raided them, and turned back some of the rearmost families. Turkomans of the Aral region struck at them, and plundered the moving human mass. The three Kirghiz hordes (Moslems and so antagonists of the Buddhist Mongols) contested their way, in turn.

By midsummer they were still passing through arid lands, and their herds had suffered. By early autumn, the Kalmuks gained the streams flowing into Lake Balkhash, and drove off the last of the hostile peoples as they passed Balkhash and entered the western frontier of the Manchu Empire, where the enlightened Kien Lung had lands set apart for them along the Ili River.

The Kalmuk clans had made this extraordinary trek [2]

---

[2] The story of this trek caught the imagination of Europeans very quickly. Thomas De Quincey wrote his *Flight of a Tartar Tribe* depicting a nomad people enduring all the horrors of war, privation and thirst, to gain sanctuary, while in reality these Western Wing Mon-

in eight months. Chinese officials estimated their number on arrival at fifty thousand tents or three hundred thousand mouths. Kien Lung himself wrote: "Their envoys were conducted with honor and without expense over the imperial post-roads to the place where I then was. I met them and spoke to them and I was glad to have them share the pleasure of a hunt with me. Afterward, their suite withdrew to Ge Ho. There I gave them a banquet of ceremony."

It was odd that these last migrations across central Eurasia should have been from west to east. No longer did the mass movements from the eastern interior threaten the west, as under Mongol and Othman Turkish dominion.

In fact Turkish central power, at Constantinople, had weakened greatly since the last unavailing siege of Vienna (1683) and the independence of Hungary and Transylvania. The Turkish horsemen had ceased to be terrible to well-drilled European regiments, and the Janizaries themselves had become more of a palace guard to luxury-loving sultans than infantry formidable in the field. With the weakening of the great Turkish army, the balance of military strength between these two empires of the east was passing to Russia, and soon to be used—the Kalmuks had already served as cavalry in such use—in a slow thrusting back of the western Ukrainian frontier, by war and treaty, to the line of the river Danube, on the way toward Constantinople.

In their trek the Kalmuks had passed from the Volga to the frontier zone of the Manchu Empire without crossing the outposts of the new Russian Empire. Those outposts still lay beyond the Kirghiz steppe, above 50 degrees of latitude.[3]

---

gols seem to have brought most of their humans and herds through safely.

By that time Siberia itself was becoming known to western readers by tales of Dezhnev's wanderings, Bering's voyage, and the exile of political prisoners. In European maps the names "Russian Tartary" and "Independent Tartary" still endured and the whole formed a welcome *terra incognita* to storytellers like Jules Verne, whose *Michael Strogoff* embodied most of the newer imagery, replacing the Cathay, the Golden Old Woman and the tent of the Grand Cham of Tartary of the centuries before.

[3] It was long before the southern frontier penetrated the barrier of the arid steppes and the nomad peoples, the Turkomans, and the great Turkic clans of the Kazaks, and branches of the Kirghiz.

In the Crimea the Tatar khans did not become subjects of the tsars until 1775. The north slope of the Caucasus was not subjected by the Russian armies until 1859–65—simultaneously with the advance into the Amur basin in the east. Russian forces occupied the plateau between the Caspian and Aral about 1820, but did not subdue the

But the frontier of the empire was being outlined, very slowly, by the extension eastward of military posts commanded directly by Moscow. The cossack *stanitzas*—the "cordon" villages—in which the men were liable for military duty, formed links in this new fortification of the Siberian frontier. These military posts changed the communal character of the early settlements.

From the Volga eastward the native peoples had not been merged into a new entity—the forest folk, Laps, Samoyeds, Voguls, existed as before.⁴ So did the older Siberians, the Ostiaks, Chukchi and Tungusi. And the plains folk, the Mordvas, Bashkirs and Cheremiss. They occupied their lands as before.

So did those in the melting pot of the Ukraine, Turks, Greeks, Poles, Tatars and even German colonists. They were merely subject to the distant control of Moscow.

---

khans of Khiva and the Bokhara region until 1864–73 (this was the territory traveled at such hazard by Jenkinson). The frontier was pushed south of Lake Balkhash along the Ili and the new lands of the Kalmuks in 1854.

⁴ A modern census of the U.S.S.R. (*Guide to Soviet Union,* Vneshtorgisdat, Moscow, 1932) lists these northern Siberian peoples as still separate.

Yakuts	240,709
Tungusi	37,546
Chukchi	12,332
Ostikas	22,306

On the other hand, in this census, the former tribal people of mid-Asia—mostly Moslems—are much more numerous. Russian ethnologists believe that the elder Siberians, existing in a hard climate on poor soil, have tended to diminish in numbers since medieval times, while the southern folk under better conditions have increased proportionally. In the seventeenth century, however, the steppe peoples were unquestionably much more numerous and powerful than the northern tribes.

Kirghiz	762,736
Turkmen	763,940
Turks	1,706,605
Kazaks	3,968,289
Uzbeks	3,904,622

(This particular handbook reminds the reader that "The Soviet Union is not only a European country; it is Eurasian. . . . The Five Year Plan contemplates a gradual shifting of the center of population and industry toward the east, with the progress of the development and settlement of the enormous regions east of the Urals. . . . Siberia, its huge mineral resources practically untouched so far, will form the basis of the future Socialist Commonwealth.")

Kamchatka to Alaska

The pioneers who found the Amur basin barred to them after 1648 made one final outward thrust. In every way this last effort toward new land conformed to the pattern of the great advance that had carried the frontier to the Eastern Ocean Sea.

It sought new hunting ground for pelts, and new fisheries; it moved to the northeast, around the forbidden zone of Chinese military strength, and it crossed over a water barrier to get at land beyond.

Russian hunters who penetrated the Kamchatka Peninsula toward the end of the century learned from the native Chukchi of islands beyond the horizon. Exploring these islands by small boat, they reached the western end of the Aleutian chain that stretched in a seemingly endless curve through mist and floating ice. Exploring past the first (Commander) group, they found seal and blubber plentiful on the islands to the east; they broke down the resistance of the Aleutian natives, reducing them to merciless slavery.

Then followed exploration by ship, in 1728–41. A vessel under the Danish captain, Vitus Bering, and another under the Russian Alexei Chirikov surveyed much of the intervening strait, the islands and outer sea, the survivors reporting their findings to Moscow.

Blockhouse posts were built on the larger islands like Unimak and Unalaska (in time a mission and a prison settlement being added to the trading posts). Boats exploring the farthest islands of the chain sighted the Alaska shore. A Russian navigator, Fedorov, landed on this coast, making certain it was no island, in 1732. He called it the "Great Land" and it was in fact the tip of America. After these explorers came the fur hunters, and finally the agents of a state monopoly.

Soon after the Russians reached this remote point in the New World, stray Spanish vessels quested up from California way, and the English navigator, James Cook, appeared on the scene under orders to search for a still possible Northeast or Northwest Passage through Arctic waters, from this communicating strait.

Curiously enough Bering's first discoveries aroused the Moscow government to examine all the Arctic coast that was becoming revealed upon its maps. Working eastward as the English and Dutch had attempted to do, from the mouth of the Ob, and taking to small boats and sleds when the ships were immobilized by the ice pack, starting again from the Lena's mouth, and questing far out from Archangel toward Spitsbergen—where they encountered English whaling vessels—the Russians sought for silver on Nova Zembla, and found troves of mammoth tusks on unknown Siberian islands. This great endeavor to probe the shores of the only Russian sea (1732–73) did not reveal a clear passage from the Pacific to the Atlantic, but it proved that the Russians, at least, could get through.

These early voyages began the long and courageous Russian survey of the polar region.

But the foothold, or rather the hunting post, on the North American coast was not maintained by the Russian government, even after its explorers had penetrated south as far as California. Such an extraterritorial province beyond the sea, with its far-flung hunting, trading and mission activity, did not fit the pattern of Russian expansion outward by zones from the heart of Eurasia. Alaska had become a commercial venture, in the hands of adventurers. Unlike the Spaniards of the earlier centuries and the English and Dutch of more modern times, Moscow never leapfrogged colonies across the seas to distant coasts. Its process of growth was to occupy the land adjoining its frontiers, and then, once occupied, to move beyond to the next strip of land.

By the middle of the nineteenth century, the course of Russian military control and colonization followed this familiar pattern from upper Siberia, down into the rich farming land of Manchuria across the Amur, toward agricultural Korea and the northern provinces of China.[5]

Alaska was sold.

[5] Oddly enough, one familiar pattern appeared in this latter-day outward thrust. In the 1860s some gold had been uncovered in Siberia, along the Yenisei and the Stanovoi range; in the resulting gold fever, there was a movement toward the iron and gold mines along the Amur. But the main impulse of the advance into China was the acquisition of an agricultural, wheat-growing region with control of the river mouths and ports opening upon a navigable sea, to give access to the Pacific.

ACKNOWLEDGMENT

MY INDEBTEDNESS for material on medieval Asia extends over many years to many individuals, but chiefly, in regard to Muscovy and the eastern expansion of the Muscovites, to these:

Professor Vasily Struve of the Institute of Ethnography at the Academy, Lenigrad (for suggestions as to the origin of Siberian clan groups), and to the unpublished notes of the historian Daniel Mordovtzev, to Professor A. Golitzin, and Professor P. Bariatinsky (contemporary accounts of Irmak and the Volga frontier).

I acknowledge the courtesy of the Historical Museum in Moscow in forwarding photographs of charts of the movements of the Golden Horde, and of pre-Mongol Russia. The work of Grum-Grzhimailo, *Zapadnaya Mongoliya*, Leningrad, 1926, has been important for the eastern Asiatic peoples —as has *Aboriginal Siberia*, by M. A. Czaplicka, Oxford, 1914.

Among the historians of Russia as a whole, there is the splendid, detailed work of Vasily Kliuchevsky, from which many observations have been quoted; the invaluable studies of George Vernadsky (especially upon the ancient Ukraine, and the recurrence of popular movements along the medieval frontiers), the summary of Professor P. N. Milyukov, and the biased but able work of M. N. Pokrovsky. The brief *Survey of Russian History* by B. H. Sumner, London, 1944, complements the work of the great Russians.

I am indebted to the narratives and the maps in John F. Baddeley's *Russia, Mongolia, China,* London, 1919.

The pioneer study of Professor Robert J. Kerner, *The Urge to the Sea: The Course of Russian History* (the role of rivers, portages, ostrogs, monasteries and furs), University of California Press, 1946, has been a guide and constant reference during the latter half of these narratives. For details of the Siberian fur traffic, use has been made of *The Russian Fur Trade*, 1550–1700, by Raymond H. Fisher, University of California Press, 1943.

The contemporary narratives pieced together in this book

are, for the most part, the following. Some are quoted directly, others indirectly. They happen to be, almost all of them, the journals and testimonies of priests, voyagers, traders, diplomats, prisoners, wanderers or simply curious minds gathering accounts of travel—being part of my own collection of the first explorers of medieval Asia, toward Cathay.

(The native Russian chronicles used in the earliest chapters include the well-known Ancient Chronicle ["Nestor's"] ending about 1116 A.D., the *Word of Igor's Arming*, 1185, the journal of Daniel, Archimandrite of Kiev, 1106–1107, and the Chronicle of Novgorod, 1016–1471.)

The journal of Benjamin of Tudela, a Spanish Jew, describes Constantinople and touches upon the Black Sea ports, 1160.

THE FIRST CENTURY OF MONGOL DOMINION

The witnesses here are captives, or monks, and merchants voyaging to the various courts of the khans. Recital of an unknown English crusader, captive of the *orda* of Batu Khan, 1243 (eastern Poland and Hungary), given, from Ivo of Narbonne, in the chronicle of Matthew of Paris, and also in Hakluyt. Friar John of Plano Carpini, 1245—his journal, like that of his brother friar, William of Rubruk, 1253, describes a passage through the Ukraine under the aegis of the Golden Horde. Both are published in the *Sinica Franciscana, Volumen I, Itinera et Relationes Fratrum Minorum Saeculi XIII et XIV,* Van den Wyngaert, Firenze, 1929; and in Hakluyt. Oderic of Portenau, published in Wyngaert and elsewhere, gives a fantastic account of the lands and legends of mid-Asia, about 1317. There is also the itinerary of Ricaldus of Monte Croce, 1296, of a journey in the Black Sea region.

By then the Italian merchants had become the chief voyagers. After the book of Marco Polo, which mentions the visit to the territory of the Golden Horde (1260–61) only briefly, there is the well-known travel journal of Ibn Batuta, 1324, which touches the Black Sea and Sarai (best edition that of C. Défrémery and B. R. Sanguinetti, Paris, 1853). Then comes the brief itinerary of the Florentine merchant Pegolotti, 1335, from the Crimea and the Don to Cathay.

With the breakdown of Mongol dominion and the closing of the transcontinental routes, the Christian missions in the farther east and the few trading posts beyond the Black Sea region were isolated or abandoned.

THE CENTURY OF THE ITALIAN AND GERMAN DIPLOMATS

One captive, Johann von Schildberger, of Munich, gives a remarkable and altogether confused recital of his wanderings among the Turks and with Tamerlane's army along the southern and eastern borders of Rus, 1396–1427, in contact with the Golden Horde. It has never been carefully edited.

Josafa Barbaro, a Venetian envoy to the Crimea, gives routes around the Black Sea, 1436, and Tabriz and the Caucasus, 1471. (Aldus, 1545.)

Nicholas of Cusa (in Treves) seems to have been well acquainted with the lands and trade of Rus, and may have drawn the first European map thereof, about 1450, used by both Sebastian Münster and Von Herberstein.

Ambrogio Contarini's journal, 1474–76, gives the first full account of a visit to Moscow. (First published 1487 in Venice, and included in many travel works since then.)

Nicholas Poppel leaves fragmentary accounts of his two journeys from the court of Frederick III to Moscow, 1486–89, in the Vienna archives. There also lies the record of the embassy of Georg von Thurn, from Maximilian to Moscow, 1491.

Sigismund von Herberstein gives the first extensive account of Muscovy—*Rerum Moscoviticarum Comentarii*—published in Vienna, 1549, and enlarged and improved in the Basle edition of 1553, which was in return revised to include the two maps in 1571. Herberstein's work was greatly sought after and often republished during the second half of the sixteenth century, and is mentioned by Englishmen who came after him—some of the young factors studied it, apparently, before going into Muscovy.

THE ENGLISH VOYAGERS, 1553–1600

From the journal of Richard Chancellor, the survivor of the discovery voyage, 1553, to the narrative of Anthony Jenkinson, and the businesslike appraisal of Giles Fletcher, as late as 1589, and the trading venture of Christopher Burrough, the embassy of Jeremy Bowes, 1582—these are given with loving care in the voluminous *Principal Navigations* of Richard Hakluyt, many of them edited and republished by the Hakluyt Society. Here are also the transactions of the English Muscovy Company, the sparse details of the polar explorations, the abstracts of letters home from young factors and traders in the east. (Horsey and Rowe are given in *Purchas, His Pilgrims,* the cruder compilation after Hakluyt's.)

With the Hakluyt voyages, the *Cosmographia Universalis* of Sebastian Münster, 1544, is important. Also the *A True Discourse of the late voyages of discoverie, for the finding of a passage to Cathaya* by George Best, 1578 (reprinted by the Hakluyt Society).

It is amusing to remember that the 1591 edition of Giles Fletcher, *Of the Russe Commonwealth*—a narrative used as a source by modern Russian historians—was suppressed by action of the Privy Council of the time.

THE DUTCH, THE DIPLOMATS, AND THE SOLDIERS OF FORTUNE

Good geographical and historical résumés are given by: Paulus Jovius, *De Legatione Basilii magni Principis Moscoviae* . . . (the text in Grynaeus, *Novus Orbis,* Basle, 1532, was used for this book), and Matthew of Michov, *De Sarmatia Asiana atque Europa.*

Toward the end of the reign of Ivan IV, and especially after the ensuing time of troubles, European narratives increase in number. These given below were used for this book.

Heidenstein, *De bello Moscoviticarum,* Basle, 1588.

Jehan Savvage, *Mémoire d'un Voiage en Russie,* published by Louis Lacour, *Archiviste,* Paris, 1855.

Jacques Margeret, *Estat de l'empire de Russie et Grand Duche de Moscovie,* Paris, 1855.

Isaac Massa, *Légend de la vie et de la mort de Demetrius,* Amsterdam, 1606. *Relatio de Siberica,* Amsterdam, 1727. (Also in Adelung, *Reisenden in Russland.*)

Oderborn, *Joannis Basilidis vita,* Vitebsk, 1585.

Possevino, *Moscovia et alia opera,* Vilna, 1587.

THE SEVENTEENTH-CENTURY TRAVELERS

Olearius, *Voyages faits en Moscovie et Tartarie, 1633–39,* Amsterdam, 1727.

Jean Struys, *Les voyages de Jean Struys en Muscovie, Tartarie, en Perse (1669–72),* Amsterdam, 1720.

Father Avril, *Travels into Divers Parts of Europe and Asia* . . . , London, 1693. (An attempt to find a new way through to Cathay, 1685.)

Avvakum, *Life of the Archpriest Avvakum by Himself,* . . . (written before 1685), translated by Jane Harrison and Hope Mirrlees, The Hogarth Press, Ltd., London, 1924.

Isbrant Ides, *Three Years Travels from Moscow overland to China* . . . (1692), London, 1706.

Father Gerbillon, *Travels into Western Tartary by Order of the Emperor of China* . . . (1689–98), published by Du Halde, and summarized in Astley's Voyages. (A detailed relation of the first meeting, at Nerchinsk, of Russian and Chinese envoys. Odd that the speaker for the Russians should have been a Pole, the language Latin, and the spokesman of the Chinese two Jesuits.)

Index by John Askling

ABOUT THE AUTHOR

HAROLD LAMB, who died in 1962, was one of America's most popular historians. His great gift was his ability to take scholarly material and weave out of it fascinating accounts of fabulous empires and their rulers. His books were eagerly awaited by his hundreds of thousands of readers.

Among his many best-selling books are *Genghis Khan: Emperor of All Men, Hannibal, Theodora and the Emperor, Cyrus the Great* and *Babur the Tiger*.